God and Money

God and Money

A Theology of Money
in a Globalizing World

Nimi Wariboko

LEXINGTON BOOKS

A division of
ROWMAN & LITTLEFIELD PUBLISHERS, INC.
Lanham • Boulder • New York • Toronto • Plymouth, UK

LEXINGTON BOOKS

A division of Rowman & Littlefield Publishers, Inc.
A wholly owned subsidiary of The Rowman & Littlefield Publishing Group, Inc.
4501 Forbes Boulevard, Suite 200
Lanham, MD 20706

Estover Road
Plymouth PL6 7PY
United Kingdom

British Library Cataloguing in Publication Information Available

Library of Congress Cataloging-in-Publication Data

The hardback edition of this book was previously cataloged by the Library of
Congress as follows:

Wariboko, Nimi, 1962-
    God and money : a theology of money in a globalizing world / Nimi
Wariboko.
        p. cm.
    1. Money—Social aspects. 2. Money—Religious aspects—Christianity.
    3. Monetary unions. I. Title.
    HG221.W345 2008
    261.8′5—dc22   2008016752

ISBN: 978-0-7391-2723-0 (cloth : alk. paper)
ISBN: 978-0-7391-2724-7 (pbk. : alk. paper)
ISBN: 978-0-7391-3034-6 (electronic)

Printed in the United States of America

Contents

Acknowledgments

This book could not have been written without the help of many people. First, I want to mention Professor Mark Taylor, theologian, who intensely reflected on money with me for two years. Professor Peter Paris, social ethicist, was also a tremendous source of inspiration, motivation, and guidance. Professor William Rodgers, an economist at Rutgers University, was invaluable for his insights on applying sound economic reasoning to ethical issues. I would also like to thank Professor Viviana Zelizer, a Princeton University economic sociologist, whose guidance and support were critical in the writing of chapters three and four. This book is richer for the insights and perspectives each of these scholars brought to bear on it. All errors are mine as their views and insights were critically filtered through my own perspective and goals for this study.

Great thanks and commendation go to Julie E. Kirsch, the executive director of Lexington Books, for your magnificent direction of the project from manuscript to publication. She also had the wisdom to have picked an anonymous reviewer whose skills, knowledge, and talents were invaluable in making the arguments of this book clearer and more forceful.

I also wish to mention my wife, Wapaemi, whose incredible love and support was the necessary ingredient for the peace of mind that engendered the reflections in this study. The love and patience of my children, Nimi, Bele, and Favor, as I undertook one study after another, were some of the strongest psychological forces in powering me forward.

Introduction

Theologians treat money paradoxically: Although money is everywhere, relentlessly connecting and desiccating all private, public, and sacred spaces, as a theological category it remains unanalyzed. The monetary system has either been outrightly neglected as if it is not theological enough or has not been addressed directly as yet. This book addresses the issue of religion and the monetary system, offering a model of rigorous and innovative scholarship for examining money as a major theological-ethical category. This theological-ethical study of the nature and role of money in contemporary societies goes beyond making ethical recommendations to providing a framework for understanding and critical reflection on the global monetary system. The study analyzes the dynamics at work in the global monetary system and argues that the monarchial currency structure of the dollar, euro, and yen may be moving toward a trinitarian structure of a democratic world currency. The overall purpose of this study is to interpret, evaluate, and aid the transformation of the global trade and payment system in the light of the dynamic relations of the triune God. Based on the inequities, ambiguities, and contradictions in the system uncovered by the framework, it makes a case for a denationalized single global currency as a means of redressing certain destructive dynamics in today's global monetary system.

At the core of the theological thinking in this book is the notion of relationality which is of interest to both scholars of religion and economics. Money is conceptualized as a social relation. Not only are monetary transactions embedded in social relations, but also social relations are constitutive of money *itself*. The notion of relationality has been a useful device in theological thinking for some time and in this work I extend the insights of relational theology to the monetary system. While many economists are aware of the social character of money, the theological and ethical reflections I bring to bear on the relationality of money will help them to think about the global monetary system in ways that are not discussed in their field.

The particular relational theology that informs the whole framework is discerned from the relational principle of coherence that posits a primarily just, close, and irreducible relations in the perichoretic communion of the Godhead. I argue that the dynamic relations of the triune God model the relationships that need to be created in the global monetary system. The ethics is in the critique of the contemporary global monetary system which exposes the values, power differentials, and the hegemonic domination of the system that are threatening the moral order of the international community. The critique also reveals the ways the monarchical currency regime of the dollar-euro-yen hinders full participation of developing countries in the global monetary system and their economic progress.

I know that bringing the triune language into monetary relations may seem like a category mistake or a conceptual move that some theologians and economists may find strange. Nevertheless, I have turned to the dynamic relations of the triune God for two reasons. For understanding the most developed Christian view of positive relations and relationships the logical place to look is the trinitarian language of the Christian tradition. Second, I am using Paul Tillich's principles of trinitarian thinking as a basis for developing the ethical principles that should guide the development of the global financial system in ways that can improve monetary relations between developing and advanced economies of the world.[1]

The triune model will help theologians, ethicists, and economists to reflect on how to nudge the structures and organization of monetary life toward creating and maintaining an embracing economic community that brings *unity-in-difference* into perpetual play and also fosters more ethical relationality without stifling its creativity and galvanizing force. Thus, this book describes an imaginative alternative to the global monetary system that is likely to foster better justice in international economic relations. It argues for a reordering of the relations in the present exclusionary global trade and payment system to secure for each country better participation and integration in an embracing economic community.

Seeing the international monetary system in terms of a model of the Trinity or using the model of the triune God as a perspective on the monetary system is not just a heuristic device. It is a significant and alternative way of thinking about the structures (current or re-imagined) of the global financial architecture and for discovering the set of relations in an ethical theory of the international monetary system. The model of the Trinity provides us with a template or screen for understanding the monetary system and for translating such a template into ethical principles. It enables us to avoid, as Bernard Lonergan would say, the "social ethicists' tendency to be content with 'vague moral imperatives' instead of figuring out moral precepts from the immanent intelligibility of economic processes."[2]

The model of the dynamic relations of the triune God is also useful when applied to the issues of power differentials that are embedded in the current global monetary system. It is particularly so when it functions as an imaginative framework for crafting an inclusive, non-hierarchical alternative to any socioeconomic system. I am interested in forging an alternative to the current structures of the global monetary system because of my sense of justice. For me the praxis of justice in the global economy, and for that matter national economy, is about drawing all nations and persons (poor and rich, powerful and not-so powerful) to share in a living communion by removing or challenging structures that thwart relationship of equality and participation.

The use of the triune model of relationality in analyzing the monetary system in this book transcends its application as a mere heuristic device in yet another way. The model informs the interpretation of the dynamics at work in the global monetary system. My analysis of the dynamics indicates that the global trade and payment system may be moving toward trinitarian structures. Before now theologians and ethicists just apply the notion of the trinity to social issues and proceed to explicate matters. They never take the time to explain if the logic and dynamics of the system they are analyzing are moving toward trinitarian structures or a perichoretic format. They do not attempt to bring to the fore the underlying values, principles, and inner conflicts that animate the system and are leading it to the solution they are proposing. They are often not patient enough to identify the bridge that covers the basic gap between the "what is" and "ought" (the expectation of the new). My approach is not just to posit trinitarian social values and expect the public to accept them on faith, but I endeavor to show that the system I am analyzing is moving toward trinitarian structures or one global currency system without special seigniorage privilege to a few nations. I cover the gap not only by providing a vision of a new system, but by also having a technical theory (by way of Tillich's trinitarian principles) which shows how and why the particular situation may or must transmute to the envisioned state. Tillich in the *Socialist Decision* emphasized the need for a technical theory to support any theological vision or symbol of hope.[3] He stated that Karl Marx followed this rule to fruitfulness and rigor in his thought. Marx had the problem of moving from the "what is" of capitalism to the "ought" of socialism. He latched on to the notion of dialectics to provide the engine for the movement of the system to its fulfillment. Thus, the theology of money being developed in this book shows the structural dynamics and logic of the global monetary system which are driving toward its transmutation into a "perichoresis of national currencies," one that anticipates the eschatological gathering of the whole people of God and makes room for poor nations to further actualize their potentials.[4] The animating power for the social practice of money—like the historical dialectics of Marx—is the typological-structural tension in the dynamics of money as an exchange medium which drives it toward a trinitarian structure of global trade and payment system. All this is not to dismiss any suggestion that voices and movements that are challenging the current imperial, monarchial global monetary system (in addition to the internal dynamics of the global monetary system itself) are also "driving it forward" and "anticipating" the eschatological gathering.

Why is this book relevant at this point in time? There is a special significance of this study for issues pertaining to Africa's and Latin America's progress and other developing regions' economic development. With the rising tide of globalization and economic integration there is an increasing debate in economic circles about the need for one global currency to replace all imperial national currencies. Paul Volcker, the former chairman of the Federal Reserve Bank of the United States has argued that a global economy needs a global currency. Robert Mundell, the 1999 Noble Prize–winner in economics and whose theory of optimum currency areas is at the bedrock of the monetary union behind the euro, has similarly called for a world currency. African economists have long called for an international currency that does not give seigniorage and other imperial benefits to the owners of key global vehicular currencies. John Maynard Keynes with his *Bancor Plan* made a similar call at the 1944 Bretton Woods Conferences that established the World Bank and the International Monetary Fund.[5] This book, for the first time, makes the case for a world currency based on theological and ethical analyses. This study by proposing an alternative logic for discussing and imagining the global monetary system provides another voice and support to the poor, developing countries who have been clamoring for a more equitable global trade and payment system.

This study for the first time provides a proper systematic theological treatment of money. Before now, Christian social teaching on economic and social justice has only touched on the monetary capital of societies as it speeds toward prophetic protest against the economic system or as it aims to arm the church for ideological combat with owners of capital. In its critique, the church's social teaching has not paid adequate attention to the paramount processes in the creation, circulation, and control of money and thus failed to come up with a set of recommendations that can engage and enlist the global monetary system for the ideals of church's notion of social justice. This study corrects this failure.

One major contribution this study makes to the field of theological ethics is the rigor with which it engages economic thoughts in the task of reimagining alternatives to the current global monetary system. As I argued in chapter two, there are many theologians and ethicists who aspire to reorganize the monetary system but offer alternatives that can only elicit disinterested yawns from economists and financial experts who will regard them as idealistic and impracticable. Many a theologian has not managed to come up with a set of recommendations that can engage and enlist economists and business leaders in order to put into effect their theological visions. We require a study that corrects this kind of shortcoming and that can stand the chance of nudging the global monetary system toward fulfilling the fullness of participation, cooperation, and justice without stifling its creativity and galvanizing force.

Theologians' call for more humane and just economic orders has to be supported with the necessary rigor and expertise of an interdisciplinary breath of knowledge. I think the beginning of wisdom in this conversation is a working definition of money to avoid talking at cross purposes. An overwhelming majority of the theologians we examined in chapter two proceeded to craft theologies of money and critique the contemporary monetary system without first answering the question, what is money? Often their understanding of what money is, is not compatible with those of non-theologians. The contributions theologians can make to monetary discourse should not involve distorting, "spiritualizing," or "theologizing" the definition of money. I intend to avoid this mistake by understanding money from solid economic and sociological perspectives and only after that to undertake a theological-ethical critique of the contemporary monetary system. There is, indeed, an urgent need for serious methodological reflection on the role of theological approach to money.

SUMMARY OF A THEOLOGICAL APPROACH TO MONEY

As already indicated above, I am using Tillich's trinitarian principles and the social trinitarianism of Miroslav Volf to develop a theological model for approaching money and its social-international system. I combine Tillich's notion of trinitarian principles with the perichoretic trinitarian theology of Volf as described in his *After Our Likeness: The Church as an Image of the Trinity*[6] to craft a unique approach to theologizing about the global monetary system. The trinitarian thinking has been worked into the warp and woof of the fabric of the theological-ethical framework presented here.

There are three principles at the foundation of Tillich's trinitarian think-ing. The first is the dialectics of the absolute and concrete elements in the idea of God. The second is the dialectics of life as symbolically applied to the divine ground of being. Finally, there is the dynamics of depth, form, and meaning. In chapter seven I explicitly show the application of the first principle to the global monetary system. There I identified the typologi-cal-structural tension (as interpreted through the theological lens of Tillich and Volf) in the dynamics of money as an exchange medium which drives it toward a trinitarian structure of the global trade and payment system.

Both Tillich and Volf are concerned with the relationship between the universal (abstract) and the particular (concrete) in certain areas of Chris-tian theology. Tillich focuses on the dynamics of the tension between the concrete and absolute elements in the idea of God as they engender trini-tarian monotheism. Volf, on the other hand, trains his analytical lens on how to achieve a delicate balance between the equally valid concerns of the universal church and the particular (local) church. Though both the-ologians are dealing with the issue concerning the universal and the par-ticular, they come at it differently. The accent of Tillich's thinking is on the dynamics and that of Volf is on the "statics" aspect of the intersection. Combining Tillich's dynamics and Volf's statics (equilibrium) considera-tions, I address the tension between the universal and the particular in the idea of a global currency which could function as an alternative (replace-ment) to the current monarchical triumvirate of dollar, euro, and yen.

Also in chapter seven, as part of the working out of the first root of trini-tarian thinking, I offered a trinitarian model of money to illuminate the path for a better organization of the global financial system in ways that could promote the fullness of participation and justice. I envision a global financial system (*Earth-dollar* system) in which the dance of exchange rates of national currencies works out "not only as a movement of each in the others but also as each offering the others 'room for movement'" [7] and economic development.

In order to avoid the common problem of premature appeals to social analogy and "dangers of idealizing and projection" common with the use of the doctrine of Trinity in social analysis, I first went through a process of intermediate argumentation based on economic theories of global money forms and exchange rate system.[8] The resulting insight was that the nature of trinitarian relationships provides for a proper reflection on economic issues. This is in the sense that the whole of my argument about money and global finance has two sides: the theological perspective is its "immanent" face and the *Earth-dollar* system is its "economic" face (or-dering the household, οικονομια, of the financial world); and the two proceeded *pari-passu*. Starting from Tillich's trinitarian principles and incorporating the ideas of Volf about the perichoretic sociality of the Trinity[9] on the theological side and those of John Maynard Keynes and Robert Guttmann on the economic science side, I conceived of a model of global trade and payment system that is likely to promote fellowship, encourage the growth of community of nations without privileges and without subjugation, and is directed toward God's eschatological future.

The use of the second principle of the Tillichian trinitarian thinking is undertaken principally in chapter five. The second principle is about life—"the structural elements of being moved divergently and convergently in every life process; they separate and reunite simultaneously."[10] I demonstrated that money separates and unites simultaneously. Money has a certain analogy with life and it has sometime been crudely described as life-blood of the economy. Once we grasp this: that is, the idea that money is not a *dead matter*, not a "dead identity," but a pulsating flow of energy in the economy, we realize that theological treatments of money up to now have been very inadequate. Theologians and theological ethicists have often treated money as matter, not as a form of energy, not as a flow. The stock concept of money and the related ethical issues dealing with the allocation and use of the quantity of money in a given political economy have dominated the theological discourse and not much has been done on the analysis of money as a *motion* (the flow concept of money). Theologians and ethicists have tarried too long on one spot; concentrating too much on giving and generosity and individual ethics to the neglect of social and systemic issues. In so doing they have largely ignored the production, circulation, and control of money, the flows of money, which actually determine who gets what quantity, when and how.

The manifestation of the divine ground of being in the appearance of Jesus as the Christ is the third root of trinitarian thinking. This is about the element of form, the *logos*, in the symbolization or in the development of the idea of God. In chapter two, among other things, I show that the logos (third-root) issues of depth, form, and meaning illuminate aspects of how money functions in the modern economy. I argue that money as a social relation is a "dynamic unity of depth and meaningfulness." The *depth* of money is the ever-expanding sphere of economic production, the ground of satisfying human needs and wants. The value of a given national currency is supported by the industrial and non-industrial productions of its country. *Meaning* stands for the *principle of form* structuring the productive activities, the satisfaction of social wants.

The third root of trinitarian thinking as applied to money is also about the manifestation of the idea of money in concrete form. How does the abstract concept of money (unit of account) "manifest" itself so that it can be used phenomenally? With the decision by government that a certain physical, historical form or medium (such as the greenback) is money, the problem of currency becomes part of form-of-money problem. What forms of money are out there? What is the real money among them? What is the best representation of that which is basically abstract? The conclusion concerning the state of the literature is that there is no one "real money" but a continuum of monies, all real, but with different scope. The argument I make in chapter four is that money is a *relational thing*. This involves two inseparable ideas. First, money is not a fixed attribute of things; rather, it is a social relation of many economic agents. Second, it is a thing that mediates, participates, and runs alongside the relationships of interpersonal exchanges. Combining these two features, I suggest that money is a *relational thing*. The social-relation part of the conception appropriately points to the universalizeable tendency of money in its roles as general equivalent and as a medium of account. The thing part particularizes it in its roles as a medium of exchange and means of payment. The thing part is also meant to capture the aspect of money which could be imbued with specific cultural and social meanings by any subset of economic agents in the society.

There are two important points, theoretical and theological, to keep in view as we reflect on this conception of money. The theoretical point of the definition of money as a *relational thing* is that the question, What is money? is not answered by equating money with money of account or with monetary media, however materialized or dematerialized the media are. The generalizable tokens (whether bills, paper, commodity, metal, or electronic circuit) are the forms money takes but they are not the "essence" of money (which I consider as social relations). There has to be first money before monetary media; first moneyness which has to be embodied in a particular form. The theological point of this definition is that it captures one of the tensions in the trinitarian thinking—the tension between the universal (abstract) and concrete. As Tillich has argued, the roots of the trinitarian thinking show up in several aspects of life. "The consideration of the trinitarian principles is not the Christian doctrine of the Trinity. It is a preparation for it, nothing more."[11]

By explicitly offering a definition of money that not only acknowledges the tension between the universal and concrete, but also shows how the tension is embraced in the instrument of money I laid the groundwork for the arguments make in chapters 6 and 7. In those chapters I identify the tension between particularity and universality that exists in the use of particular national currencies as key, vehicular currencies in the global trade and payment system. The need for a balance between the forces of particular national interests and the concern of a global economy which needs a global currency drives the system of currencies, as I argued, toward a trinitarian structure of the global monetary system. I proposed that the solution to the tension is a single world money that can really claim ultimacy and be uncontrolled by local (national) interests without losing the concrete element in the idea of money. It is a form of money in which the universal and concrete (for each participating country in the system) are united. The upshot of my analysis is to re-imagine an ethical alternative to today's global monetary system.

HERMENEUTIC SELF-IMPLICATION

It would be beneficial to help the imagination of the readers by placing this book in its context. I will register how this study relates to some of my efforts to comprehend the nature of the connection between extreme poverty, monetary system, and economic development in Africa.

Tillich once wrote "for a quarter of a century I have wanted to write a systematic theology. It always has been impossible for me to think theologically in any other than a systematic way. The smallest problem, if taken seriously and radically, drove me to all other problems and to the anticipation of a whole in which they could find their solution."[12] For me it has been twenty years since I wanted to write a systematic treatise on money. Since the fall of 1987, when three of us, young economists (the others are Ashikiwe Adione-Egom and Ikechi Emenike) were working as financial journalists, regularly discussing the connection between money and economic development,[13] and feeling the urgency to overcome the cloud of poverty that had settled over the black man and woman, I wanted to thoroughly understand money. At the turn of this century, about one in two people (46.4 percent) in sub-Saharan Africa are living on less than one dollar a day. A third of the population suffers from malnutrition, and life expectancy at birth is only 46 years.[14] This is extreme poverty. As the United Nations' *Millennium Project 2005: Investing in Development* puts it:

> Extreme poverty can be defined as "poverty that kills," depriving individuals of the means to stay alive in the face of hunger, disease, and environmental hazards. When individuals suffer from extreme poverty and lack the meager income needed even to cover basic needs, a single episode of disease, or a drought, or pest that destroys harvest can be the difference between life and death.[15]

I longed to tell the story of Africa's underdevelopment from the point of view of the imperial monetary system. I long desired to reveal the ways the global monetary system hinders the participation of the poor countries of Africa, Latin America, and Asia in the international trade and payment system and inhibits their economic progress. I wanted to understand money systematically and thoroughly.

So I went from being a financial journalist to being a commercial banker. After less than two years as a banker, I came to the United States and studied finance and accounting (M.B.A.) at Columbia University and subsequently worked as an investment banker in Lagos, Nigeria and New York City. I taught Advanced Mergers and Acquisitions" and "Security Analysis at New York Institute of Finance. As an adjunct assistant professor of social sciences at New York University, I taught a history course, African Civilization. After five semesters at NYU, I went over to the business school at Hofstra University, in Long Island. I served as a senior pastor of an immigrant church in Brooklyn for over nine years. During these years, I have come to see, first hand and sometimes too closely, the sufferings of immigrants who were thrown into new and often hostile environments. One cannot fully account for why they left their places of birth to seek their fortunes in far away places without taking into account the role of the global monetary system, whose critical involvement in their plight most of them are unaware of.

I have published seven books and several scholarly articles in finance, accounting, management, sociology, anthropology, and African history. In all these callings and endeavors I have tried to systematically understand money and economic development.

The choice to embark on this study at this point in time was triggered by my reaction to Michael Hardt and Antonio Negri's *Empire*,[16] which I read in the fall of 2004. I felt their treatment of empire ignored the role monetary systems play in defining and sustaining empires and glossed over the involvement of the today's global monetary system in the poverty of the Global South. This work, however, is not all against Hardt and Negri's viewpoint. In the development of my arguments, I am thinking *with* them as well as thinking *against* them. When I am thinking *with* them, I am in support of their view of empire as "totalizing." But when I am thinking *against* them, my overall experience leads me, by conscious choice in this book, to present the discourse of empire and globalization from a subaltern perspective.[17] Thus, my vision of a new global monetary system—as oriented to subaltern communities[18]— is geared to increase the participation of poor, developing countries and to subject the current global financial architecture to the demands of justice. I would not say, however, that I have accomplished my goal of systematic understanding of money. For instance, I have not laid out a philosophical system in which the various concerns about money, especially money and economic development, could find their solutions. In this work I am only systematically dealing with money principally at the international level from a theological perspective.

ORGANIZATION OF CHAPTERS

I have structured the study into two main parts. First, I set the context and define the crucial understanding of money I will deploy for the theological-ethical imagination. In the second half of the study, the trinitarian model of the global monetary system is investigated in detail. Chapters 1 to 4 constitute Part One and chapters 5 to 8 make up Part Two. The opening chapter of Part One ("Modeling Money on God") describes the model of the dynamic relations of the triune God as it will be applied to the international monetary system. Chapter 2 ("Money and Theology: A Review and A Direction") engages with the discourse on theological analyses of money. Since this book is about the monetary system, the conversation will be limited to theological works that systematically treat the monetary system. Besides, the dialogue will be limited to the analysis of the existential questions that are embedded in the contemporary monetary situation. Selected works of the following theologians, Mark C. Taylor, Philip Goodchild, Kathryn Tanner, Craig Gay, W. Taylor Stevenson, and Jacob Needleman meet these criteria and therefore will form the main focus of this chapter's review.[19]

It is germane, in addition to the theological understanding of money, to explore the socioeconomic understanding of money. The combination of theological and sociological perspectives is necessary for crafting a rigorous and robust definition of money that will enable us to uncover the ambiguities, ethical tensions, and ethos embedded in monetary relations. Thus, in chapter 3 ("Money and Society: Socioeconomic Interpretations"), I examine the interpretations of money by economists and sociologists in order to identify the key characteristics of money in the twenty-first century.[20]

Building on the knowledge gained from the theological and sociological understandings of money, I craft a definition of money that will be used in this study. Chapter 4 ("Money as a Social Relation") not only argues that all monetary phenomena are socially contingent, but also posits that social relations are constitutive of money *itself*.[21] The definition, which acknowledges the tensions inherent in the monetary process, will set important groundwork for our later turn to Tillich's trinitarian principles in chapter 7 and clarifies how the principles can help form the basis of an ethical reflection on the monetary system. The definition also clarifies how those principles apply to national currencies and how those currencies can be conceived in trinitarian terms. It is germane to mention that this analogy has to be handled with circumspection as we cannot reasonably conceive of national currencies in strict correspondence to the trinitarian persons.

The first four chapters, basically provide a working understanding of the nature of money in contemporary society and provide us with the critical social analysis necessary for theological-ethical reflection on the monetary system. Part Two begins the theological-ethical analysis of the contemporary monetary situation. In chapter 5 ("Discerning Distortions in Monetary Relations") I employ another concept from Tillich that anticipates his view of trinitarian relations and that is helpful for the analysis at this point: his concept of "the demonic."[22] This does not concern a supernatural world of demons, but is used by Tillich to refer to destructive distortions of human relationality. I use the term for naming certain general "demonic" distortions and twists that are caused by money in societal relations.

The overall result of the analyses in chapter 5 is the unveiling of the basic existential questions and conflicts implicit in the social practice of money—essentially showing where the ethical questions are situated in the structures and organization of monetary life. The next logical task is how the existential questions will be mutually and critically correlated with theological-ethical discourse. Thus, in chapters 6 and 7, I show how the trinitarian symbolization can provide a theological-ethical response to the existential questions and ethical conflicts relating to the monetary system. This task is accomplished in two steps.

First, in chapter 6 ("Money and Empire") I empirically examine the structural character and tensions of relationships in the international monetary system and patterns of "demonic" distortions and twisting of money at the global level, showing how the severe imbalance of power between rich and poor countries in the global trade and payment system severely undercuts the ethical quality of the system. The imbalance inhibits especially the full participation of sub-Saharan African economies and other developing economies in the ongoing globalization process. The disparity in power reveals the presence of *empire*. The current global monetary system itself, in fact, represents a form of *empire* with a powerful center, contrary to the theorizing of Michael Hardt and Antonio Negri who see *empire* today as having no center.[23] To the contrary, the current global monetary *empire* has a center insofar as the dollar, euro, and yen are the major imperial, vehicular, and reserve currencies of the global monetary system standing over the plebeian rest of the national currencies.[24] I will demonstrate that anywhere and anytime there is a monarchical arrangement of national currencies there is *empire* which has a nerve center.

Second, in chapter 7 ("A Trinitarian Model of the Global Monetary System"), I show how the structural tensions in the dynamics and crisis of money could be addressed by reimagining and outlining possible ethical alternative to the international monetary system. I draw on the practical consequences of the trinitarian principles and doctrine of the Trinity based on the perichoretic interpretation to show how the global monetary system can be used to draw nations more generally into a mutually participative life. This is the point at which I articulate the kind of system of trinitarian principles and relations that is at work in Tillich's model of relations in the triune God. The resulting re-imagined system highlights the importance of relationality in monetary interactions, giving us a perspective on how to redress certain destructive dynamics in today's monetary system.

Here I will use Tillich's first root of trinitarian thinking to show how "poly-mediastic" national currencies can become "mono-mediastic," that is, giving way to one global money form. I will argue that the tension between the universal and particular as played out in the global trade and payment system is an underlying principle that drives particularistic national currencies toward universal and total integration as one global currency and then defines the patterns of interaction between them. According to Tillich, there is a tension of the elements in the idea of God: the dialectics of the need for concreteness (particularity) and absoluteness (ultimacy and universality). The trinitarian principle is what structures the balance between the concrete and absolute drives so that they are united in a living God. He sees trinitarian monotheism as the ultimate realization of this principle. He argues that the Trinitarian God has overcome the typological-structural tension between particularity and universality. The triune God who claims universality and ultimacy, is uncontrolled by local interest, and yet does not lose that God's concreteness. The triune God is absolutely concrete and particular (in Jesus the Christ) and yet is absolutely universal at the same time.[25]

This trinitarian principle is important for looking at the global monetary system. The structural tension in the dynamics of money as an exchange medium in the international monetary system is expressed in two ways: first, particularistic national currencies aspire to transcend their national borders, and second, the present global vehicular currencies (such as the dollar, euro, and yen) are unable to transcend national interests even while they claim ultimacy and universality in the global trade and payment system. The need for a balance between these forces of particular national interests and a global system calls for a trinitarian structure. Following this Tillichian line of reasoning, I will propose that the solution to the tension is a universal currency that can really claim ultimacy and be uncontrolled by local interests without losing the concrete element in the idea of money. In this way, I seek to transcend the tension between the particular and universal tendencies of all current legal forms of money and imagine an ethical alternative to today's global monetary system. What is at stake is not only the re-imagination of a system, but also the fact that, by imagining a new, proper system, I point out the weak spots of the current global monetary system, the one that is supposedly serving global capitalism well.

Finally, chapter 8 ("Payoff for Poor Countries") discusses the study's payoff for poor economies. Here I would attempt to show, only briefly, how the *Earth-dollar* monetary system addresses some of the radical economic needs of the dominated Global South. It also brings the work to a close by highlighting the study's contributions to Christian theology and social ethics and pointing to areas of further research.

NOTES

1. See Paul Tillich, *Systematic Theology*, vol. 3: *Life and the Spirit, History and the Kingdom of God* (Chicago: University of Chicago Press, 1965), 283–85, 421–22; Tillich, *Systematic Theology*, vol. 1, *Reason and Revelation, Being and God* (Chicago: University of Chicago Press, 1951), 157, 221, 228, 241–43, 252.

2. Frederick G. Lawrence, Patrick H. Byrne, and Charles C. Hefling Jr., eds., "Introduction," in Bernard Lonergan, *Collected Works*, vol. 15, *Macroeconomic Dynamics: An Essay in Circulation Analysis* (Toronto: Lonergan Research Institute, 1999), lxxi.

3. Paul Tillich, *The Socialist Decision*, trans. Franklin Sherman (New York: Harper & Row, 1977), 71.

4. It appears that this claim, as a statement, is full of optimistic and harmonistic presumption about the global monetary system. I really think that given the pace of globalization and the forces driving it forward it would not be long before we have a global currency like the way the Europeans have the euro. Tillich is not one that easily falls for harmonistic presumptions but he was to assert that dynamic forces inherent in the ideas of God (the Trinitarian principles) "pushed" religious thinking to the concept of Trinitarian monotheism. In the same way, as I will show in chapter 7, the inherent tensions in current global currency system are likely to move it toward a one-currency system. I am not ignorant of the fact that this move will be resisted by the nations that benefit most from the current monarchical system, but I hope that other agents will work together to nudge the system to the place-of-one-currency system that will usher in an era of greater justice and balance of opportunities to seek wealth for all countries and peoples.

5. For Paul Volcker's statement see Robert Mundell, "Currency Areas and International Monetary Reforms at the Dawn of a New Century," *Review of International Economics* 9, no.4 (2001): 595–607; Mundell, "A Theory of Optimum Currency Areas," *American Economic Review* 51, no. 4 (1961): 509–517; Mundell, "The International Monetary System and the Case for a World Currency," Leon Kozminski Academy of Entrepreneurship and Management (WSPiZ) and Tiger Distinguished Lecture Series 12, Warsaw, October 23, 2003; Robert Guttmann, *How Credit Shapes the Economy: The United States in a Global System* (Armonk, NY: M. E. Sharpe, 1994); Peter Alexander Egom, *NEPAD and the Common Good* (Lagos, Nigeria: Global Market Forum, 2004); *Globalization at the Crossroads: Capitalism or Com-*

munalism (Lagos, Nigeria: Global Market Associates, 2002); *Money in the Theory of International Economic Activity: An Inquiry into the Nature and Causes of the Wealth and Poverty of Nations* (Guderup, Als, Denmark: Adione, 1977), and John Maynard Keynes, *The Collected Writings of John Maynard Keynes*, vol. 25, *Activities 1940–1944: Shaping the Post-War World, The Clearing Union*, ed. D. Moggridge (London: Macmillan, 1980).

6. Miroslav Volf, *After Our Likeness: The Church as the Image of the Trinity* (Grand Rapids, MI: William B. Eerdmans Co., 1998).

7. Stanley J. Grenz, *Rediscovering the Triune God: The Trinity in Contemporary Theology* (Minneapolis, MN: Fortress Press, 2004), 83.

8. For a critique of the use of doctrine of Trinity for social analysis see Collin E. Gunton, *Father, Son and Holy Spirit: Toward a Fully Trinitarian Theology* (London: T & T Clark, 2003), 23–25.

9. For a thorough introduction to contemporary theologies of the Trinity see Stanley J. Grenz, *Rediscovering the Triune God: The Trinity in Contemporary Theology* (Minneapolis, MN: Fortress Press, 2004). For insights on how some Christian theologians have attempted to interpret the doctrine to non-Christians see Veli-Matti Kärkkäinen, *Trinity and Religious Pluralism: The Doctrine of the Trinity in Christian Theology of Religion* (Aldershot: Ashgate, 2004).

10. Tillich, *Systematic Theology*, vol. 3, 241–42.

11. Tillich, *Systematic Theology*, vol. 1, 251.

12. Tillich, *Systematic Theology*, vol. 1, vii.

13. This connection will be made explicit in chapters 6, 7, and 8. Here it suffices to just say that poor countries are exposed to virulent, violent exchange rate movements that are generated by financial systems outside their control. Also with the use of the key imperial vehicular currencies, the locus of control of the major vehicle of global economic relations is monopolized and placed outside African economies.

14. United Nations, *UN Millennium Development Goals Report 2005* (New York: United Nations, 2005), 6–7.

15. United Nations Millennium Project 2005, *Investing in Development: A Practical Plan to Achieve the Millennium Development Goals* (New York: United Nations Development Program, 2005), p. 4.

16. Michael Hardt and Antonio Negri, *Empire* (Cambridge, MA: Harvard University Press, 2000).

17. Simply put, by "subaltern perspective" I mean the perspective of people considered outsiders by those in centers of global power structures and as such their voices are suppressed by modernity's project of privileging some groups and some forms of knowledge. The purpose of the subaltern perspective is to challenge the hegemonic and monopolist orders of knowledge production that suppress the voice and viewpoints of the underprivileged.

18. Communities are rendered "other"/*alter* to the global system and subordinated within it, thus sub-*altern*.

19. Taylor, *Confidence Games*; Goodchild, "Capital and Kingdom"; Goodchild, "Debt, Epistemology and Ecotheology"; Tanner, *Economy of Grace*; Craig M. Gay, *Cash Values*; Stevenson, *Soul and Money*, and Needleman, *Money and the Meaning of Life*.

20. Nigel Dodd, "Reinventing Monies in Europe," *Economy and Society* 34, no. 4 (November 2005): 558–83; and Viviana Zelizer, "Missing Monies: Comment on Nigel Dodd, 'Reinventing monies in Europe,'" *Economy and Society* 34, no. 4 (November 2005): 584–88.

21. See Geoffrey Ingham, *The Nature of Money* (Cambridge, MA: Polity Press, 2004); and "The Nature of Money," *Economic Sociology, European Electronic Newsletter* 6, no. 1 (October 2004): 18–28.

22. He also refers to the same concept as the "social demonry." See Paul Tillich, *The Interpretation of History* (New York: Charles Scribner's Sons, 1936), 91–116.

23. Hardt and Negri, *Empire*.

24. Or should we say three centers with the U.S. dollar as the overall leader and the epicenter of the triumvirate?

25. Tillich, *Systematic Theology*, vol. 1, 16–17, 221–30; *Systematic Theology*, vol. 3, 283–94.

PART ONE

1

Modeling Money on God

INTRODUCTION

This book provides a basic framework for theological and ethical reflection on the global monetary system. It makes the case for a denationalized single global currency based on theological and ethical analyses in order to aid the transformation of the global trade and payment system in the light of the dynamic relations of the triune God. My reflections on the global trade and payment system seek to replace the binary logic of the imperial vehicular currency system[1] (the monarchical triumvirate of dollar, euro, and yen against the plebeian currencies of the rest of the world) with a relational and communitarian logic that posits a close and irreducible relation between all national currencies. Therefore, I will work out a model of the dynamic relations of the triune God for the international monetary system that is likely to foster a fuller participation of relatively less dominant economies in the world in the ongoing globalization process. Here the model of the dynamic relations of the triune God functions as an imaginative framework for an understanding of an inclusive, non-hierarchical alternative to the global monetary system.[2] This imaginative framework is important to develop even if political and economic realities block its immediate implementation. A certain realism, such as the ability of the nations whose currencies serve as the global currencies of trade and central banks' foreign reserves to block moves toward a denationalized global currency, compels us to acknowledge this skepticism.

What is the theorectical problem that has also necessitated this study? The problem can first be focused by commenting on certain gaps in the theological literature. The works of Mark C. Taylor, Kathryn Tanner, Philip Goodchild, Craig Gay, W. Taylor Stevenson, and Jacob Needleman that deal with theological-ethical analyses of money show one or both of two problems.[3] First, often little or nothing is said about structures and organization of the monetary relations that condition the ethical responses of Christians. There is also silence on how the content of some fundamental Christian values and doctrines might influence the possible reorganization of the structures of the monetary life.[4]

Second, these theological writers ignore the highly important dual nature of money. The source of this duality in the monetary system is what can be termed the dialectical paradox of money: the "hyphenating"[5] movement of money that simultaneously binds and separates economic agents in the monetary system.[6] This paradox is the most vexing problem for harnessing the vitality of money for economic growth and social development. As a table relates and separates the persons who are sitting around it; so, too, does money relate and separate subjects, at the same time, who come together in an economy.[7]

Money is relational[8] and inclusive in that it opens up persons, industries, and nations outwards to the other. It binds persons, corporations, groups, and regions together into communities through its social practice of exchange. Money's relational practice of inclusion feeds on its persistent tendency of exclusion.[9] Money also disconnects. Money creates differences as necessary conditions for market exchange and valuation.[10] These differences that money creates cause systematic crises, discrimination, deprivation, despoliation, separation and segregation among classes, races, and regions. Indeed, money in a broad sense is a dynamic union of exclusion and embrace. It seems that every one of its movements toward embrace is denied by a powerful centrifugal force toward exclusion. Thus, the task of ethical thinking on money is to show how the structures and organization of monetary life can be nudged toward creating and maintaining an embracing economic community that brings *unity-in-difference* into perpetual play and also fosters more ethical relationality without stifling its creativity and galvanizing force.

I argue that the dynamic relations of the triune God model the relationships that need to be created in the global monetary system in order to deal with its ambiguities and certain key destructive tendencies.[11] Specifically, I develop the idea that the perichoretic communion of the Godhead is a model for how nations should relate to one another in the global monetary system. In doing this I draw from Paul Tillich's trinitarian principles. Tillich's trinitarian thinking is informed and guided by what he calls the trinitarian principles or the three roots of trinitarian thinking. The trinitarian symbolization[12] for Tillich is not limited to the Christian doctrine of the Trinity but is a theological response to existential questions.

He argues that the principles are not just for theological discussions, but are also relevant in interpreting human reality and events. He believes that the trinitarian principles are the most inclusive answer to the questions implied in human predicaments.[13]

Overall, the Tillichian principles work to structure the development of the study and even function at a more significant level as my own hermeneutics. In the following section, I will give a description of the three Tillichian principles.

TILLICH'S TRINITARIAN PRINCIPLES

Paul Tillich (1886–1965) was one of the towering theologians of the twentieth century. His many theological works have profoundly influenced and vigorously stimulated thinking in diverse areas of contemporary religious thought, as well as engendering a methodological approach (the method of correlation).[14] This German-American was forced by Nazi Hitler's government to migrate to the United States in the early 1930s. He fell out of favor with the Nazis because of his scholarship that criticized the government for "absolutizing" the state. As a professor (a Christian of Prussian parentage) and dean at the University of Frankfurt, he publicly defended Jewish and left-wing students at the same time demanding the expulsion of Nazi youths known for causing violence on campus. When he came to America, he taught at Union Theological Seminary and Columbia University, New York. He later also taught at Harvard and University of Chicago.

I have turned to Tillich for my study of money because of his theology of culture. This is his systematic attempt to use theological and philosophical skills and multidisciplinary perspectives to analyze forms of cultural existence. His method of theological-cultural analyses seeks to uncover how the structures and dynamics of culture are pervaded by religious meaning. Second, he would correlate the existential tensions and questions and ambiguities, creative and destructives forces, from such thoroughgoing analyses to theological concepts in order to formulate a religious response. His thought system is relevant to understanding the social practice of money because it enables one to see and lift up for investigation the *tension between structure and ecstasy* in the ambiguities of the monetary system. As he indicated in his book, *The Socialist Decision*,[15] the analysis of a religiocultural situation should attempt to bring to awareness the underlying values and principles that animate the situation, reveal its inner conflict, and are likely to lead it to a solution that lies within the symbols of religious (Christian) tradition. The animating power for the social practice of money is the typological-structural tension in the dynamics of money as an exchange medium which drives it toward a trinitarian structure of global trade and payment system.

Tillich's trinitarian thinking is informed and guided by what he calls the trinitarian principles or the three roots of trinitarian thinking.[16] The trinitarian symbolization for Tillich is not limited to the Christian understanding of Trinity but is a theological answer to existential questions relating to being, existence, and life which are not unique to Christians.[17] He posits that:

> One can distinguish at least three factors which have led to trinitarian thinking in the history of religious experience: first, the tension between the absolute and the concrete element in our ultimate concern; second, the symbolic application of the concept of life to the divine ground of being; and third, the threefold manifestation of God as creative power, as saving love, and as ecstatic transformation.[18]

For Tillich, these three principles (which he also calls roots) are not just for theological discussion; this is how reality is to be interpreted.[19] They are not inanimate abstractions or a mathematical identity between three and one but are dynamics of life. He believes the trinitarian symbols are the most inclusive answer to the questions implied in human predicaments.[20] For the Trinity has a *fundamentum in re*, a foundation in reality. As he puts it:

> These aspects [the three roots] are reflections of something real in nature of the divine for the religious experience and for the theological tradition. They are not merely different subjective ways of looking at the same thing. They have a *fundamentum in re*, a foundation in reality, however much the subjective side of man's experience may contribute. In this sense we can say that the trinitarian symbols are a religious discovery which had to be made, formulated, and defended. [21]

The three roots arise from tension in the development of the idea of God. The first tension is between the absolute and the concrete elements and arises because humans want concreteness in their ultimate concern which drives them to polytheistic structures, but the reaction of the absolute element (ultimacy) initiates a movement toward monotheistic structures. The need for balance between the concrete and the absolute drives them toward trinitarian structures. The Christian triune God is concrete monotheism, the affirmation of the living God in whom the ultimate and the concrete are united.[22]

The second root of Tillich's trinitarian monotheism is the symbolic application of the concept of life to the divine ground of being. Tillich argues that God must be conceived as life, a living being. For without this principle God would be a "dead identity." A living God, according to Tillich, must include an element of otherness or a form of non-being in his being. God (power of being-itself) embraces non-being (which belongs to finitude) and God is not threatened by it. The otherness (non-being) is not only within God, it is also between God and God's relationships to other centered selves or finite beings. "The Divine Life then would be the reunion of otherness with identity in an eternal 'process.' This consideration brought us to the distinction of God as ground, God as form, and God as act, a pretrinitarian formula which makes trinitarian thinking meaningful."[23] As will be shown below, this way of conceptualizing God as ground-form-act—the triad connection and dynamics—is useful for economic analysis. The ground-form-act triad, as will be shown in chapter 2 below, can be used to conceptualize production and exchange in an economy.

Tillich does not leave the explication of the second trinitarian principle at the abstract philosophical level. He brings it down to a very concrete, mundane level with his concept of life, which I find even to be more applicable to a robust conceptualization of money in the contemporary economy. He uses the term "life" in a way that it not only provides connection with the first and second roots of the trinitarian thinking, but it also helps us to understand money's character of simultaneously separating and uniting economic agents in the marketplace.[24] Tillich writes:

> Life is a process in which potential being becomes actual being. It is the actualization of the structural elements of being in their unity and in their tension. These elements move divergently and convergently in every life process: *they separate and unite simultaneously*. Life ceases in the moment of separation without reunion or of union without separation. Both complete identity and complete separation negate life. If we call God the "living God," we deny that he is a pure identity of being as being; and we also deny that there is a definite separation of being from being in him. We assert that he is the eternal process in which separation is posited and is overcome by reunion. In this sense, God lives. Few things about God are more emphasized in the Bible, especially in the Old Testament, than the truth that God is a living God. Most of the so-called anthropomorphisms of the biblical picture of God are expressions of his character as living. His actions, his passions, his remembrances and anticipations, his suffering and joy, his personal relations and his plans—all these make him a living God and distinguish him from the pure absolute, from being-itself (italics added).[25]

Tillich insists that the application of the concept of life to God is only done at the symbolic level because there are key distinctions between God and other lives. For instance, in God there is no distinction between potentiality and actuality, but the life of humans is a process in which potential being becomes actual being.[26] The symbol of "divine life" is applied to God only to indicate or imply that there is "an analogy between the basic structure of experienced life and the ground of being in which life is rooted."[27]

The manifestation of the divine ground of being in the appearance of Jesus as the Christ is the third root of trinitarian thinking. In more general terms, it is the principle of God's self-objectification whereby God manifests and reveals himself as "the inner movement of the divine life as an eternal separation from itself and return to itself."[28] This is about the element of form, the *logos*, in the symbolization or in the development of the idea of God. Tillich conceives this as introduction of the presence of the other and the overcoming of estrangement of otherness in the Divine Life. Overall, the third root refers to the creativity of the divine ground which gives form, meaning, and structure to the dynamic processes of life. It is the logical character of life.[29]

Tillich, though focusing on revelation, argues that in all attempts to understand human reality and events we must apply all three roots of the trinitarian thinking (the abysmal character, the spiritual character, and the logical character). He writes:

> If the abysmal character of the divine life is neglected, a rationalistic deism transforms revelation into information. If the logical character of the divine life is neglected, an irrationalistic theism transforms revelation into heteronomous subjection. If the spiritual character of the divine life is neglected, a history of revelation is impossible. The doctrine of revelation is based on a trinitarian interpretation of the divine life and its self-manifestation."[30]

It is germane to mention that my concern with Tillich's trinitarian thinking and with modeling (trinitarian modeling) structures the whole development of the study.

METHODOLOGICAL ISSUES: MODELING A
THEOLOGICAL APPROACH TO ECONOMICS

The primary methodological issue of our study is the attempt to combine Tillich's trinitarian principles with the social trinitarianism of Miroslav Volf [31] to forge a new look at the relational character of money. A creative synthesis of the ideas of the two theologians enables me to develop my arguments about the monetary system and monetary flows (not monetary stock or uses and stewardship of money[32]) better than either of them alone. The synthesis of Tillich (trinitarian principles) and Volf (perichoretic trinitarian theology) enables me to provide a theological model that is adequately supported and informed by a technical theory which shows that the logic and dynamics of the current monarchical currency system are moving toward trinitarian structures. This is not an approach usually taken by theologians and ethicists who use the doctrine of the Trinity in social analysis. Often their theological reflections on social issues are not supported by a technical theory which shows that the system or phenomenon they are analyzing has a built-in dialectics to move in the direction they are pointing out to us.

Beyond this consideration, I need to explicitly justify why I am using Volf alongside Tillich. According to Tillich, the resolution of the tension between the particular (concrete) and the universal (the abstract) in the idea of God led to the trinitarian monotheism. There is also a tension between universal (global vehicular currency) and particular (national currency) in the international monetary system. Tillich's trinitarian principles or "theory of the trinity"—when carefully and adeptly transposed into a model for reflecting on an international monetary system—is valuable in helping us to think through the dynamics of the objective trend of the global monetary system. However, there is a shortcoming in Tillich's theory. His falls short of telling us what to do once the tension is resolved—that is, when the idea of God has come to rest at trinitarian monotheism, what is then the nature of the ongoing relationship in the union (in the Trinity). Put differently, Tillich's does not give us the principles of coherence operating in such a communion. Tillich's theory of the trinity is about ontology, it is about the structure and dynamics of a certain monotheism without a theory of relation, a *logic*.[33] I do not only need to explain that the objective trend in the global currency system is leading to a single currency, but I also need to describe the nature of the relationship between currencies once we arrive there. This is where Volf's perichoretic ideas become useful for our study. Volf's doctrine of the trinity is a theory of the relation between the "parts" in the union (communion). The social trinitarianism that Volf advocates is principally about defining the logic (the theory of relation) peculiar to the triune God. Volf's theory of the trinity as exemplified in his theology of the church shows how the tension of the particular and the universal is resolvable in a concrete, static church situation. The value of my turn to Volf's theory is that it makes explicit the logical operations that I will be using in my monetary model that would otherwise remain implicit or opaque.

Now let me relate all of this to our concern with modeling, the move from theological vision to economic model. I need to note that one cannot just make the move to economic modeling with ontological conception alone (a la Tillich) without a "minimal theory of relation." The ontology of being, once you push it toward economic modeling of money as a social relation and to properly structuring notion of monetary situation at the global level, requires an engagement with a *logic*. Tillich's ontology by itself cannot articulate this logic. On the other hand, logic (theory of relation) alone is also not enough. How one organizes a given situation or defines a system of belongings is determined by the established ordering function internal to it. It is this combinatorial necessity, if you will, that has led me to Tillich and Volf, to integrate ontology and logic in the theo-philosophical dimension of this study. This choice, for me, is axiomatic—in the sense that it is a foundational move that guides and structures the nature and presentation of the arguments and deductions in this book.

As stated above, I will interpret the current global monetary system in ways that highlight the underlying values and principles that animate monetary relation, that highlight its inner conflict, and then show how one can address that inner conflict from the standpoint of a particular understanding of the dynamic relations of the triune God. Thus, I am using Tillich's trinitarian principles to clarify the basic ethical conflicts in the monetary system and to forge some ethical guidelines that point toward an alternative structure of relationships in the global trade and payment system.

Economic analyses often implicitly or explicitly presuppose norms and models, which assume, for example, that profit-maximization and competition provide sound bases for ordering society. Normative analysis has a legitimate and indeed necessary role to play in the global monetary policy process. The ethical guidelines discerned from the dynamic relations modeled in the triune God serve both evaluative and prescriptive purposes. The guidelines will be used to either evaluate the normative properties of the current global monetary system or recommend courses of action as an input into collective decision-making process and economic models.

My attempt to use the model of the triune God as a perspective on the monetary system is not just a heuristic device. It is a significant and alternative way of thinking about the structures (current or re-imagined) of the global financial architecture and acquiring a resourceful template for translating the immanent processes of international monetary system into ethical principles. In this way I avoid, according to Bernard Lonergan, the "social ethicists' tendency to be content with 'vague moral imperatives' instead of figuring out moral precepts from the immanent intelligibility of economic processes."[34]

Of course, one does not proceed directly from the observation of economic flows and processes to ethical theory without the critical aid of models. Models like the Trinity show us how we can lift up the activities, processes, and relationships between nations in the international monetary system for one possible interpretation of global social relations. By juxtaposing our familiar and conventional understanding of the monetary system with the unfamiliar and unconventional trinitarian model of monetary system I set two ways of being in the economic world in tension with each other. The juxtaposition manifests the tension between the current acceptable modes of nations relating to one another in the global monetary system and a possible new way that can be imagined. The model of the triune God provides us with structure and insight into the unknown and unfamiliar alternative to the current monetary system, enables us to investigate its immanent processes, and also suggests new ways of talking about it and influencing attitudes toward it. And by this creative re-imagination we may constitute, according to Lonergan, "an ethos that at once subtly and flexibly provides concrete premises and norms for practical decisions."[35]

The triune model of money does not only serve a constructive purpose. As long as we do not make the illegitimate move of identifying the global monetary system with the Trinity (as we are wont to do with the use of metaphors in theological discourse, if we are not careful), the juxtaposition enables us to critique the current system and press it toward greater justice and equality. Every theological model, as theologian Sallie McFague, states is always a judgment of similarity and difference between two worlds or thoughts. It is shot through with the tension of the "is and is not." To think of "this" as "that," that is, to think of monetary system in terms of a model of Trinity, is to become "less comfortable in the world, aware of the difference between things as they are and things as they ought to be."[36]

I am aware of such difference in the global monetary system. The monetary relationship between the advanced countries and the poor, developing countries—in other words between the power of the advanced economies and that of the poor countries—is *dualistic* and *asymmetrical*. The question that arises now is this: In what models should we re-conceive of advanced economies' currencies which are related to those of poor countries in a *unified* and *interdependent* way? What I am doing in this study is to critique and contrast the monarchical imperial-currency model of the global monetary system with a perichoretic trinitarian model of the global monetary system in an attempt to address the issues and crisis[37] of today's monetary system.[38] I am not claiming that the trinitarian model is the only viable way to re-imagine today's global monetary system. Other experiments with other theological models are appropriate and are indeed necessary for a richer understanding of the monetary system.[39]

What is, indeed, the motivation for turning to an ethical model in trying to understand the monetary system? I will soon show that various models are often deployed and used by economists themselves and that now I am meeting them with another kind of model for consideration, namely one informed by trinitarian thinking.

The use of models is widespread in the social sciences, especially in economics. As the German economist and philosopher, Julian Reiss puts it:

> Social scientists pursue a wide variety of different ends with their model-building practices. To name a few, data models are built for measuring complex social phenomena; forecasting models are built for predicting the future values of target variables of interest; explanatory models are built for gaining a deeper understanding of phenomena of interest; policy models are built for analyzing the likely effects of intervention.[40]

Models in general seek to explain by identifying a pattern of relationships that pertain to the whole economic system or parts of it. Economists whether in academe or on Wall Street create theoretical models by tracing analogy between the structure of certain observable behaviors they want to explain and structure of another phenomenon or behavior they are familiar with.[41] It is believed that when the definitions and assumptions that go into a model are realistic the performance of the model often mirror the economic system in a simple form.

Let me give an actual example of modeling in economics. Economists explain the movements of stock prices by drawing an analogy between stocks and molecules. They posit that variation in security prices is similar to the random movement of molecules and they argue that the behavioral model of molecules represents the behavior of any group of stocks in an efficient stock market. They call this model the "random walk" or "Brownian motion." Since the mathematics of random movement shows that the path of movement of molecules cannot be predicted, the economists also go on to say movement of stock or security prices are not predictable.[42] They argue that investors take into account all public information relating to the securities in valuing them. Put differently, it means all relevant information is impounded into the price of financial assets. This means that only the radically new can affect prices and this by definition is not knowable in advance. Such bold assertions are made with languages that have strong religious or theological undertones. For instance, Paul Samuelson, the first U.S. economist to win the Nobel Prize in economics science wrote:

> We would expect people in the marketplace, in pursuit of avid and intelligent self-interest, to take account of those elements of future events that in a probability sense may be *discerned* to be casting their *shadows* before them. (Because past events cast *their* shadows after them, *future* [coming] *events can be said to cast their shadows before them*).[43] (italics added, except "their")

In general, the nature of modeling (and thinking) money, valuation and prices in economics is future oriented. In addition, I would say it is "theological and eschatological." I plan to support this assertion by looking at a possible intersection of the doctrine of eschatology and monetary (financial) economics: the discounted cashflow model, arguably the most popular monetary valuation method in economics.

Money in a capitalist system is always a good place to talk about eschatology. Money—value of assets and liabilities—is always "eschatological in its structuring," that is, "the present is created from the future."[44] The value of assets or liabilities in the market system depends on anticipated flows of income, anticipated returns, promises of expansion in an imagined better future. Asset allocation decisions (deployment or withdrawal from the market) are always on the basis of projections about value and income flows from assets in the future. Yet when this imagined future arrives the value of the asset would still be based on expectations of what it will be in a further imagined future. Capital, as if, is trapped in a web of eschatological expectation of a better future—a being that is eternally becoming.[45] Thus the British theologian Philip Goodchild aptly observed:

> Capital is not merely a flow because it is always an anticipation of an imagined future—whether we are concerned with speculation or credit, it is always an anticipated rate of return that determines how much there will be. What there is now is dependent upon what we believe there will be: our eschatology determines our mode of being, whether one adopts the Enlightenment eschatology of perpetual progress that is essential to economic growth, the American eschatology of creating the kingdom of God on earth by force, the Augustinian eschatology of human imperfection supplemented by divine grace, or the environmentalist eschatology of imminent apocalypse. Once credit is linked to fiat, an eschatology is capable of calling matters into being.[46]

Let us deepen our understanding of this connection between the eschatology of money and biblical eschatology. After my M.B.A. from Columbia University's Business School in New York City, I worked as an investment banker on Wall Street and one of the things I did for years was develop valuation models for assets and companies in the process of acquisition or merger. The most scientific and artful technique used and still in use on the Street is the Discounted Cashflow Model (DCF). Under this methodology, the value of an asset is a function of its projected stream of net cashflows, dividends from time, t_1 to t_n . . . perpetuity. (The projection is based on probabilistic readings of the future state of a firm's market, economy, marginal tax rate, just to name a few.) The sum of the stream is then discounted to the present, t_0, by the appropriate discount (interest or return) rate. The resulting value is called the present value and it is taken as the monetary value of the given asset, stock, bond, or corporation at t_0 (time zero, today).

If one stepped back and looked at this combination of mathematics and economic reasoning that stands behind the projection of the income stream and the whole DCF model with an eye of a philosopher, instead of that of banker or economist, this is what one will see. Complicated economic systems (firm to industry to economy to world to market) give rise to emergent cashflows, financial "properties" which are captured as values (quantitative numbers representing money, some aspect of the flux of production and consumption genie captured in a bottled tagged "asset" or "security"). These values, discounted cashflows, "supervene" on the economic systems that give rise to them. And because those who work on the models try as much as possible to make sure that the "properties" and the "systems" are related as much as possible (after all, this is what good modeling or projection is about), it is proper to say that if the economic systems are re-created or repeated exactly in t_{n+1}, an identical cashflow would be ipso facto re-created in exactly the same way. Nothing would be lost.[47]

There is a process of sociality in the way the periodic projections or forecasts are related to one another and as a whole to economy. Each cashflow (that is, cashflow of a particular time, t) is part of a series of creativity. The whole is a "series of moments of concrescence or creativity, each one ending and bequeathing the creative task to the next generation of occasions [projections are accumulative—forecast at time t_{n+1} is $t_{n\ cashflow}$ (1+growth rate, r]"[48] and thus every successive stage includes those preceding it. This is not all. The cashflows as a whole are related to the economy in this way. Each cashflow (say at t_n) "experiences" the economy (the ground of the projected cashflow at t_{n+1}) as an other, "comprehends" within itself the economy's "response to it and then internalizes this response into itself, and thereby becoming more than it was before."[49] This is a kind of "self-reflexivity in communion" that mimics many areas of "subjectivity" (a la Hegel) in human existence or fundamental sociality.

Now that I have shown the importance of imaginative models in economics for understanding economic and monetary systems, I will turn to show how ethical modeling is deployed in this book. It is important to remind the reader that the goal of doing this is to forge a path that can move ethicists and economists from dualistic and asymmetrical models of the global monetary system to one that is unified and interdependent.

NATURE AND NECESSITY OF ETHICAL MODELING OF THE GLOBAL MONETARY SYSTEM

In this book I will be using the knowledge of the tension between the concrete and universal elements in the idea of God as developed by Tillich, and the insights that I discern from the perichoretic understanding of the relationship and relatedness in the Godhead as developed by Volf, to inform the building of a model that would help me to re-imagine an alternative to the current global monetary system. The *unity-in-difference* deriving from the dynamic relations of the triune God provides me with a fruitful and suggestive way of reflecting about the structuring principle of global monetary architecture. The model I am developing is important not because it gives a picture of what the monetary system is like *in se*, from which all else emanates, but rather because it specifies how the various aspects of the global trade and payment system might hang together if we are to encourage the fullness of participation and justice in the comity of nations.[50]

It may be asked: Why do you not just indicate the religious symbols that correlate with the existential questions, and if possible then draw out some ethical principles from such a mutually critical correlation to guide policy actions? Why bother to translate ethical principles in a theological framework into concrete proposal or policies? It was the indefatigable philosopher Alasdair MacIntyre who once said that "we have not fully understood the claims of any moral philosophy until we have spelled out what its social embodiment would be."[51]

In addition, the modeling of the international monetary system as a support for my ethical arguments and reasoning in this book is germane for another reason. I want to "liberate" "goods internal" to the social practice of money from their submersion under and subservience to "external goods." MacIntyre defined a social practice as:

> any coherent and complex form of socially established cooperative human activity through which goods internal to that form of activity are realized in the course of trying to achieve those standards of excellence which are appropriate to, and partially definitive of, that form of activity, with the result that human powers to achieve excellence, and human conceptions of the ends and goods involved, are systematically extended.[52]

In pressing MacIntyre's concept of social practice to our use there are two crucial notions that we must bear in mind. First, there is the notion of goods that are internal to a form of activity and external goods. "Internal goods are those that can be realized only by participating in the activity well, as judged by its standards of excellence."[53] External goods, in contrast, include prestige, status, honor, and power and can be achieved without excellence in the activity in question and when achieved are always some individual's property or possession. "External goods are therefore characteristically objects of competition in which *there must be losers as well as winners*. Internal goods are indeed the outcome of competition to excel, but it is characteristic of them that their achievement is *good*

for the whole community who participate in the community" (italics added).[54]
In order to illustrate this, MacIntyre gave the example of chess-playing.
Goods such as prestige, status, and money are externally and contingently
attached to the game. Internal goods include excellence in performance
and experience of participating in the practice of chess-playing.

I think that the *goods internal* to the social practice of money include the
distribution of work and its rewards equitably across space and time and
the giving to every citizen the opportunity to raise her human capability
and freedom so she can fully participate in economic activities. Participation has to involve not only individuals, but also regions and nations.
Money, monetary structures, and monetary policies have to spread development across geographic spaces. The current *imperial, monarchical currency* system does not equitably spread development around, within, and
among countries. People in the areas deprived of dynamic development
are led to the areas of surplus—and this might very well explain the migration of Global South workers.[55] The logic and dynamics of underdevelopment of economies and migration of labor from the poor countries
to the rich economies are intertwined with the logic and dynamics of imperial currencies that generate discriminating spatial demographics. We
will see in chapter 6 how the imperial currency regime corrals and channels savings of the world (of even poor countries) to the global cities like
New York, Frankfurt, Tokyo, and London.

It is obvious that the pursuit of goods internal to the social practice of
money in the global economy is threatened by goods that are external to
it. In other words, the external goods defined by the powerful nations prevent pursuit of internal goods by members of poorer countries. The whole
issue of managing money in a more just way, both at local and international levels, is often related to how to subordinate external to internal
goods. "The relation between goods internal to a practice and goods external to it tends to be morally problematic."[56]

We can illustrate this moral problem by examining international banking practice. The internal goods of banking include excellence in technical
banking and marketing skills and the financing of economic development. The external goods, such as profits and power which are sought in
order to stay ahead of competitors, lead to several moral problems. In the
1970s and 1980s many poor countries were loaded with massive loans so
that bank officers could increase their loan portfolios as their banks com-
peted for market share. The result is that many years after many countries
in the Global South are carrying heavy debt burdens. Susan George in her
article, "How the Poor Develop the Rich,"[57] revealed that between 1982
and 1990 poor debtor countries in the South transferred $6.5 billion in in-
terest payments alone to creditors in the North each and every month for
108 months. Debt has become, even if originally unintended, a "prof-

itable" enterprise for financial houses in the North. This is so because the poor countries cannot pay off the principal and are just making interest payments. The hapless Global South countries have been put in debt peonage.[58]

Someone may argue that my whole discussion of internal and external goods in the social practice of money presupposes without warrant that there are goods internal to the social practice of money. Such an interlocutor may argue in this way: Money being the chief representative of market capitalism, which strives in cutthroat competition for maximum gain at the expense of any virtue cannot have any intrinsic virtue in its practice. I have three responses to the interlocutor. First, in the Tillichian viewpoint of this book I will state that money may be demonic, but it is not a pure negative and destructive evil. Tillich once wrote that the purpose of understanding social demonry is to liberate the good in it:

> Only when this dialectics is understood, is a fundamentally correct attitude in social affairs possible. Otherwise we find either the will for improvement in progressive attitude or will for preservation in the conservative. The first sees everywhere material which at some time or other will be formed in correspondence with the ideal; the second sees everywhere the unconquerable sinfulness which renders a decisive change impossible. The perception of the demonic dialectics leads one beyond this contrast, and to the recognition of something contra-positive which is to overcome, neither progress, nor through mere revolution, but through creation and grace. It leads at the same time to the comprehension of the particular demonry at every point in society so that it may be isolated and opposed. The battle against the demonries of a time becomes an unavoidable, religious-political duty. Political activity gains the deeper meaning of religious activity. Religious activity gains the concreteness of a struggle against the principalities and powers.[59]

This book was partly motivated by my desire to understand the peculiar dialectics of the great monetary structures and forces that frame existence and actively confront Africans and their economies in their task of seducing development both from their environments and from the international economy in a fallen world. My interest is not only to understand the "what is" of the monetary situation, but also to forge policies and ways of overcoming the social demonry of international money—all to better grasp what "ought to be."

Let us now go to my second response. Many twenty-first-century ethicists and moral philosophers may have forgotten that eighteen-century Adam Smith, the moral philosopher who made the concept of *invisible hand* popular, was, by means of it, pointing to some internal goods in entrepreneurial competition for profits. The point of the concept was that as business persons compete, in spite of their search for maximum profits, they might excel at meeting the public good. Smith argued that the satisfaction of the public good is intrinsic in the whole market competition. He wrote in *The Wealth of Nations*:

> It is not from the benevolence of the butcher, the brewer, or the baker, that we expect our dinner, but from their regard to their own interest.
> [E]very individual necessarily labors to render the annual revenue of the society as great as he can. He generally, indeed, neither intends to promote the public interest, nor knows how much he is promoting it. . . . He intends only his own security; and by directing that industry in such a manner as its produce may be of the greatest value, he intends only his own gain, and he is in this, as in many other cases, led by an *invisible hand* to promote an end which was not part of his intention. Nor is it always the worse for the society that it was no part of it. By pursuing his own interest he frequently promotes that of the society more effectually than when he really intends to promote it. (italics added)[60]

Adam Smith's notion of the invisible hand is at the heart of modern understanding of market. He is deservedly famous for the phrase, "invisible hand" in his 1776 book, *The Wealth of Nations*. What is rarely recognized is the origin of this idea is traceable to John Calvin and Saint Augustine of Hippo. Unlike many scholars, I am tracing the source of the idea of invisible hand to both Calvin and Augustine rather than to Calvin alone. What many have not recognized is that there are two grand ideas in the image of the invisible hand. First, there is the idea of a kind of "providence" and self-organization which is traceable to Calvin. The other idea of harnessing and transforming passions and vices into something constructive that works toward the general welfare which, according to Albert O. Hirschman, is traceable to Augustine.[61]

Calvin had written about God's providence sustaining order in the world and referred to it as an invisible hand. Smith translated this image of invisible hand into economic language.[62] Instead of the world being organized by God, an external agent imposing order from without, Smith reasoned that the market is self-organizing because of the automatic harmony in the relationship between agents in the market. For Smith, order grows from within, endogenous and spontaneous. Each human actor pursuing her own interest serves the public good. This is not the only way Smith developed his economic version of the divine providence. "Just as traditional Calvinist theology distinguishes general and special providence, so Smith draws a distinction between the *general* tendency toward [market] equilibrium and *special* cases of equilibrium. The overall framework Smith established continues to set the terms for much of analysis today."[63]

Smith appropriated Calvin's idea first through aesthetic.[64] He had used the image of the invisible hand in his *The Theory of Moral Sentiments* (1759).

In the section, "Of the beauty which the appearance of UTILITY bestows upon all production of art, and the extensive influence of this species of Beauty," he wrote:

> They are led by an invisible hand to make nearly the same distribution of the necessaries of life, which would have made, had the earth been divided into equal portions among all its inhabitants, and thus without intending it, without knowing it, advance the interest of the society, and afford the means to the multiplication of the species. When Providence divided the earth among few lordly masters, it neither forgot nor abandoned those seemed to have been left out in the partition. . . . The same principle, the love of system, the same regard to beauty of order, of art and contrivance, frequently serves to recommend those institutions which tend to promote the public welfare.[65]

Recently, Lisa Hill has joined a rising chorus of scholarly voices to argue that the image of the invisible hand not only has a theological origin but expresses Smith's hidden theology. Anthony Waterman in 2002 put forward the suggestion that Smith could be read as offering a kind of Augustinian theodicy of the market. According to him, Smith's idea could be interpreted as thus: just like God put governments in place to restrain sin, the institution of the market also restrains sin.[66]

Hirschman traces the origin of the image of the invisible hand to St. Augustine. The fourth-century theologian cautiously spoke of the possibility of using one vice to check another—the desire for wealth could be suppressed by the desire for glory, love of praise. In the hands of later writers, the cautiousness was thrown overboard and the love of glory was purported to have "redeeming social value." It was in this appropriation and adaptation of Augustine's idea that image of the invisible hand emerged in the medieval time.

The points to note here in linking the idea of invisible hand as developed by Smith to Augustine are these: as stated earlier there are two grand ideas in the popular image of the invisible hand. There is one idea of "providence" and self-organization, and the other idea of harnessing and transforming passions and vices into something constructive that works toward the general welfare. What Hirschman is saying is that the second idea is traceable to Augustine. The early Christian scholar had condemned the three human drives or passions of lust for money and possessions, lust for power (*libido dominandi*), and sexual lust. But he noted that there could be circumstances when one vice could be used to check another. For instance, in the love of fatherland the desire of money and possessions may be suppressed for the strong desire or vice of praise and glory. This cautiously stated simple idea was taken far beyond his teachings and the striving for possessions, honor, or glory made the touchstone of public virtues and greatness in the hands of the spokespersons for what Hirschman calls "the chivalric, aristocratic ideal." Hence, noting the role of the great medieval scholar Montesquieu in this transformation of the Augustinian limited endorsement of glory-seeking, Hirschman writes:

> In fact, the idea of an "Invisible Hand"—of a force that makes men pursuing their private passions conspire unknowingly toward the public good—was formulated in connection with the search for glory, rather than with the desire for money, by Montesquieu. The pursuit of honor a in monarchy, so he says, "brings life to all the parts of the body politic;" as a result, "it turns out that everyone contributes to the general welfare while thinking that he works for his own interests."[67]

The Princeton University economist's point is that it was in this "adulterated" form that the idea of the invisible hand (rather one of its two component parts) reached the eighteen century and got incorporated into Smith's thinking. One does not need to state that it is difficult to prove ancestry or genealogy of ideas as they move from one period to another.

Be that as it may, Hirschman also noted that Blaise Pascal and some of his Jansenist contemporaries also anticipated Smith. They argued that self-love in spite of being sinful is workable and can hold society together better than charity.[68] The point I am trying to make is that there is *some* internal good redeemable in market competition, however distorted it might appear today or hidden in the form of market theodicy.

Now this is my third and last response to the interlocutor. It has been a well-known fact in economics that structures are important for the functioning of capitalist markets in order for them to achieve the good internal to them. Economists decry monopoly capitalism for its distortion of market structures, arguing that it presents a serious departure from perfect competition. Similarly, collusion between producers to fix prices and restrict output is considered socially unacceptable, unethical, and unjust because it hinders the proper functioning of the market. The antitrust laws in the United States were enacted, among other considerations, to reduce the concentration of excessive powers in the hands of relatively few firms, promote competition, and limit monopoly. One of the most famous of the antitrust laws and the first of the federal government actions to limit monopolies is the Sherman Acts passed in 1890 and amended in 1974 and is codified in 15 U.S.C.§1 through 15 U. S. C.§7. The thrust of the 1890 Act lies in following two sections:

> Sec.1. Every contract, combination in the form of trust or otherwise, or conspiracy, in restraint of trade or commerce among the several states or with foreign nations, is hereby declared to be illegal. Every person who shall make any such contract or engage in any such combination or conspiracy shall be deemed guilty of a misdemeanor . . .

Sec. 2. Every person who shall monopolize, or attempt to monopolize or combine or conspire with any other person or persons, to monopolize any part of trade or commerce among the several states, or with foreign nations shall be deemed of a misdemeanor.

With the 1974 amendment the violations were made felonies rather than misdemeanors.

It is important not to lose sight of the fact that the whole purpose of the body of antitrust legislations in the United States is to protect the structures of the American economy as informed by some imagined nature of perfect competition. So when I undertake to reimagine the structures of the global financial architecture I am in line with this venerable tradition of protecting the system for greater efficiency and equity. Good behavior is somewhat dependent on good structures or polity. Aristotle imagined a polity that would support his virtue ethics. University of Chicago's 1982 Nobel laureate in economic science, George Stigler, once said "any industry which does not have a competitive structure will not have competitive behavior."[69] In addition, I am interested in forging an alternative to the current structures of the global monetary system because of my sense of justice. For me the praxis of justice in the global economy, and for that matter national economy, is about drawing all nations and persons (poor and rich, powerful and not-so powerful) to share in a living communion by removing or challenging structures that thwart relationship of equality and participation.

NOTES

1. This phrase is well described in chapter 6. It refers to the current global monetary exchange system whereby three national currencies (dollar, euro, and yen) dominate the global trade and payment system to the disadvantage of almost all other countries. They constitute the international currencies of exchange and savings. Almost all foreign exchange reserves of central banks or nations are kept in assets denominated in these currencies. The economically dominant countries/bloc that have these three currencies collect a form of tax, called seigniorage, from every user of their currencies, which is practically the whole world. This tax and its unfair nature will be amply examined in chapter 6.

2. This study may appear to some as too ambitious in its scope. It obviously requires a systematic explication and knowledge of multiple areas of theology and social sciences. The very nature of money and its significant place in contemporary society demand that any serious theoethical analysis of money draw from many academic disciplines. This necessity carries its own risk. The analyst may be carried too far afield such that comprehensiveness and complexity, rather than revealing truth, may just conceal or complicate it. In order to avoid this obvious pitfall, I have carefully developed a rubric that will bring order to the various discourses at work in this book.

3. See Mark C. Taylor, *Confidence Games: Money and Markets in a World Without Redemption* (Chicago: University of Chicago, 2004); Philip Goodchild, "Capital and Kingdom: An Eschatological Ontology," in *Theology and the Political: The New Debate*, ed. Creston Davies, John Milbank, and Slavoj Zizek (Durham, NC: Duke University Press, 2005), 127–52; Goodchild, "Debt, Epistemology and Ecotheology," *Ecotheology* 9, no. 2 (2004):151–77; Kathryn Tanner, *Economy of Grace* (Minneapolis, MN: Fortress, 2005); and Craig M. Gay, *Cash Values: Money and the Erosion of Meaning in Today's Society* (Grand Rapids, MI: William B. Eerdmans Co., 2004); W. Taylor Stevenson, *Soul and Money: A Theology of Wealth* (New York: Episcopal Church Center, 1991); and Jacob Needleman, *Money and the Meaning of Life* (New York: Doubleday, 1991).

4. Tanner is the only one that asks this question, but there is more force and insight in her question than in her answer.

5. A hyphen, unlike the plus sign, connects and separates two words.

6. One of the ways the idea of money as something that attaches and cuts came to me as through a reflection on and the working out of philosophical ideas (proverbs) of Kalabari women (of the Niger Delta region of Nigeria) about money that I imbibed as a boy in the Kalabari town of Abonnema. There are two proverbs about money that I heard the women of Kalabari say often: "igbigi oyibo and igbigi ane ma toru ogiye." They mean, "Money is a man" and "Money is a double-edged knife" respectively. They have always fascinated me because of the paradoxicality and boldness of the imagery in them. In the traditional patriarchal cultural context man, maleness is synonymous with domination and domineering. Maleness stands for defense and the ability to accomplish a lot. Man is also a metaphor (synecdoche) for the male reproductive organ that is always considered an ambiguous object in female conversation. The phallus is a source of creativity (semen and pregnancy), but it is also a source of fouling matter. Money goes between the sublime and the excremental. Like the phallus its creativity creates and distributes work and prosperity. Urination brings something out of our interior, exposes innermost intimacy, and also key destructive tendencies. Here one can see why money is considered a double-edged knife. This metaphor in Kalabari refers to a person or object that can cut or attach, nurture or destroy, support or undermine, love or hate, loyal or disloyal all at the same time. The male reproductive organ is a channel of pleasure and if given a different circumstance it can be bludgeoning instrument of violence and rape.

7. Hannah Arendt made this metaphor of table famous in her book, *The Human Condition* (Chicago: University of Chicago Press, 1958), 52, 59–60. For an extension of Arendt's idea to public law, see Antoine M. Hol, "Adjudication and the Public Realm: An Analysis based on the work of Hannah Arendt," *Utrecht Law Review* 1, no. 2 (December 2005): 40–55.

8. More precisely, money is εκ-*static*. This means there is nothing private about money. Money is by definition, as we will see later in this book, "ex-centric, directed outward, beyond the limits" of a merely private possession and use (what I am quoting is from Peter Hallward in another context. See his *Badiou: A Subject to Truth* [Minneapolis: University of Minneapolis Press, 2003], 129). This notion of relationality, collectivization or anti-privatization should not be construed to

mean or imply uniformity. There are clearly many different ways of relating or maintaining connexion to the collective dimension of the monetary system.

9. There is another way we can present the dual tendencies of money: simultaneously forging participation and posing a threat of exclusion from participation. Money has two components in a fundamental sense: *power* and *wonder*. The social practice of money is *power* as it enables us to acquire power over properties, appropriate them, and take them into possession. The more money you have the more things or properties you can conquer and dominate. In fact, the Bible rightly says money is a defense. But money does not only defend, it also throws a person into a belonging, into a fellowship and forces one to open oneself for others and give oneself to its overwhelming flow that connects and draws all persons into mutual participation. In this sense, money in modern society—money as a social practice—works to overcome possessive, isolated, monad-individualism. (In actual fact, in the sense of money as a social relation—an idea we are going develop in subsequent chapters—isolated, monad-individualism is not really an option.) The power of money—the freedom of disposal over property, the liberty to act as a center of activity, the "I"—can only be understood in the light of the "other." The "I" does not merely decree and dispose, it must also receive and adapt. Money is a social relation—a social practice. By and through the social practice of money we all participate in the lives of one another. The person, even the richest one among us, participating in the social practice of money cannot transform it into his or her property but is rather forced to be a participant in it. As Otto A. Piper puts it, "there is no private money. As a means of exchange, money has its place [only] within a community." See his "That Strange Thing Money," *Theology Today* 16, no. 2 (July 1959): 219. Money, thus, confers fellowship and the social practice of money is participation in *wonder*. It is wonder because as Jurgen Moltmann states, "in wonder the subject opens himself up to the overwhelming impressions." See his *The Trinity and the Kingdom* (Minneapolis: Fortress Press, 1993), 5.

10. These differences occur at least in three ways. Market or voluntary exchange exists because each partner in a bargain gives up something she values less for another thing that she values more at the point of exchange. Second, the buyer and the seller attribute different values to the particular goods in exchange because of differences in personal preferences. Third, the whole equilibrating movement by and through which price formation occurs depends on differences in valuation of buyers and sellers. There is always someone trying to sell short or long a good (service). If all should become sellers or buyers at the same time no exchange can occur.

11. As a general comment, I need to say that it cannot be overstated that my use of the Trinity is metaphorical because, otherwise, it can easily appear that my argument moves toward an idolatry, that is, the equation of money with the Trinity.

12. In this work, the word "Trinity" (and some other familiar religious words) would often be referred to as a symbol. It is necessary for me to explain how the word "symbol" is used in this book, especially for those who are not familiar with theological language. A religious symbol is a word or thing that participates in and signifies what transcends its own particularities and the world of its users. Theologians see the word or thing as standing for something else. When we

ordinarily say God is a father, the symbol of father does not merely point to a "spiritual father," but we are really and truly saying that God is father. But for the ologians, in recognizing that father is a symbol applied to God, they also acknowledge the relevant distance between image and reality. They are also indicating that when we transfer our earthly linguistic and social concept of father to God, Being-Itself, it cannot fully express who and what God is—even the best model of fatherhood on earth does not and cannot approximate what fatherhood is in God and how it is expressed by God. Simply, by symbols theologians mean earthly, temporal words that point to the transcendental dimension of God. These words or terms can never truly and fully capture the attributes or characteristics of God that they are calling us to observe; hence they are called symbols. "Trinity" is a symbol not because God is a symbol or myth, but because our human terms cannot really portray who God is, the one who is the source of all being and value.

13. Paul Tillich, *Systematic Theology*, vol. 3, *Life and the Spirit, History and the Kingdom of God* (Chicago: University of Chicago Press, 1965), 283–85, 421–22; Tillich, *Systematic Theology*, vol. 1, *Reason and Revelation, Being and God* (Chicago: University of Chicago Press, 1951), 157, 221, 228, 241–43, 252.

14. For a discussion of Tillich's influence and life, see Mark Kline Taylor, *Paul Tillich: The Theologian of Boundaries* (Minneapolis, MN: Fortress Press, 1991); and Wilhelm and Marion Pauck, *Paul Tillich: His Life and Thought*, vol. 1, *Life* (New York: Harper & Row, 1976).

15. Paul Tillich, *The Socialist Decision*, trans. Franklin Sherman (New York: Harper & Row, 1977), 71.

16. It is germane to note that Tillich is not always very consistent in his use of the phrase, "the trinitarian principles." Sometimes he refers to them as aspects of the divine life or moments within the process of the divine life. When used in this sense, which somewhat differs from the use as roots of trinitarian thinking in the history of religious experience, he is referring to three moments. They are first the *Abyss*, the principle of vitality in the divine life; second, *Form* (the *Logos*)—the abyss-manifesting form. The first has the polar ontological elements of individualization, dynamics, and freedom; the second has participation, form, and destiny. The third principle is the Spirit that eternally unites the Abyss and Form, the first and second principles, such that balance between dynamics and form is never disrupted. The positing and return of the first and second principles in the divine life is simultaneous. But it must also be noted that all the uses of the principles are related, if one is patient enough to examine the changing contexts of their usage. Abyss is related to the first root of trinitarian thinking, form ties in with the third root and spirit as the ecstatic unity of first two principles points to the simultaneity of life, the second root. As Tillich puts it in a critique of Nietzsche, "we must say that God is living because he is Spirit." Tillich, *Systematic Theology*, vol. 1, 245–51. For an excellent study of Tillich's thought on the Trinity see Ronald Bruce Maclennan, "The Doctrine of the Trinity in the Theology of Paul Tillich," unpublished PhD dissertation (Chicago: Lutheran School of Theology at Chicago, 1991).

17. See Tillich, *Systematic Theology*, vol. 3, 283–85. See also *Systematic Theology*, vol. 1, 251, where he declares that "the consideration of the trinitarian principles is not the Christian doctrine of the Trinity. It is a preparation for it, nothing more. . . . The trinitarian principles appear whenever one speaks meaningfully of the liv-

ing God." It is important to note that in spite of this assertion he emphasizes the Christological focus of the third root. He considers the saving love, the third root, as "the manifestation of the divine ground of being in the appearance of Jesus as Christ." *Systematic Theology,* vol. 3, 285.

18. Tillich, *Systematic Theology,* vol. 3, 283.

19. There are other functions Tillich wanted his principles to serve. They are to serve not only to inspire individuals and societies to work through conflict arising from creative and destructive forces, but also to inspire the process of spiritual transformation of societies. For Tillich God is an ecstatic union of opposites. Paul Tillich, *The Courage to Be* (New Haven, CT: Yale University Press, 2000), 34; *Systematic Theology,* vol. 1, 251. For a discussion of these other purposes behind Tillich's formulation of the trinitarian principles see Randall B. Bush, *Recent Ideas of Divine Conflict: The Influences of Psychological and Sociological Theories of Conflict upon the Trinitarian Theology of Paul Tillich and Jürgen Moltmann* (San Francisco: Mellen Research University Press, 1991), 71–143.

20. Tillich, *Systematic Theology,* vol. 3, 285.

21. Tillich, *Systematic Theology,* vol. 3, 283.

22. Tillich, *Systematic Theology,* vol. 1, 221, 228.

23. Tillich, *Systematic Theology,* vol. 3, 284.

24. In chapter 5, I will undertake a sociotheological analysis of money using this second principle as my organizing framework.

25. Tillich, *Systematic Theology,* vol. 1, 241–42.

26. Tillich, *Systematic Theology,* vol. 1, 243.

27. Tillich, *Systematic Theology,* vol. 1, 156.

28. According to Tillich, "the doctrine of the Trinity does not affirm the logical nonsense that three is one and one is three; it describes in dialectical terms the inner movement of the divine life as an eternal separation from itself and return to itself." *Systematic Theology,* vol. 1, 251; for this quote see p. 56.

29. Tillich, *Systematic Theology,* vol. 3, 285, 421–22.

30. Tillich, *Systematic Theology,* vol. 1, 157.

31. Miroslav Volf, *After Our Likeness: The Church as the Image of the Trinity* (Grand Rapids, MI: William B. Eerdmans Co., 1998).

32. The stewardship approach to money focuses too narrowly on rules for distributing surplus money or wealth and little or nothing on the process of producing money. Theology in this way has been banished from the economic scene and allowed to only occasionally come in, when the money has been made and reinvested, to work in the severely limited sphere of helping their owners to spend it charitably. See M. Douglas Meeks, *God the Economist: The Doctrine of God and Political Economy* (Minneapolis, MN: Fortress Press, 1989), 20–21; Andrew Carnegie, "Wealth," *North American Review* 148, no. 391 (June 1889): 653–64; and Max L. Stackhouse, *Public Theology and Political Economy: Stewardship in Modern Society* (Grand Rapids, MI: William B. Eerdmans Co., 1987).

33. Please note that I am using the word *logic* in the fashion of Alain Badiou and Peter Hallward (see Hallward, *Badiou,* 294–95, 301–02). Logic here means the kind of relations that are permitted in a given universe. Logic describes what operations or relations are permissible by the orientation of a particular universe; what operations among elements, entities, or structures in a particular category can be

legitimately executed. In short, it means "the principle of coherence operating" in a universe (301). For instance, given a set of positive whole numbers the logic of permissible relations dictates what kind of operations (e.g., equation, subtraction, negation, sum, product, the exponentiation of one by another, etc.) is valid and can be recognized. In the complicated kinship system of a traditional society, logic or theory of relation tells its members, for instance, who can marry whom and who to avoid as a suitable partner. What the social trinitarian scholars are doing with the notion of perichoresis is defining and interpreting the perceived logical relations in the triune God. Is there equality or hierarchy, subordination, subjugation, or parity and mutual indwelling? Badiou has this to say: "I call 'logic' that which is a theory of relation as relation, relation between elements, between parts, etc" (295).

34. Frederick G. Lawrence, Patrick H. Byrne, and Charles C. Hefling Jr., "Introduction," in Bernard Lonergan, *Collected Works*, vol. 15, *Macroeconomic Dynamics: An Essay in Circulation Analysis* (Toronto: Lonergan Research Institute, 1999), lxxi.

35. Bernard Lonergan, *Insight: A Study of Human Understanding* (Toronto: Toronto University Press, 1992), 248.

36. Sallie McFague, *Metaphorical Theology: Models of God in Religious Language* (Philadelphia: Fortress Press, 1982), 51, 65.

37. By "issues and crisis," I mean the ambiguities and certain key destructive tendencies of money. I have carefully explained them in chapters 5 and 6.

38. What I am trying to accomplish here is different from Sallie McFague's project. She tries to develop models of God that are additions and alternatives to the classical, hierarchical, and monarchical model of God. But I am using an already developed model of God as a basis, as a root metaphor, to develop an alternative to the current imperial-currency model of the global monetary system. See McFague, *Models of God: Theology for an Ecological, Nuclear Age* (Philadelphia: Fortress, 1987); *Metaphorical Theology*.

39. In a sense, what I am doing in this book is akin to what theologians like Douglas Meeks, John Cobb, and Marion Grau did in using theology to provide alternative perspectives to key economic concepts, systems, and practices. See Meeks, *God the Economist*; Herman E. Daly and John B. Cobb Jr., *For the Common Good: Redirecting the Economy toward Community, the Environment, and Sustainable Future*, 2nd ed. (Boston: Beacon, 1994), and Marion Grau, *Of Divine Economy: Refinancing Redemption* (New York: T & T Clark, 2004).

40. Julian Reiss, "Explanatory Mechanism and the Aims of the Social Science," http://reiss.org/papers.html.

41. Mark Blaug, *The Methodology of Economics or How Economists Explain* (Cambridge: Cambridge University Press, 1992); Daniel Little, *Varieties of Social Explanation: An Introduction to the Philosophy of Social Sciences* (Boulder, CO: Westview Press, 1991); and Alexander Rosenberg, *Philosophy of Social Science* (Boulder, CO: Westview Press, 1995).

42. Peter L. Bernstein, *Capital Ideas: The Improbable Origins of Modern Wall Street* (New York: Free Press, 1992), 103–06; *Against the Gods: The Remarkable Story of Risk* (New York: John Wiley & Sons, 1996), 144–49, 200.

43. Paul A. Samuelson, "Proof that Properly Anticipated Prices Fluctuate Randomly," *Industrial Management Review* 6 (Spring 1965): 44.

44. This nature appears akin to life as conceived by Colin E. Gunton, *Father, Son and Holy Spirit: Toward a Fully Trinitarian Theology* (London: T & T Clark, 2003), 134–37. See also Wolfhart Pannenberg, "The God of Hope," *Basic Questions in Theology* 2 (1971), 234–49.

45. Alternatively, one can argue that money's being is not in its becoming. For the fact that it refuses to pass away (when the imagined future arrives the value of the asset would still be based on expectations of what it would yet be in a further imagined future), the being is in its coming. Value as conceived in valuation techniques of assets is always on the move and coming toward the asset owner. As the coming value, the present and past are set in the light of the future. Value (the present value of assets as calculated by the discounted cash flow method) "flows" out of the future into the present. It has the future in its being, so to speak with my tongue in cheek. For a theological play on the words, "coming" and "becoming" by Jürgen Moltmann, see his *The Coming of God: Christian Eschatology*, trans. Margaret Kohl (Minneapolis, MN: Fortress Press, 1996), 13, 23–24.

46. Goodchild, "Capital and Kingdom," 143.

47. Philip Clayton, "Eschatology as Metaphysics under the Guise of Hope," in *World without End: Christian Eschatology from a Process Perspective*, ed. Joseph A. Bracken, S.J. (Grand Rapids, MI: William B. Eerdmans Co., 2005), 140, n17.

48. Clayton, "Eschatology as Metaphysics," 143.

49. Clayton, "Eschatology as Metaphysics," 145.

50. I have borrowed Karen Kilby's peculiar phrasing for my use here. See Karen Kilby, "Perichoresis and Projection: Problems with the Doctrines of the Trinity," *New Blackfriars* 81, no. 956 (October 2000): 444.

51. Alasdair MacIntyre, *After Virtue* (Notre Dame, IN: University of Notre Dame Press, 1984), 23.

52. MacIntyre, *After Virtue*, 187.

53. Jeffrey Stout, *Ethics After Babel: The Languages of Morals and their Discontents* (Boston: Beacon Press, 1988), 267.

54. MacIntyre, *After Virtue*, 190–91.

55. Peter Alexander Egom, *NEPAD and the Common Good* (Lagos, Nigeria: Global Market Forum, 2004), 102.

56. Stout, *Ethics After Babel*, 272.

57. Susan George, "How the Poor Develop the Rich," in *The Post-Development Reader*, ed. Majid Rahnema with Victoria Bawtree (London: Zed Books, 1997), 207–13.

58. Susan George put the massive transfer of resources in perspective for us. Within the same period, 1982–1990, the total resources transfer flows to developing countries amounted to $927 billion compared to the total of $1,345 billion in debt service and principal repayments made by the developing countries. The monthly number for both interest and principal payments is $12.45 billion for each and every month for 108 months. "The income-outflow difference between $1,345 and $927 billion. . . is $418 billion in the rich countries' favor. For purposes of comparison, the U.S. Marshall Plan transferred $14 billion 1948 dollars to war-ravaged Europe, about $70 billion in 1991 dollars. Thus in the eight years from 1982 to 1990 the poor have financed six Marshall Plans for the rich through debt service alone." George, "How the Poor Develop the Rich," 209–10.

59. Paul Tillich, *The Interpretation of History* (New York: Charles Scribner's Sons, 1936), 115–16.

60. Adam Smith, *The Wealth of Nations*, Bantam House Classic Edition (New York: Random House, 2003), 23–24, 572.

61. Albert O. Hirschman, *The Passions and the Interest: Political Arguments for Capitalism before Its Triumph* (Princeton, NJ: Princeton University Press, 1977).

62. For a discussion of Smith's Calvinist leanings see Robert H. Nelson, *Reaching for Heaven on Earth: The Theological Meaning of Economics* (Savage, MD: Rowman & Littlefield, 1991), 278–90; Robert H. Nelson, *Economics as Religion from Samuelson to Chicago and Beyond* (University Park, PA: Pennsylvania State University Press, 2001), 95–106.

63. Taylor, *Confidence Games*, 239.

64. Actually, he first used the phrase in his book, *The Principles which Lead and Direct Philosophical Enquiries Illustrated by the History of Astronomy*, vol. 3, in *Essays on Philosophical Subjects* ed. W. P. D. and J. C. Bryce (Oxford: Oxford University Press, 1980), 49. He used it to mean supernatural agency ("the invisible hand of Jupiter"), which less civilized people used to explain irregular or alarming natural events. I got this reference from James Buchan, *Frozen Desire: The Meaning of Money* (New York: Welcome Rain, 2001), 176.

65. Adam Smith, *The Theory of Moral Sentiments*, ed. D. D. Raphael and A. L. Macfie (Oxford: Clarendon Press, 1976), 185; quoted in Taylor, *Confidence Games*, 85.

66. See Lisa Hill, "The Hidden Theology of Adam Smith," *European Journal of the History of Economic Thought* 8 no.1 (2001): 1–29; James Alvey, "Lisa Hill's Discovery of Adam Smith's 'Hidden Theology,'" paper presented at the Australian Political Studies Association Conference, University of Adelaide, Adelaide, September 29–October 1, 2004; Anthony M. C. Waterman, "Economics as Theology: Adam Smith's Wealth of Nations," *Southern Economic Journal* 68 no. 4 (2002): 673–86; *Political Economy and Christian Theology Since the Enlightenment* (New York: Palgrave Macmillan, 2004); and Paul Oslington, "Natural Theology as an Integrative Framework," St Marks Day Public Lecture, St Marks National Theological Center, May 2005. For an interesting view of the connection between Christian ideas and theologies and the rise of capitalism and science, see Rodney Stark, *The Victory of Reason: How Christianity led to Freedom, Capitalism, and Western Success* (New York: Random House, 2005).

67. Hirschman, *Passions*, 10.

68. Hirschman, *Passions*, 17ff.

69. Quoted in Edwin Mansfield, *Managerial Economics: Theory, Applications, and Cases* (New York: W. W. Norton & Co., 1990), 541.

2

+

Money and Theology:
A Review and a Direction

INTRODUCTION

This chapter reviews theological analyses and interpretations of money and monetary relations that illuminate features and moral issues of monetary system through the lens of the doctrinal and conceptual resources of the Christian faith. For our limited purposes here, I will restrict the discussion to analyses that either explicitly use trinitarian themes[1] or reveal the deeply theological character of the monetary system. This restriction of scope is necessary because this study is about explicating the urgent ethical questions about the contemporary monetary system and illuminating the nature of today's monetary relations through the explicit use of the trinitarian principles. The discussion will proceed as follows: Section 1 discusses aspects of the symbol of Trinity and money—how Christological themes inform the understanding of money. Section 2 will focus on theological interpretations of monetary relations in the market economy.

It is necessary to mention that in reviewing the theologies of money of writers in both sections I will critique them in ways that give an indication of my own alternative approach to the study of money. Some of my criticisms are couched in the thought process and language of Tillich. I have incorporated Tillich's system of thought into my own economic reasoning. At some point this may require that I discuss some of the philosophical concepts and ideas of Tillich in order to show how they will be working in my conversations of money with the theologians. What I will be saying about their works is crucial to my own approach and the construction of my trinitarian model of the global monetary system.

SECTION 1: CHRISTOLOGICAL
THEMES IN MONETARY DISCOURSE

W. Taylor Stevenson, a philosophical theologian, in his book, *Soul and Money*, provides a provocative theological understanding of money by interpreting the role of Jesus Christ as "coin and surplus." His book is about how money as a symbol mediates the union of the finite and infinite by the way of the soul (enigmatic center of imagination and projection). His thesis about seeing Jesus as a kind of divine exchange medium and money as a symbolic unity of the finite and infinite is developed in three closely related arguments.

First, money is a sacrament of divine-human unity. As he explains it, money is condensed energy and time. The money in your bank account or wallet is a condensation of all the energy and time you have expended. With that condensed energy and time you can purchase the energy and time of others in the present to enable you meet your needs in the present and realize your dreams of the future. In this way money (condensed energy and time) manifests the presence of the past and the presence of the future. "In money the past, the present, and the future meet to inform one another . . . history and eschatology meet and inform one another."[2] Positing that all energy, life force, comes from the Creator, Stevenson avers that money, which is a repository of energies, has an aura of the sacred of which it is a sacrament. Life force as energy both points and makes present the gift of God. Reposited energies can be transferred from one generation to another.

Second, money as a condensed energy of the past is really a gift of the ancestors and is a surplus to be invested in the future. The investment is necessary so that life and our future may continue and we may continuously give a gift to the future. Though coming from the past as gift from the ancestors, it provides the energy that enables present sustenance as well as giving the fillip to future life and development to go on. This investment in the future which has its foundation in the past unites ancestors with descendants and represents a sacrament of the intersection of time and eternity. This is what, according to him, makes money sacred.

Third, from this assertion, he connects his thoughts about money to Christology. Jesus Christ as the meeting point of humanity and divinity in whom time and eternity intersect is also a "coin" to Christians.[3] He states:

> For Christians Jesus Christ is the coin of God, given for us and to us, and therefore is our own coin, our surplus. That surplus was offered originally

upon the spit of the cross, just as analogously the Greeks offered it upon another kind of spit over another kind of flame. In both situations, it is that surplus which energizes the imagination of the community, unites us with the ancestors [the communion of saints living and dead within whom Christ lives and mediates our connection with God in heaven], and makes manifest the intersection of time and eternity which is always present.[4]

This insight that Stevenson has about Jesus as a form of divine "coin" that supplies energy to believers so that life and future may continue is not as dramatic or revolutionary as it appears at first notice. Several scholars both in the past and the present have arrived at similar conclusion, albeit from different starting points. For instance, Marc Shell in his book, *Art and Money*, exploring the vexing relation between visual art and money, also sees a close parallel in his understanding of Christ and money. Jesus is both divine and human and money is both an ideal thing and a real thing, a symbol and a physical entity. "This makes money disturbingly close to Christ as a competing architectonic principle."[5]

Medieval Christianity appears to have made a similar connection. The form of the bread used in the Eucharist, the communion wafer, was round and embossed as a stamped coin and by the nineteenth century, "the wafer had changed into an actual coin, which was used in Protestant churches for admission to communion." Some of those Christian wafer coins had the dollar sign. Today in many countries, currencies bear this sign, perhaps indicating their religious origin.[6]

By making the Eucharist wafer in the form of a coin, this holiest of the sacraments came to assume some of the characteristics of actual money. Just as a worthless piece of paper is turned into money by the fiat of a state, the priest's word performatively "transforms a worthless bread into the priceless body of Christ." Both paper and bread are symbols of something else. In this sacerdotal economics of the sanctuary, the *use value* of the bread becomes less important in comparison with its *exchange value*—its value is suddenly being measured by the relative worth of exchanged grace. According to those who hold the view of transubstantiation, the bread, as a "currency of exchange" and a point of contact with efficacious divine grace, plays a mediating role between the spiritual and the physical.

Karl Marx, in trying to grapple with the relationship between use value and exchange value of money, repeatedly turned to Christological language to gain insight into money. Commenting on James Mill's discussion of money as the medium of exchange, he states that money is the "mediator" that has "become an actual god."[7] Just as Christ who as the incarnation of God does the work of reconciliation between sinful humans and God and between humans themselves, Marx also sees money as "the

incarnation of exchange value"[8] which is also capable of reconciling conflicts between individuals in the market place. It is germane to fully quote
Marx here:

> Christ originally represents: (1) man before God; (2) God for man; (3) man for
> man. Likewise, money originally represents by its concept: (1) private prop-
> erty for private property; (2) society for private property; (3) private property
> for society. But Christ is God *externalized*, externalized man. God has value
> only insofar as he represents Christ; man has value only insofar as he repre-
> sents Christ. It is the same with money.[9]

Although Marion Grau's work *Of Divine Economy: Refinancing Redemption* is not a theological analysis of the monetary system and not even of
the economic system *per se*, it contains flashes of brilliance about economic symbols of redemption and monetary terminologies in theological
understanding of Christ's salvific work that it pays to give some attention
to her work at this juncture of our literature review. Take for example this
statement: "In the Christological negotiations of the fourth century, the
term *homoousios*—a monetary term describing several coins as having
made from the same metal, and thus genuine—comes to stand for the
consubstantiality of Father and Son"[10] (italics in the original). Or this:
"Christ the ransom paid, by the formulations of orthodox divine economy
became the ultimate price and gift. Christ was minted as the currency that
explodes the terms of the old contract/testament, and became the new
coin that bought out previous exchanges between God and humanity."[11]

Grau appropriates the ancient, patristic Christological motif of the *commercium*, or "the deal with the devil," for a theology subversive to neoclassical economics. Hers is a postcolonial reading of a divine commerce
that describes a salvific exchange in which trickster-like Christ mimics
and mocks boundaries of *ousia* (that which is one's own: substance, property, wealth, money, being[12]) and false, demonic claims to ownership of
humanity, and reminds us that spheres of God and Mammon are deeply
related. She argues that *commercium* and *conubium*, the counterfeit currency of Christ's ransom, and Christ as trickster (*a la* Gregory of Nyssa)
provide tools to theologize redemptive departures from economic op-
pression and divine moves toward just trade.

As stated above her book is not about the modern economic or monetary system, despite the abundance of economic terms in the title. They,
perhaps, function to direct our attention to the connection between God's
economy and our economy. The book is really about *oikonomia theou*. She
deals with how economic soteriologies, economic symbols of redemption—in all their ambivalences—can contribute to a contemporary understanding of a coredemptive *soteria*. She appropriates the layers of mean-

ing of the term "economy" (as originating from the theological and Greek term *oikonomia*) and the play between them for theological reconstruction of divine economy. At the end, she did not quite explain how one can go from theological reconstruction of divine economy to theological reconstruction of the modern economy.

At the core of either the theological interpretation of money by Marx or the economic interpretation of the mediator incarnate as the "currency of exchange" in the divine economy of salvation is a notion of transcendence. Money mediates the relationship between commodities. The relation between any two economic agents in the market is mediated and not direct. Just as God is transcendent to the self-world structure, money is transcendent to the subject-subject economic transaction. The presence of transcendence can be revealed from another (Christian) perspective—that of the signified and signifier. The value of a human being is not grounded in herself—her value as a human being and as believer is in reference to God; she bears the *imago dei*. Eucharist bread or wafer coin is a sign referring beyond itself to the divine presence. Similarly, there was a time when a mental coin or paper currency was a sign that either referred beyond itself to gold, which was the "real money" and the anchor of currencies circulating in the marketplace, or to some state power which stood above economic exchanges and guaranteed the value of money. Either in the realm of the spiritual or the market the "real" was transcendental or there was a transcendental referent which secured the realm's foundation. But what if the real is not transcendental or what if there is no foundation as in a relational network? If everything is relative because all things are related what is the specific point that anchors everything?

These questions also apply in full force to Stevenson's notion of Jesus Christ as a divine exchange coin. In the spiritual realm where life forces, energies are exchanged, the coin as the medium of exchange makes redemption possible. Similarly, money is what makes redemption of debts or claims possible for economic agents. But what if there is no possibility of redemption, security, or closure, but only constant openness as in a complex adaptive network system? What if there is no transcendental referent to bring closure or to make a "buy back"?

These are the type of questions raised by postmodern theologian, Mark C. Taylor in his 2004 book, *Confidence Games: Money and Markets in a World without Redemption*. He argues that as exchange (market) has moved from commodity-money to representational-money (gold or some metal serving as transcendental signified) to *virtual money* (dematerialized, spectral money) in an economy where relativity is "absolute" and all general equivalents have disappeared, the concepts of "foundation" and "redemption" are no longer conceptually viable way of thinking about money and markets. The general equivalent (gold, which he says is the economic equivalent of God) has disappeared in "relational play of float-ing signifiers backed by nothing other than themselves."[13] There is no possibility of closure in this system as self-organizing, self-regulating, and coevolving interconnections increasingly create ever-expanding webs of countless relations. Hence, we are in a brave new world of no redemption where order is not imposed from outside by either a providential God or an institution. Taylor sums up his argument in these terms:

> Since redemption presupposes closure as well as satisfaction, however it is figured, the ceaseless flux of life in network culture renders redemption im-possible. Rather than the sign of certain death, the impossibility of redemp-tion is the mark of endless life. To affirm this life is to embrace the infinitely complex networks that make us what we are and are not. . . . In the final analysis, the problem is not to find redemption from a world that often seems dark but to learn to live without redemption in a world where the interplay of light and darkness creates infinite shades of difference, which are in-escapably disruptive, overwhelmingly beautiful, and infinitely complex.[14]

With this kind of argument, what Taylor is positing, if I understand him accurately, is that theological models, or specifically Christological mod-els, which emphasize mediation, transcendence, or redemption are no longer adequate lenses with which to view historical events and they are also no more viable metaphors for interpretation of historical reality. Tay-lor also argues that market or indeed the flux of economic activities do not have any meaning or purpose at all. But I think that there are aspects of the Christological model and its associated trinitarian principles[15] that can still be recovered, retrieved, and pressed into service to yield a new un-derstanding of the contemporary monetary system. I also think that money and markets have "depth and meaning." I will show that, with a more careful and nuanced engagement with what Tillich calls the trini-tarian principles, "Virtuality"[16] could be seen as not the only form or con-struct of the sacred or God that can help us to make sense of our world to-day. This will be executed in two steps.

First, let me explicate what the governing assumption behind Taylor's theory is by drawing insights from the work of Jean-Joseph Goux, *Sym-bolic Economies*.[17] Following Marx's notion of general equivalent, Goux ar-gues that the idea of God in a society corresponds to its stage of the gen-eral equivalent, the abstract norm of value. So a society where gold, locked away in a vault, functions as a general equivalent and guarantee of currency in circulation, such a society is likely going to have a tran-scendent God hidden in a heavenly realm and standing behind all of this-worldly transactions. From here, it is not difficult to see how Taylor's idea of God and no redemption could emerge once he posits the economic sys-tem as in the historical stage of "absolute relativity" and "Virtuality."

Goux's theory helps us to both better understand Taylor's idea and at the same time critique it.

We can see that Taylor's attempt to link the stages of monetary development to the theological notions of redemption and God is beholden to Goux's general theory of symbolization.[18] Taylor's theory, like that of Goux's, harbors the historicist assumption that there are structural parallels across spheres of society (arts, monetary, entertainment, and religion) in any given historical period. The question that arises is: does the idea of God and God's work of redemption correspond with the stage of historical development of the general equivalent? To insist that this must be so, as Taylor has affirmed, appears to me as falling into the pits of crass functionalism where all things must function for social cohesion and integration. The critique Kathryn Tanner put forward against Goux's theory may well be directed at Taylor. She writes that Goux is unable to avoid the "totalizing of historical periods, in which the same structural features are thought to recur in all fields of society . . ." but if he has seen "society and historical periods not as wholes but as made up of competing status groups and classes" he would have avoided the totalizing idea that all spheres mirror one another in their basic structure.[19]

For the second step, let me now turn to Tillich's conceptualization of the trinitarian principles of the living God in order to more frontally counter Taylor's *Virtuality-God*. My limited purpose here is to use Tillich's understanding of the trinitarian principles to critique Taylor's view of the market and retrieve some Christological theme (the third root) for interpreting and understanding money and markets in today's world.

Money as a social relation is a dynamic unity of *depth* and *meaningfulness*. The *depth* of money is the ever-expanding economic production, the ground of satisfying human needs and wants. What supports the value of a given national currency is the industrial and non-industrial productions of its country. Every currency is rooted *in* the depth of a country's economic and military power relative to the rest of the world. The preposition "in" points to the inability of money anywhere to exist without the supporting power of production (industrial and service alike) and the "immanence of creative potentiality" of the nation's people at the supporting depth of production.[20]

Production is regarded as the depth of money because of its element of power. Production (the whole gamut from extraction of raw materials and services to distribution and consumption) is the power of the economic life, which enables it to resist chaos, "non-being," and social solipsism. Production gives the "power of being" to every exchange transaction. To have a place as an economic agent in the social practice of money is to exist in an economic sense, and this means above all to have an economic space (be a node of production, exchange, and consumption beside others) among the spaces of all other agents and to resist the threat of losing one's economic space and perhaps with it existence altogether.[21] A person does not just occupy this space, but occupies it in order to transcend it in creativity. To occupy is also to act, to move from individuation to participation and back as living being in anticipatory actualization of potentials (what Tillich also calls fulfillment). In fact, the aim of production and that of history in general is the fulfillment of humanity in every person.

Now that we have got some sense of connection between money and its depth (and power) of production, let us try to explicate how *meaning* is implicated in the social practice of money. By "meaning" I am referring to the individualistic, personal connection to this ground of production, which is to say a person's engagement in projects of worth. If the *production grounding* (*character*) of money is neglected, an irrationalistic financialism ("casino capitalism") transforms economic exchange into heteronomous subjection, an external agency capable of granting economic life or death to human sociality. If the *meaningful character* of money is neglected, a rationalistic, dispassionate invisible hand sphere transforms all agents' decisions into mere revelation of information or mere making distinctions only of price and quantity in the market. For one to step into the social practice of money (to engage in exchange) without *meaning* is to wholly objectivize oneself and block the path to all sensuous interpersonal relationships—both of these are impossible to do. If the *social practice* (*relation*) *character* of money is neglected, not only the social meaning of money is impossible to understand, but also money as a realm where the divine Spirit of God can impact and transform individual and social lives becomes difficult, if not, impossible to conceive.

There are three related ways I am using the word *meaning*. These senses of the word are important in critiquing Taylor's thesis that modern economic processes have no meaning. First, *meaning* expresses the urge of a woman to fulfill herself, to actualize her potentials. It is from here the animus of creativity feeds into the production process. Meaning in this sense is very connected with the idea of monetization as rationalizing process. When some scholars describe money as the spearhead of rationalization, as an instrument or as a reification of means they are often conceiving money as a mere means for agents who got their ends from "somewhere else." As it were, money is simply only a tool. The idea of looking at money (and market) as a mere tool is naïve, to say the least. Money (market) does not just operate or participate from the outside in the production process. Money (market) creates the production and distribution in which it participates. This is an idea that can be worked out more fully but which we will not be tempted to undertake here and now. I have brought this up to substantiate my point that money is by no means a mere tool in the production-consumption process. Besides, the view of money as mere tool ignores a crucial point. *Meaning (purpose) determines ends and only then the means.* Sociologists and economists may separate means from *meaning* in their analyses or the temporality of production and exchange may give the impression that means and reasoning about means are separated from *meaning* and reason. But they are not really separated. This is so because means is used to fulfill the demands of *meaning.*

Second, where there is money there are a self and a world of production in interdependence. The function (a la Tillich) of the person through which she actualizes herself and grasps and shapes this world is *meaning.* *Meaning* expresses the notion that every economic transaction is a "syndrome (i.e., a running-together) of facts and interpretation."[22] There is nothing like naked money or pure transaction. Money as a social practice always bears in it a historical consciousness. Social practice unites the events of metal, paper, or electron exchanges with symbolic interpretations.[23] Social practices transcend the satisfaction of immediate needs, and they combine actions with purposes for an animal species that has both self-awareness and historical consciousness. There is no social practice of money without factual transactions, and there is no money without the reception and interpretation of factual transactions by historical consciousness of a group or that of an individual.

Third, *meaning* also stands for the *principle of form* structuring the productive activities, the satisfaction of social wants. Here one does not need to agree with Adam Smith's notion of invisible hand with all its implications to accept the fact that market structures, organizes, and reconciles countless productive activities. There is somewhat of a compulsive drive to *form* as "chaotic" production (myriad uncoordinated, individualistic decisions) has to express and complete itself in market as the meaningful and orderly moment in the socioeconomic life. (The exchange value of a product is expressed, realized, and validated only in the market.) It is only in this meaningful market framework that the antimony between chaos and order, individual and collective decisions can be partly balanced by the social practice of money as the precondition and possibility of their synthesis[24] in social life.

Now that we understand what *depth, power,* and *meaning* mean when applied to the economy as a whole, we may venture to say that social practice of money is the ultimate unity of both the power and meaning in the process of social-economic life. Social practice of money is not only a unity of power and meaning, but also of the static and dynamic. It is through the social practice of money that one can easily explain the self-separating and self-returning activities of production. Through the social practice of money, a commodity or capital investment goes out of itself,[25] proceeds from the ground of production and gives actuality to the potential value in the production ground. Put differently, the ability of a log of wood to become a table is activated when an entrepreneur puts out her capital and steps into the social practice of money and exchange. It is in this process of exchange and value creation in producing a table, for example, that a potential log is made to yield an actual table. Through the social practice of money the fullness of monetary value is realized from production as something definite, and at the same time it is reunited in the production ground as new investment. As Marx puts it, "circulation itself returns back into the activity which posits or produces exchange values. It returns into it as into its ground."[26] This self-reflexive process Marx famously described as C–M–C or M–C–M.[27] Marx's famous formula adequately captures the self-separating (C–M) and self-returning (M–C) activities of production I am trying to describe here. In a capitalist production process, the entrepreneur invests his capital to earn return by putting it into the circulation process. This is the separation phase. The invested capital, if all goes well, comes back with a profit. This is the return phase which has the original capital and the new (earned, augmented) value. It is also important to note as Marx explained that as the original product (*self-identity*) goes into the market, its form is *altered* (C→M); it turns to money, and the investor uses the money to buy another commodity (M→C, *self-identity* again) which will be put into circulation again—and the whole process starts all over.

In the whole process from production to *meaning* to social practice, separation is posited and overcome by reunion. But there is *nothing automatic* about it. The separation of potentiality (invested capital) from actuality (earned value) that defines and comprises the economic life embeds within it the possibility of a disruption. Thus, the whole process of dynamics and form requires redemption and reconciliation from time to time—as the history of business cycle and capitalist crisis management has demonstrated. The visible hand, rather than the invisible one, is needed from time to time to set it on the right course. The prophetic voice is also needed to point this process, its polarities, the splits and disruptions, and attendant injustice, to the kingdom of God or any other symbol of social transformation.

While I may not have totally succeeded in refuting Mark Taylor's thesis of a economic world without the possibility of redemption, I have certainly shown that Tillich's trinitarian symbol of *logos* enables us to interpret the modern economic system. Understanding *logos* as that which gives meaning and form to all human activities, enables us to avoid the non-living,[28] dead-identity, Virtuality-God of Taylor and still conceive of an economic world with the possibility of meaning and redemption.

Before bringing this section to a close, I would like to bring in a "theological perspective" on money offered by a non-theologian, Gil Anidjar of

Columbia University, New York. His view on Christ and money provides yet another interesting dimension to the whole issue we have been examining here. His Christological perspective on money is taken from the analogy between the blood of Jesus and money as the social blood of the economy. I will distill his somewhat complicated and not always succinct argument to five steps. First, he argues that capitalism is actually the out-working of tendencies inherent in Christianity. It is either a parasite of Christianity or the realization of the task of Christianity. "Money—which is to say, blood money—is the true spirit of capitalism made flesh, the incarnation *and* liquefaction of flesh and blood" (italics in the original).[29]

Why does Anidjar conceive of money in this rather strange way, you may say? This takes us to the second layer of his argument and throws us right back into history of the Eucharist wafer. We have already seen the ancient association of blood and money; how communion bread was turned into stamped coin during the Middle Ages, and how bread was transformed into the flesh of Jesus by pious priest's word. The bread mysteriously incarnated or coagulated into the priceless body of Christ. This bread took yet another metamorphosis (from flesh to blood) that we have not previously mentioned. "The [priest's] word became flesh, and the flesh became blood (since the wafer, and no longer the wine, quickly became the only species which Christians were allowed to consume)."[30]

This association between money and liquid is carried over to the present day—in the form of the language we use for money. The French word for cash is *liquide*. On Wall Street the availability of cash in a corporation's accounts is measured by "liquidity ratios." When a corporation is strapped for cash but awash with hard assets it is often advised to "liquefy" some of its abundant hard assets. *Species* in the Roman Catholic Church refers to the elements in the Eucharist meal and *species* in English (*espéces* in French) is "Eucharistically" designated as coined money. We *speculate* in the market when we venture into risky deals. The words "speculate" and "species" and "spectral" ("spectral money" for that matter) come from the same Latin root, *spek*.[31]

Third, Anidjar posits that blood is an intermediary step to the modern dematerialization and spectralization of money—incarnation, liquefaction to its becoming-spirit.[32] What Anidjar means is that once the idea of money became associated with blood or liquid, it is just a short step to its spectralization. Specifically, he states that:

> Clearly, the religious origins of money go back to the very beginnings of history, yet, the singular transformation of Christ's blood into an ever more significant object of worship affected the no less ancient association of blood and money. Thus, the "historically momentous change" that takes place with the modern dematerialization of money, the invention of electric money can

be located on a continuum with the earlier transformation in the history of money and within economic theology, as a series of "processes that moved *Christendom* from the age of electrum coins toward the age of electric money" (italics in the original).[33]

Fourth, he argues that the Christian community is a "community of blood"—believers are unified by the blood of Jesus as an immanent, organic whole. The liquefaction of money and its circulation, he argues, is behind the conception of the state as a monetary community. Money was conceived in the medieval era as the blood of the state. Blood was seen as the center of the economic, political, and divine systems in a civilization that weaved state, society, and church into *Corpus Christianum*. From William Harvey who discovered the circulation of blood in the human anatomy, and his friend Thomas Hobbes who saw money and commerce flowing in the veins of the state to John Law who declared money as the blood of the state, money and blood served as the basis of Christian economic theology.[34]

Finally, once commodity money was seen as liquefied and circulating as blood does in our bodies it is only a short step toward its floating—"money was beginning to float (a phenomenon that was slowly generalized but only finalized on August 15, 1971)."[35] With this "dematerialization," the specter of money floated to the surface of our monetary thinking. Though the specter was, in this manner, set loose it has refused to ascend into heaven so we can "buy and eat without money and without price"[36] but rather it remains to haunt the economic community as the ghost of Hamlet. As Marx reminded us about one and half centuries ago, this *phantasmagoria* "is nothing but the definite social relations between men themselves which assumes here, for them, the fantastic form [*dies phantasmagorische Form*] of relations between things."[37]

Anidjar has, indeed, given us a provocative view of the relationship between money and Christianity and by so doing he has drawn our attention to the intimate relations that exist between money and religion. I, however, think that he has drawn the relationship between Christianity and money or even Christian theology and money too close. The intimate connection between religion and money preceded Christianity as even a cursory reading of the "biography" of money would reveal to anyone. I will simply make my case by briefly presenting the history of money in its early days in the temples.

Following Igor Kopytoff, I am going to sketch the "cultural biography" of money.[38] This is the story of the various historical forms it has taken in different political-economic systems and periods. Money has a fascinating life story which will enable us to better understand its process of dematerialization. Although money is today largely in the form of digital codes of 0/1 floating freely in the complex networks of computer and economy, there was a time it was a concrete and tangible object. It was expressed as cowry shell, salt, tobacco, cattle, copper, silver, gold, paper, etc. The English word, *pecuniary* comes from Latin *pecunia* (*pecus*=cattle) and our word *salary* is from the Latin word for salt (*sal*).

The English word for money comes from the Roman goddess *Moneta*.[39] Religion and money strive on trust and faith and it is conceivable that the temple may have lent some of these precious "assets" to the emerging form of money. It is important to note that as the earliest forms of money crawled out of its "primordial soup" in the temple in the remote recesses of time, it was hard material that formed its "vertebrae" and the *pneuma* (wind) that inflated its "lungs" was confidence, generalizable confidence. The power of deity or rather of belief, peace, and security were needed from the beginning to launch money forward in the turbulent world of trade where the aleatory can erupt.[40]

Let us explore the money-god (religion) connection further. It is not difficult to conceptualize monetary exchange as a sacrifice. Each party in the exchange gives up something and if it is a reasonable transaction they each hope to get something in return. The German word for money *Geld* meant sacrifice; the Greek *drachma* meant handful of sacrificial meat.[41] In fact, contrary to the trade-by-barter tale of origin of money usually disseminated in introductory economics textbooks, an increasing number of economists believe that money first originated in the sacrificial economies between humans and deities.[42] Many economists now question the familiar tale of money having originated through barter in the private sector rather than in the public sector.[43] Michael Hudson states that "in recent years a more historically grounded alternative view of money's early evolution has emerged. Historians of ancient Mesopotamia who deal with cuneiform records—Assyriologists—have found that the monetary role of providing a general unit of account and store of value appears to have been introduced initially in the temples and palaces."[44] And Georg Simmel insists in his monumental *Philosophy of Money* that:

> All Greek money was once sacred; it emanated from the priesthood, as did other generally valid concepts of measure referring to weight, size and time. The priesthood represented at the same time the unity of the various regions. . . . The shrines had a non-particularistic centralizing significance, and money expressed this by bearing the symbol of the common God. The religious social unity, crystallized in the temple, and became active again through money that was put in circulation, and money acquired a basis and function far beyond the significance of the metal content of the individual coin."[45]

No matter who is right or wrong in the debate about the evolutionary history of money, the fact remains that since money emerged from its "primordial soup" as a structure of mediation that forever displaced the spatial and temporal immediacy of barter, it has needed more and more trust or confidence to hold human beings together in an ever-expanding network of economic activities. As money has stretched the barter impulse over an increasing expanse of work, it has also elongated time[46] and become time. According to Taylor, "as money emerges and develops, the face-to-face of the local market gives way to anonymous relations mediated by increasingly abstract media and distributed over ever-expanding geographical areas. Insofar as money is a standard of deferred payment, time is introduced into the economic system. Rather than having to be consummated in the present moment, the circuit of exchange can be completed at an indefinite future date. Not only is time money . . . money is time."[47]

The form of money as it left its temple environs has not remained the same. Its history has been the story of changing forms, material to immaterial—dematerialization of substance and channels of exchange. It has changed from stuff such as shells, clothes, and gold to bytes and simulacrum. The trajectory of this movement has been motivated by changing technology and broad cultural developments. With the invention of digital technologies and their use in finance from the 1960s, money or currency became bytes of information registered in computer memories. Money became the sign of other signs grounded in nothing beyond itself. President Richard Nixon made this painfully clear to the financial community when on August 15, 1971 he de-linked the dollar from gold, moving the whole global monetary system from the gold standard to the information standard.

We will argue in chapter 4, after we have dealt with the key properties of money in today's economy in chapter 3, that in all these changes and metamorphoses something about money has remained unchanged. That is, money is always constituted by social relations.

SECTION 2: THEOLOGICAL CHARACTER OF THE MONETARY SYSTEM

The theological analyses in the last section have emphasized convergence between certain views of Christ's life and salvific work and the function of money. In various ways they interpret the world of money (general equivalent) in the light of the hypostatized divine world of salvation and universality. The analyses in this section, which focus on social relations, show how divergent human interactions are from God's relations with humans. The issue is no longer about analogy between "monetary life" and divine self-manifestation, but about how the structure of experienced sociality could be lifted up to approximate God's generosity toward humans. If the first set of discourse brought Christ down to our level to make sense of human earthly experience, then the second set attempts to raise earthly relations, structures, and organization of economic life to God for their transformation. In either case we have an implicit tension between the particular and the universal at play. When a particular national currency is juxtaposed with the Christ symbol it is to universalize that particular currency by its very placement. On the other hand, when a particular human institution is being lifted up to approximate God's graciousness, the universal is about to be particularized at a given historical moment. This tension of the particular (concrete) and the universal (the ultimate) is not dissimilar from the first root of the trinitarian thinking. As Tillich has said, the trinitarian principles play themselves out in several aspects of life.

Let us now examine the studies that focus on the theological character of monetary relations and how divergent they are from God's relation with humans. The first work we will consider is that of Jacob Needleman's, 1991 book, *Money and the Meaning of Life*. He begins his study by tracing lines of similarity in the conception of money and God. The psychological feelings aroused in us by money are akin to those stirred by the idea of God. Money captures our imagination as an "absolute means" almost as God captures our imagination as an "absolute agent." Georg Simmel has made a similar point in his magisterial book of 1907, *Philosophy of Money*. Money like God "rises . . . above the whole broad diversity of objects; it becomes the center in which the most opposed, the most estranged and the most distant things find their common denominator and come in contact with one another."[48] But Needleman goes further to say that in money the spiritual and physical natures of human beings coincide—sort of the transcendence and immanence meeting together; nature and spirit intimately touching each other as money becomes the "will" of the modern person.

Needleman's book is about deciphering the relationship between the human quest for meaning of life and the quest for money. His explanation of the connection proceeds in four steps. First, he presents an ontological expose of human nature. He argues that the human being or life has two natures: physical and spiritual, outer and inner realms. These two natures are related by the will. He then argues that in money as a social technology all the physical and spiritual forces of human life encounter one another. For in the monetary exchange there is "the encounter between the striving of man to make contact with God and the needs of man to survive in the world of nature and society."[49] Second, he makes the argument that the challenge of living adequately with these two opposing natures is to make the material life serve the spiritual one. The question then arises, how can money, a principal representative of the material nature, be brought under the influence of spiritual ideas so it can take its proper place as a secondary thing in human life? (He regards physical body as secondary to spiritual life.) Money will be secondary if it is made to serve the search for self-knowledge which is an aspect of the spiritual life.

Third, he posits that dealing with money should be approached or studied as an instrument for seeing ourselves.[50] Disavowing any radical distinctions between the two natures of humans, he states that the human search for self-knowledge and inner development takes place in the midst of ordinary life. Money is a way of life in which the two natures encounter one another or by which human beings attempt to harmonize the spiritual and material impulses within them. How is this so? Money maintains a relationship between human's spiritual and material needs. It is a principle of reconciliation, of harmonization of disparate elements. According to him, money is not just an instrument of exchange of material goods, but also an instrument of exchange between material (external life) and internal life (human relationship to God). Money is essentially "an instrument both for organizing the social/survival life and for making 'space and time' available for man to grow inwardly as well."[51] Thus, money in so connecting the two natures, the inner and outward lives, acts like the will of modern persons by harmonizing all the impulses in ourselves.

> [The] word *will* really means—the power to live and be in two opposing worlds at the same time. . . . For us, in our culture, will is understood mainly as the power to do what we want in only one world. But if you really look at what passes for the will, you'll see that it is often only one desire dominating the others, no matter how it is dressed up in religious or moral language it is not development of a consciousness that harmonizes all the impulses in ourselves (italics in the original).[52]

Fourth, money is, therefore, an instrument for self-study in the midst of ordinary life. Money has taken on the face and function of the will within the modern person—there is a false sense of I. The man is not the king of his own life. Money is, insofar as it has usurped his will. Humans, through money, have tapped the vast material energy for relationships and exchanges but have left a void for divine energy without which life has no meaning. In this absence of divine energy, that is in this domination of the outer (material) life over the inner (spiritual) life in the money economy, interpersonal relationships and human-divine relations become twisted, contorted, and distorted:

> Man must ultimately choose between the inner and outer world, between God and the devil. . . . In order to chose, in order to move towards either "good" or "evil," it follows of necessity that man must be aware of both

movements, both directions; that he has within him which can be in contact with God *and* money, good *and* evil, being *and* nonbeing (italics in the original).[53]

How might we protect ourselves from moving in the wrong direction? Canadian theologian Craig M. Gay suggests how we might "protect our souls from the anomie intrinsic to capitalism's 'creative destructive process'" and from its tendency to atomize and relativize all meanings and values. He links both (tendency and process) to the use of and reliance upon money. The solution, according to him, lies in crafting a Christian theological perspective that will enable us to comprehend the money economy from beyond its own dynamic. The solution is to recover the world's capacity to apprehend and experience grace; to recognize that "our life and work in this world are ultimately the *gifts of God*" (italics in the original).[54]

This is how Gay developed his argument. He posits that modern human preoccupation with money is driven by fear. Modernity's project is premised upon the notion that fate must somehow be mastered if we are to seduce development from nature and to survive in this world. To make his case, he points the reader to Niccolo Machiavelli's argument that the world was something that had to be forced to serve human interests. He also recalls Descartes' contention that the genius of the scientific method was such that it might finally render us "the masters and possessors of nature."[55] Given this deep-seated fearfulness, modernity's use of money extends beyond simply utility to a belief that it is the only thing humans can really rely on. Gay maintains that there is a *spirituality* implicit in modernity's preoccupation with money.[56] He considers as sin the surrender to anxiety and fear and the consequent reliance on money as the security which is "apart from and all too often against God." For him, this kind of yielding to the fallen world renders humans incapable of placing faith in God, blinds them from even the possibility of trusting in God. "Service to money insidiously empties the world of grace, leaving it full of 'unbelief and caprice.'"[57] The solution to all this, he states, is a proper response to God's gift of life and world to us. We are to emulate the graciousness of God and put our hope in God's goodness and graciousness. With this kind of proper response, he maintains, things in the world will ultimately assume meaning and become purposive not because we desire them enough to spend money on them but because we use them in the service of love and we act to create and sustain fellowship by our generosity. He concludes by saying that this kind of response to God's gift is not only good for human relations, but it is also the way for the redemption of the social order. "In short gracious generosity is absolutely subversive of the power of money as 'mammon'" [money culture].[58]

In general, when the various theological analyses discussed above are considered as a whole they show one or both of two problems. First, often little or nothing is said about structures and organization of the monetary relations that condition the ethical responses of Christians. There is also silence on how the content of some fundamental Christian values and doctrines might influence the possible reorganization of the structures of the monetary life.

Second, they ignore the highly important dual nature of money. By the dual nature, I mean that there are two sides to money. Money is a flow, and money is a stock. The two are one—there are no two natures of money, but one. Money is a dialectical identity of these two sides. Whether viewed from stock or flow perspective, you are looking at one and the same phenomenon. It is like the famous ambiguous duck-rabbit drawing by the American Gestalt psychologist, Joseph Jastrow. From one point of view it is a series of flows and events; from another point it is a stock. It is just a shifting perspective on one and the same object. It is not two objects brought together in the form of a synthetic identity. The linear quantity is the embodiment of flows and the flows are the stock in process. The object is not changed, but there are two different takes from two angles of vision. The flow and stock are not parts that add up to a greater whole. It is one complex indivisible whole, with parts that overlap and cohere with one another, that can and must be looked at from multiple standpoints. You cannot get the richness of the subject matter or its theology from only a single standpoint. But it appears theologians have rested contentedly focusing only on a single perspective.

The theological literature is all too steeped in the discourse of money as a *matter* (the stock concept of money and the related ethical issues dealing with the allocation and use of the quantity of money in a given political economy) with little or nothing to say on the analysis of money as a *motion* (the flow concept of money). Theologians and ethicists are all too concerned with the stewardly use of acquired money and its uneven distribution, and have ignored the production, circulation, and control of money, the flows of money, which actually determine who gets what quantity, when and how.[59] Production, circulation, and control—the motion of money—precedes its stock and use, that is, the *matter* of money. Owing to this lopsided attention, theological scholarship has focused more on personal moral transformation than on the structures and organization of monetary relations. Also attention has principally been on the redistribution of monetary capital as the solution to national poverty in poor countries—all this to the neglect of the role of structures, dynamics, and function of money creation in the underdevelopment of economies. Thus, there is a dearth of ethical studies on how the logic and dynamics of the global trade and payment system (the monetary systems) impact the economic development of Africa and other poor regions of the world which are in the penumbra of what many would see as the current globalization sunshine.

We require new kind of studies that can shine a bright theological-ethical light on the motion of money at both national and global spheres so as to highlight the serious ethical and theological issues that pertain to the production, circulation, control, and use of money in the global structures and organizations of economic life. This new kind of work should at the minimum involve studies that address the *structures and organization of the monetary life* at national and global levels. Kathryn Tanner is one theologian that has started doing this new kind of work.

Tanner, in her book, *Economy of Grace*, theologically addresses the structures and organization of the modern economy. She argues that theological economics should move away from primarily focusing on how belief and commitment function in people's economic lives and from excessive concern with moral transformation of individuals engaged in economic transactions to concentrating on structures and organization of economic life. She posits that theological economics should concern itself with answering these kinds of questions: (1) how might the fundamental structures of economic life be reorganized in accordance with fundamental Christian values?, and (2) what are the ways the content of Christian beliefs might themselves be outlining possible structures for economic affairs?[60]

She then uses a framework, informed by her sensitivity to these issues and questions, to offer a very preliminary and rough analysis of money and the financial system. Like the Canadian theologian Gay, the American Tanner wants to "redeem" the current economic order. Unlike him, her arguments rely not so much on tinkering with capitalism at the edges or constraining exclusive enjoyment of property rights as on making a bold attempt to re-imagine the economic system, "to develop a theological alternative to capitalism of the strongest sort." In this alternative framework the idea of grace ("unconditional giving") is the exclusive organizing principle of an economy. She argues that unconditional giving can produce a new structural character of social relations that are defined by the properties of inclusiveness, non-competitiveness, and mutual fulfillment.[61]

> If human relations are structured in a way that reflects the character of God's own giving, they should be marked by unconditional giving—that is, giving that is not obligated by the prior performance of the recipients and that is not conditional upon a return being made by them. This principle marks all these relations off from *do ut des* giving or "I give so that you will give," the alternative principle of conditional giving that covers barter, commodity exchange, and debtor-creditor relations of all sorts.[62]

The new economic system she envisages is named "theological economy." This economy is organized around four basic principles. First, there is the principle of universal inclusiveness which is to be operative in the production and distribution of economic goods. This is her own way of saying economic interdependencies and intensification of globalization should benefit all across the board. Second, there should be no cutthroat competition in this envisioned economy. Competitions that increase disparities in wage and income levels and job opportunities between individuals and nations are to be avoided. Third, she advocates for universal entitlement (unconditional giving), sensitive only to needs. Resources are to be distributed in a way that enables people to develop and realize their capabilities. Finally, the new economy should uphold the principle of mutual fulfillment of all economic agents in all transactions. This may be partially achieved by increased levels of employment and poverty reduction.[63]

Using these four principles as corner stone of a framework, she analyzed the global financial system. She declares that financial markets are a problem on the score of the four principles. Given the present organization and structures of the global financial architecture, she argues, it is difficult to allow grace its distinctive voice in global economic intercourse. Yet "grace has everything to do with money because in grace money finds its greatest challenger and most obstreperous critic."[64]

Tanner offers some practical ideas on how to bring the international monetary system in line with her theological vision of a new economy. Some of her suggestions include a return to something like the pre-1970s fixed international exchange rate system in order to eliminate currency speculation, a world financial authority to influence the movement of investible funds from surplus to deficit areas, and a dampening of the competitive character of financial markets. Tanner offers these supposed solutions without giving us a palpable sense of how they might come together as a concrete system or how exactly the global financial architecture will be transformed. At the end, even though she vowed not to sound utopian, her whole project appears to me as something that would not be taken seriously by professional economists. There is really no conversation between theology and economics. All this is not to downplay the importance of Tanner's work. She has pointed out new directions in the theological study of money. Her work as much as any other work in most recent memory has shifted our attention from the issues about moral transformation of individuals engaged in monetary transactions ("the overly individualistic approach to complicated structural issues") to those of structures and organization of international financial system. Like Tanner, I am interested in the transformation of structures and organization of the global monetary systems in ways that can aid economic development, especially that of the poor nations which are not fully engaged in the ongoing globalization process.

Whereas all the previous scholars we have examined so far have sought to develop a theology of money or economic life, Philip Goodchild aims to deconstruct "theology of money." He begins from the presupposition that "the roots of the contemporary ecological crisis demand theological redescription: economic globalization, driven by debt, is founded on a poor epistemology constructed around a theology of money."[65]

He lays out how the monetary process "creates" and exacerbates the clash between ecology and economy in this way. Modern money, he writes, is principally a credit-debt relation created apart from the production of goods and services. Money is simultaneously a debt and a credit;[66] so in order to pay back one's loans one has to acquire money created elsewhere in the system by another economic agent taking out a loan. This cycle of debt creation and repayment, he argues, controls the activities of individuals and businesses. In order to service such debts (which are daily skyrocketing) economic growth, which invariably requires an increasing use of the ecological resources, is needed. "The automatic results of a money-system based on debt and interest are that it encourages competition, it continually fuels economic growth, and that it concentrates wealth."[67]

The problem of debt is compounded by an epistemology that misrepresents the intimate relationship existing between humans and their natural environment so much so that it vitiates any ecological consciousness consisting of identification with the non-human environment. After laying out the connection between debt, economic growth, and epistemology, he examines what he calls economists' "theology of money." One is able to identify five aspects of this theology as he critiques it. First, money is self-referential and all values are measured in terms of money. Second, economists consider money to be a neutral tool in the exchange process—it is only a veil for real goods and services. Third, all assets hold value only in proportion to the value of the currency in which they are denominated and value exist only in the economic sphere of exchange. Fourth, the exchange process is blind to inequalities in power relations in the marketplace. Fifth, trade (exchange) creates wealth and whatever hinders free trade limits the potential for economic growth and development.

This "theology of money," he maintains is not innocent and is fundamentally against the Christian thinking. This idea of self-referential, interconnected parts of a value system presupposes a certain view of the world and time. The theory of self-referentiality (as we saw in Taylor's theology of money) in modern epistemology is built upon the secular order—which is "the sphere of the present age untrammeled by obligation to repeat the past, or anxious expectation of the judgments of the future, where all causes are mediated to their consequences by our knowledge."[68] He then argues that other money systems (that are not based on debt and interest) be devised to serve different purposes and express other theologies. A money system based on the secular vision of the good life is insufficient and threatens the ecology and survival of humans on earth and we thus need a "theological vision of the good life." Informed by this non-secular vision, he offers an alternative to the current monetary system. He wants the creation of "local and partial" monies (not a universalizing and totalizing general equivalent) and they are to be managed by religious organizations such as churches and mosques.[69] He claims that this new system will create a collective spiritual environment in which virtues will be encouraged. He opines that:

> Churches could discover an extraordinary vital role and new relevance if they were to act as the effective conduits of trust, credit and cooperation within society. For this is the essential role that churches always had, until they were replaced by banks in modernity. Such are the promises afforded by the possibility of intelligent in money [in contrast to debt-money].[70]

Once again we have a theologian who wants to reorganize the monetary system but offers an alternative that can only elicit disinterested yawns from economists and financial experts who will regard it as idealistic and impracticable in a globalizing world that needs a global currency. I do not think that either Tanner or Goodchild has managed to come up with a set of recommendations that can engage and enlist economists and business leaders in order to put into effect their theological visions. We require a study that corrects this kind of shortcoming and that can stand the chance of nudging the global monetary system toward fulfilling the fullness of participation, cooperation, and justice without stifling its creativity and galvanizing force.

The theologians' call for more humane and just economic orders has to be supported with the necessary rigor and expertise of an interdisciplinary breath of knowledge. According to theologian Matthew Lamb, "the increasingly interdisciplinary approach toward economic and human values . . . and the teachings of religious institutions suggest that it is time to develop categories capable of promoting a more adequate dialogue between economics and theology."[71] I think the beginning of wisdom in this conversation is a working definition of money to avoid talking at cross purposes. The theologians we had examined proceeded to craft theologies of money and critique the contemporary monetary system without first answering the question, what is money?[72] Often their understanding of what money is, is not compatible with those of non-theologians. The contributions theologians can make to monetary discourse should not involve distorting, "spiritualizing," or "theologizing" of the definition of money. I intend to avoid this mistake by understanding money from solid economic and sociological perspectives and only after that to undertake a theological-ethical critique of the contemporary monetary system.

I think a further critique of the theologies of money we have reviewed in both sections of this chapter is that they do not adequately theorize what precisely is theology's contribution to the analysis of money and the monetary system. There is a need for methodological reflection on the role of theological approach to money. In this study, I will be using a theological approach—informed by Tillich's trinitarian principles—to set up a model for reconfiguring an understanding of money.

LOOKING AHEAD

The next chapter presents socioeconomic study of money as a precursor for a definition of money as a social relation. It will investigate the key properties or characteristics of money and present the debates about the definition of money as they revolve around three key properties: unit of account, monetary media, and interpersonal transactions (the social character of money). The chapter will touch on the major authors, problems, and schools of thought in the debate.

NOTES

1. I will specifically concentrate on Christological themes. The Christological question is basically at the core of the trinitarian question—at least there is a reciprocal relationship between them. As Paul Tillich puts it: "With the statement that the historical Jesus is the Christ, the trinitarian problem became a part of the Christological problem, the first and basic part, as indicated by the fact that the trinitarian decision in Nicaea preceded the definitively Christological decision of Chalcedon. This sequence was logical, but in terms of motivation the sequence is reversed; the Christological problem gives rise to the trinitarian problem." See Paul Tillach, *Systematic Theology*, vol. 3, *Life and the Spirit, History and the Kingdom of God* (Chicago: University of Chicago Press, 1965), 285.

2. Taylor Stevenson, *Soul and Money A Theology of Wealth* (New York: Episcopal Church Center, 1991), 7.

3. Stevenson, *Soul and Money*, 149.

4. Stevenson, *Soul and Money*, 152–53.

5. Marc Shell, *Art and Money* (Chicago: University of Chicago Press, 1995), 8.

6. Mark Taylor, *Confidence Games: Money and Markets in a World without Redemption* (Chicago: University of Chicago Press, 2004), 67–68; Shell, *Art and Money* (Chicago: University of Chicago Press, 1995), 16–19. Some other scholars, like

cultural anthropologist Jack Weatherford, state that the dollar sign has its origin in the Spanish imperial iconography. The pillar dollar minted by Spain had two large columns on its obverse side. There was a banner hanging from the columns that had the words *plus ultra*. According to him, "some people say that the modern dollar sign is derived from this pillar dollar. According to this explanation the two parallel lines represent the columns and the *S* stands for the shape of the banner hanging from them" (italics in the original). See Jack Weatherford, *The History of Money: From Standstone to Cyberspace* (New York: Three Rivers Press, 1997), 118.

7. Karl Marx, *Writings of Young Marx on Philosophy and Society*, trans. Lloyd Easton and Kurt Guddat (New York: Doubleday, 1967), 266.

8. Karl Marx, *Grundrisse: Foundations of the Critique of Political Economy*, trans. Martin Nicolaus (New York: Penguin Books, 1973), 225.

9. Marx, *Writings of Young Marx*, 267.

10. Marion Grau, *Of Divine Economy: Refinancing Redemption* (New York: T & T Clark International, 2004), 155.

11. Grau, *Divine Economy*, 212.

12. Grau, *Divine Economy*, 46, 106.

13. Taylor, *Confidence Games*, 326.

14. Taylor, *Confidence Games*, 330–31.

15. "The consideration of the trinitarian principles is not the Christian doctrine of the Trinity. It is a preparation for it, nothing more. The dogma of the Trinity can be discussed only after the Christological dogma has been elaborated. But the trinitarian principles appear whenever one speaks meaningfully of the living God." Paul Tillich, *Systematic Theology*, vol. 1, *Reason and Revelation, Being and God* (Chicago: University of Chicago Press, 1951), 252.

16. Taylor avers that "virtual reality is the current guise of what once was called sacred or perhaps even god. Virtuality, however, is a strange God. In a world where reality is virtual, nothing is certain or secure. Purpose and meaning are as elusive and shifty as the constantly morphing networks in which they emerge" (Taylor, *Confidence Games*, 331).

17. Jean-Joseph Goux, *Symbolic Economies: After Marx and Freud* (Ithaca, NY: Cornell University Press, 1990).

18. See Taylor's comment about gold being the equivalent of God in *Confidence Games*, 326. On p. 357, n12, he states how his project differs from that of Goux. This notwithstanding his comment on p. 326 shows that he drinks heavily from the wellspring of Goux.

19. Kathryn Tanner, *Economy of Grace* (Minneapolis, MN: Fortress Press, 2005), 17.

20. For our existence is rooted in ground of being, see Tillich, *Systematic Theology*, vol. 3, 421–22.

21. I have crudely paraphrased Tillich here. See his *Systematic Theology*, vol. 3, 315.

22. Tillich, *Systematic Theology*, vol. 3, 302.

23. I will explore this connection among thing, relation, and interpretation further in chapter 4 where I conceptualize money as a relational thing.

24. John Dourley, "Tillich's Appropriation of Meister Eckhart: An Appreciative Critique," *Bulletin of the North American Paul Tillich Society* 31, no.1 (Winter 2005),

14. I really got to understand the crucial role of the logos in the trinitarian principles that Tillich set forth in the three volumes of his systematic theology on reading Dourley's essay. This means money or product is invested to yield more surplus value. Going out of itself is a way of saying that the capital or commodity is put to the market, into the circulation or investment process to yield more value. This way of describing the process of capitalist investment sounds like something out of Hegel's book. It is so because I am using Marx's beautiful way of describing things. Marx was a student of Hegel.

26. Marx, *Grundrisse*, 255.

27. Note that M–C–M also ultimately has to return to its ground. See Robert C. Tucker, *The Marx-Engels Reader* (New York: W. W. Norton & Co., 1978), 329–36.

28. By "non-living" I mean that it has no physical, spiritual, or symbolic life applied to it as Christians usually attribute to their God. Taylor's Virtuality, which stands in the place of God in the world of relativity, is a mere mechanism. See Taylor, *Confidence Games*, 331.

29. Gil Anidjar, "Christians and Money (The Economic Enemy)," *Ethical Perspective: Journal of the European Ethics Network* 12, no. 4 (2005), 497–519. See quote on p. 500.

30. Gil Anidjar, "Christians and Money," 501.

31. Taylor, *Confidence Games*, 323.

32. On this process, see also Jacques Derrida, *Specters of Marx: The State of Debt, the Work of Mourning, and the New International*, trans. Peggy Kamuf (New York: Routledge, 1994).

33. Anidjar, "Christians and Money," 501.

34. Anidjar, "Christians and Money," 501–6.

35. Anidjar, "Christians and Money," 506. On August 15, 1971, U.S. President Richard Nixon de-linked the dollar from gold and allowed the dollar to freely float in the foreign exchange markets.

36. Isaiah 55:1.

37. Karl Marx, *Capital*, vol. 1 (London: Penguin, 1976), 165.

38. Igor Kopytoff, "The Cultural Biography of things: Commoditization as Process," in *The Social Life of Things: Commodities in Cultural Perspective*, ed. Arjun Appadurai (Cambridge: Cambridge University Press, 1988), 64–90.

39. Taylor, *Confidence Games*, 66.

40. The holy has always been implicated with money. "Bad money" can go through a process of sublimation and used to serve deity. In the ritual practices of many religions, money can stand in place of the human or animal sacrifice. Salvation is also often viewed as the payment for ransom.

41. Taylor, *Confidence Games*, 66.

42. Taylor, *Confidence Games*, 66. I will say more on this in chapters 3 and 4.

43. The debate is known in the economic history literature as chartalism (public-sector, state origin of money) and metallism (private sector, market-oriented evolution, and use of money) in the theory of money. See Stephanie A. Bell and Edward J. Nell, eds. *The State, the Market and the Euro: Chartalism versus Metallism in the Theory of Money* (Cheltenham: Edward Elgar Co., 2003).

44. Michael Hudson, "The Creditary/Monetarist Debate in Historical Perspective," in *The State, the Market and the Euro*, 41.

45. Georg Simmel, *The Philosophy of Money*, trans. Tom Bottomore and David Frisby (New York: Routledge, 1978), 187.

46. In a sense, modern economy has made time shorter by increasing the speed of economic transactions. This is not the sense in which I am using the concept of elongation. Money has enabled economic agents to better temporally spread economic activities and feel less constrained by the here and now in economic production and distribution.

47. Taylor, *Confidence Games*, 59–60.

48. Simmel, *Philosophy of Money*, 236.

49. Needleman, *Money and the Meaning of Life* (New York: Doubleday, 1991), 67.

50. In much more secular and less philosophical terms, James Buchan sees money as incarnate, frozen, congealed desire, an object of desire, and the expression of the wishes and desires of humans that can be made to fulfill any mortal purpose. As a result its pursuit has become the point of life in the modern era when there is more faith in credit than faith in God. Buchan, *Frozen Desire*.

51. Needleman, *Money and the Meaning of Life*, 161.

52. Needleman, *Money and the Meaning of Life*, 118.

53. Needleman, *Money and the Meaning of Life*, 162.

54. Craig M. Gay, *Money and the Erosion of Meaning in Today's Society* (Grand Rapids, MI: William B. Eerdmans Co., 2004), 84. See also pp. 75, 76, and 83.

55. Gay, *Cash Values*, 84–87.

56. Gay, *Cash Values*, 87–89. On a discussion on the spirituality implicit in the use of money see Jacques Ellul, *Money and Power* (Downers Grove, IL: Intervarsity Press, 1981), 81.

57. Gay, *Cash Values*, 89.

58. Gay, *Cash Values*, 96. See also pp. 94–95.

59. For example, see Daniel W. Handy, *Finding the Church: The Dynamic Truth of Anglicanism* (London: SCM Press, 2001), 114–26; Otto A. Piper, "That Strange Thing Money," *Theology Today* 16, no. 2 (July 1959): 215–31.

60. Tanner, *Economy of Grace*, 3–5. Tanner's notion of unconditional giving is what Daniel Handy calls "theology of generosity" in his book, *Finding the Church*, 122–26. Peter Selby had arrived at similar thought before, though not worked out with the same clarity and sophistication as Tanner. See his *Grace and Mortgage: The Language of Faith and the Debt of the World* (London: Darton, Longman & Todd, 1997).

61. Tanner, *Economy of Grace*, 34, 49, 62–63, 75–78, 84–85.

62. Tanner, *Economy of Grace*, 63.

63. Tanner, *Economy of Grace*, 92–101.

64. Tanner, *Economy of Grace*, 29.

65. Philip Goodchild, "Debt, Epistemology and Ecotheology," *Ecotheology* 9, no. 2 (2004): 151–77; quote on p. 151.

66. For those who are not very familiar with the modern notion of debt as used in the financial accounting world, the distillation of the concept as offered by theologian Paul Hassert will be very helpful. "Debt, in connection with usury, was something to be paid off as quickly as possible. It was a constant threat to life. But debt in connection with credit and interest is something to be employed and en-

joyed. Debt is the ledger page opposite assets: they increase and decrease together." "Theology and Money," *Explore* 4, no. 2 (Fall 1978): 21–32, quote on p. 28.

67. Goodchild, "Debt, Epistemology and Ecotheology," 170.

68. Goodchild, "Debt, Epistemology and Ecotheology," 166.

69. Goodchild, "Debt, Epistemology and Ecotheology," 172, 175.

70. Goodchild, "Debt, Epistemology and Ecotheology," 175.

71. Matthew L. Lamb, "Theology and Money: Rationality, Religion, and Economics," *American Behavioral Scientist* 35, no. 6 (July 1992): 735–55, quote on p. 735.

72. A notable exception is Goodchild in another of his work. In his 2005 "Capital and Kingdom: An Eschatological Ontology," he attempts to answer the question, what is money? in passing. The exact nature of his discussion is too complicated to go into here. His account is far from adequate. His view of money is more of a postmodern philosophical discussion rather than a theological account that relies on one of the major Christian doctrines. While his discussion is very helpful in understanding the ontology of money as mediated by practice, it is not, in my opinion, designed to encourage conversation across interdisciplinary boundaries.

3

Money and Society: Socioeconomic Interpretations[1]

INTRODUCTION

Three properties of money, unit of account, monetary media, and inter-personal transactions, have emerged as key to understanding the changing nature of money in the extant literature on the sociology of money.[2] This understanding of money has emerged after more than a century of debates and refinement of analytical tools.[3] Within this time period, the nature of scholarly contributions has passed through several stages with the early formulations focused on either critiquing, complaining against conventional orthodox economic analyses, or providing the social context of money. Today, economic sociologists have liberated themselves from mainly reacting to economic analyses to formulating social bases of monetary phenomena.[4]

Before proceeding further, I would like to provide working definitions of the three properties of money: unit of account, monetary media, and interpersonal transactions. *Unit of account* or *money of account* is the abstract numeraire, the official currency. In the United States the money of account is the dollar. "The money of account provides the accounting system in which prices are calculated."[5] *Monetary media* relate to the medium, the objects that are used as money. The money of account can be embodied in various material forms like metal coins, paper, or credit cards. The dollar, the money of account, is embodied in a range of objects: gold and silver coins, greenbacks, credit cards, various kinds of e-money, and so forth. The two qualities or properties of money can be seen in this way: "The first [the money of account] being the title or description and the second [monetary media] the thing that answers to the description."[6] The third property (interpersonal transactions) refers to money's ability to mediate interactions between people, to "the connections among persons and groups involved in monetary transactions," and to the way they use money to differentiate one relationship from another.[7]

In this paper, I will review the literature on money with the order of exposition determined by the three properties of money. My approach is to start with the neoclassical economics[8] definition of money in section 1 and progressively reshape it by bringing to bear on it various sociological analyses of the properties of money. In this way, I will trace the general contribution to monetary analysis that the sociological perspective has made to the scholarly understanding of money as well as clarify the distinctions between unit of account, monetary media, and relational differentiation (interpersonal transactions). I will end by providing a conclusion concerning the state of the literature and point attention to the some of the shortcomings in the current state of scholarship.

SECTION 1: THE NEOCLASSICAL
ECONOMIC CONCEPT OF MONEY

Neoclassical (mainstream) economists have a simple definition of money, in spite of their ever-raging debates about how to measure and account for fluctuations in the demand and supply of money and how to specify the appropriate quantity of money an economy needs to generate and sustain inflation-free, full employment. Money is any convenient commodity (good, paper, thing, etc.) that serves the following functions: acts as a medium of exchange, a unit of account, a store of value, and a standard of deferred payment.[9] This is a very functionalist definition of money—for money is what money does. Economists consider money as anything that performs the functions of money. In this way, economists link the existence and nature of money to functions of money.

The theoretical understanding of money in modern capitalist economies is centered around the "intrinsic" commodity nature of money; that is, money as representing only exchange ratios, as a neutral veil, and as only a medium of exchange. In the mainstream (neoclassical) economics view, money is essentially either a natural commodity or a symbol of a natural commodity; a commodity that can be traded for all other commodities. Whether this commodity is gold, cigarette, or paper is not really the issue; whatever it is, it merely symbolizes the underlying exchange ratios between tradable commodities. It is a veil over the "real" economy, having no economic force *sui generis*. Eminent economist and Nobel laureate Paul Samuelson writes: "even in the most advanced industrial economies, if we strip exchange down to its barest essentials and peel off the obscuring layer of money, we find that trade between individuals or nations largely boils down to barter."[10]

In order to further deepen our understanding of this way of thinking about money, let us examine some aspects of its historical origin. William Stanley Jevons, in his highly influential book, *Money and Mechanism of Exchange* (1875), put forward the idea that the use of money originated from repeated bilateral exchanges between commodities, with one commodity eventually emerging as the most cost-effective one with which to trade. This emergent liquid commodity became the medium of exchange which has an exchange ratio with all other commodities.[11] Money is only a neutral veil that overcame the inconveniences of crude barter and eliminated the need for "double coincidence of wants."[12] Thus money is said to have originated in the private sector. In this model of bilateral exchanges the "exchange ratios of commodities actually express their 'real' values." Besides, the object that serves as the medium of exchange must be "a thing that is useful and has exchange value independently of its monetary function."[13] The medium of exchange could also be *numéraire*, a pure number, a representative basket of commodities, or a device that allows the system of barter to be carried out. The *numéraire is* mere "neutral veil," a symbol of "real" good that does not have an autonomous force of its own. So with this focus on "real" economy all models of the modern economy, irrespective of their levels of sophistication, boil down to barter-economy models involving no endogenous money.[14] This is what Samuelson is really saying in the quote above. Joseph Schumpeter summarizes the focus on the "real" economy in this way:

> Real analysis proceeds from the principle that all essential phenomena of economic life are capable of being described in terms of goods and services, of decisions about them, and of relations between them. Money enters the picture only in the modest role of a technical device that has been adopted in order to facilitate transactions. This device can no doubt get out of order, and if it does it will indeed produce phenomena that are specifically attributable to its *modus operandi*. But so long as it functions normally, it does not affect the economic process, which behaves in the same way as it would in a barter economy: this is essentially what the concept of Neutral Money implies. Thus, money has been called a "garb" or "veil" of the things that really matter. . . . Not only can it be discarded whenever we are analyzing the fundamental features of the economic process but it must be discarded just as a veil must be drawn aside if we are to see the face behind it. Accordingly, money prices must give way to exchange ratios between the commodities that are the really important thing 'behind' money prices.[15]

In this view of the "real" exchange, no social relations or agent-agent relations are seriously acknowledged apart from agents haggling for prices.

What is important are the exchange ratios between commodities and the individual utility calculations as agents relate to particular commodities. This neoclassical economic perspective that regards money as a given and as nothing more than a lubricant between "real" goods has been subjected to scathing criticism. One of the most dramatic contributions of the new behavioral economics, the study of "mental accounting," has challenged the orthodox, neoclassical economics view of money from a psychological perspective. Mental accounting is the individualistic version of the sociological earmarking argument made by sociologists like Viviana Zelizer (we will come to it below). Individuals use mental accounting, according to Richard H. Thaler of the Graduate School of Business, University of Chicago,

> to keep trace [sic] of where their money is going, and to keep spending under control. Mental accounting is a description of the ways they do these things. . . . Mental accounting violates the economic notion of fungibility. Money in one mental account is not a perfect substitute for money in another account. Because of violations of fungibility, mental accounting matters [and money is not just a veil].[16]

Sociologist Geoffrey Ingham says it is "radically *a*historical and *a*social in the sense that particular forms of economic organization are deemed to be epiphenomenal or merely 'contextual'; complex social structure—banks, productive enterprises, etc.—is reduced to purely abstract relations between rational maximising agents" (italics in the original).[17]

In the preceding paragraphs, I have provided an overview of the neoclassical economic view of money. The sociological analysis of money arose principally as a reaction to this orthodox neoclassical view of money. The result now is that three properties have emerged as key to the definition of money. They are unit of account, monetary media, and interpersonal transactions.

In the next section, I will review the debate on money as a unit of account. It is important to state that the separate treatment I am giving to each of these properties is not meant to indicate that the three properties are independent of one another. Everywhere that money exists it exists with the three key properties of unit of account, medium of exchange, and interpersonal transaction. Zelizer puts it well:

> "each property acts on the others. . . . The type of medium . . . impacts on how 'people use and think about money in relation to their own lives and circumstances.' In the same way, how money integrates into interpersonal relations rebounds to affect other properties of money: monetary media and unit of account."[18]

SECTION 2: MONEY AS UNIT OF ACCOUNT

British sociologist Nigel Dodd has recently drawn attention to the failure of economic sociologists to make proper distinctions between money as a unit of account and monetary media in their scholarly analyses of money. Challenging the notion of "real money" and "quasi-monies," he argued that it is no longer analytically valid to make distinctions between monies based on issuing authority or insisting that only one form of money in a given geo-political space can perform the role of money of account. There is now multiplicity of money and each form of money has its own two qualities (unit of account and medium of exchange). He points out that there are specialized circuits of monetary exchange and each separate circuit is distinguished by a monetary medium, specific money of account, or by a mixture of both.[19]

In reaching this conclusion, Dodd draws heavily from Zelizer's analysis of the multiplicity of money using the concept of "circuits of commerce." In this work, she suggests that, and as noted by Dodd, "money is multiple as *an entity in its own right*, not just in social meaning" (emphasis in the original). Each circuit has its own localized tokens which serve as a medium of exchange and as a separate money of account.[20]

While I agree with the view of Dodd and Zelizer on the crucially important point that money in every circuit of exchange carries within it the two qualities and in so doing I disagree with the view of Geoffrey Ingham[21] who posits that monetary media are unimportant, one must note that their argument does not adequately deal with role of unit of account in establishing the "moneyness"[22] of money in a given economy. Certainly variations in monetary media matter greatly and are very relevant to a sociological understanding of money, but it is another matter to see every form of monetary medium as having its own form of "money" or unit of account.[23] Besides, the question of "what is money?" does not necessarily translate into an inquiry into monetary media. This is where one needs to introduce other voices to balance those of Zelizer, Dodd, and Keith Hart who have conflated the issues of money of account and money as a medium.[24] Particularly, Dodd shows his confusion on this matter when he sought to understand the "concept of money itself." He states that Simmel's "pure concept of money" is what money really is but fails to realize that the pure concept of money in Simmel's work is the abstract unit of account (money of account).[25] He makes this assertion about the pure concept of money after he has stridently argued that every form of money has its own unit of account.[26] It is true that every form of money has the dual qualities of money of account and medium of exchange, but it is another matter to argue that every form of money has the unit of account on its own. The unit of account is conferred by the abstract money of account in a given monetary space.

The question, "what is money?" is not answered by equating money with monetary media, however materialized or dematerialized the media might be. The generalizable tokens (whether bills, paper, commodity, metal, or electronic circuit) are the phenomenal forms money takes but are not the moneyness of money. There has to be first money before monetary media; first there has to be moneyness which has to be embodied in a particular form. Philip Grierson got it right when he stated that "money lies behind coinage."[27] Georg Simmel, seeing money as a form of *sociation* constituted by the social relation of credit, posits that money is "only a claim upon society."[28] Moneyness is found in the abstract money of account, the unit of account. Keynes calls the unit of account *"description or title."* And it precedes media, which is the money-stuff, money as a means of payment. In Keynes' words it is "the *thing* which answers to the *description*."[29]

Let us try to deepen our understanding of the concept of unit (money) of account. I would like to organize the sociological literature on the subject around three types of discourse in order to make it manageable for our limited purpose in this chapter. First is the discourse that seeks to uncover the origins of money as a money of account and not as a medium of exchange. The question is: what is the source of the money of account/measure of value? It may have arisen from *wergeld* ("worth payment"), the precise scale of tariffs and compensations for injuries and damages that ancient community, political authority, or temples imposed on wrong doers. It also may have come from sacrifice (primordial, fundamental debt) of the living to appease god, spirits, and ancestors in order to expiate transgressions or to maintain the long-term continuity of society.[30]

In the *Wergeld* system we can find the two basic elements (moral and utilitarian, long- and short-term spheres) of the social structure that Jonathan Parry and Maurice Bloch talked about in *Money and the Morality of Exchange.* "*Wergeld* symbolically represented society's two faces. On the one hand, it attempted to quantify the functional contribution of social roles by the imposition of payments for the loss or impairment of the individual incumbents. On the other hand, these scales were informed by a codification of the values without which the attribution of functional worth to society would have remained anomic and anarchic."[31]

Economic historian, Michael Hudson also traces the money of account to the *Wergeld* institutions as substantive, specific payments that gradually became decontextualized, and to developments in bookkeeping. "The monetary use of silver and other metals emerged in the context of the weights and measures developed in the Sumerian temples and palaces [public institutions] as part of their account-keeping and administered prices. Money was a 'public good,' used to price rations and other resources flows."[32] Georg Knapp argues that the state is the source of money, and it did not originate in the private sector and that "money is a creature of the law."[33] Keynes in his early writings supported this view, asserting that "Money of Account, namely that in which Debts and Prices and General Purchasing Power are expressed is the primary concept of Theory of Money" and the source of it is the state or community.[34] According to him, if money has only a medium of exchange function then transactions have scarcely emerged from the stage of barter. The test for knowing if exchange has emerged from the stage of barter is the emergence of measure of value, according to numismatist Philip Grierson. "Unless the commodities used for exchange bear some fixed relation to a standard, we are still dealing with barter. . . . The parties in barter-exchange are comparing their individual and immediate needs, not values in the abstract."[35]

The second type of discourse is about the crucial difference between money of account and medium of exchange. The medium of exchange is the asset or commodity that creditors are willing to accept to extinguish debts or what sellers of goods (services) are willing to accept to complete a sale (purchase). It needs not have a physical embodiment as it can be gold, bookkeeping entries or computer magnetic traces. The standard in which prices or debts are quoted is the medium or unit of account. The unit of account in the United States is the dollar and in the days of the gold standard it was defined as certain grams of gold. In fact, it should be stated that any thing may be "accepted as representing this abstract value of the unit of account."[36] So in history we have had metals, commodities, animals, shells, vegetables, etc., which are forms of money-proper representing this *abstract* money of account, measure of value, purchasing power. There are many sociologists and economists, as we shall see below, who argue that the quality of "moneyness" comes from and is embedded in the social and political arrangements that create and sustain this common, stable yardstick, and not in the forms of money-proper and their circulation. For instance, banker A. Mitchell Innes writing in 1914 states that:

> the eye has never seen, nor the hand touched a dollar. All that we can touch or see is a promise to pay or satisfy a debt due for an amount called a dollar. That which we handle may be a dollar certificate or a dollar note or a dollar coin; it may bear words promising to pay a dollar or promising to exchange it for a dollar coin of gold or silver, or it may merely bear the word dollar. . . . The theory of abstract standard is not so extraordinary as it first appears, and it presents no difficulty to those scientific men with whom I have discussed the theory. All measures are the same. No one has ever seen an ounce or a foot or an hour.[37]

The question now is why is it important to differentiate the money of account from the actual social or phenomenological forms of money? The

issue is not whether money exists anywhere today without simultaneously being *unit of account* (money of account) and *medium* (monetary media). All forms of money have these two qualities. The defining issue in
the debate is whether the function of medium of account is historically
and logically prior to the development of the medium of exchange. If one
of them is not always or have not always been reducible to the other, can
we identify "the different causal trajectories involved in the emergence"
of the two properties and in their development in today's globalizing
world? Understanding how they came into being is important not only
for interpreting the history of money, but also for analyzing money as a
sociological category.

Neoclassical economists, working from the insights of two nineteenth-
century economists, Stanley William Jevons and Carl Menger, on the evolution of money, argue that medium of exchange came first in order to
transcend the inconveniences of barter. It was the process of searching for
a generally acceptable medium of exchange that produced the abstract
concept of the money account.[38] Not everybody agrees. Economists like
Tyler Cowen and Randall Kroszner and many sociologists sternly reject
this view.[39] Sociologist Ingham writes: "the very *idea* of money, which is to
say, of abstract account for value, is *logically anterior and historically prior to
market exchange* (emphasis in the original).[40] If the abstract concept of
money of account is prior to the phenomenological form, then moneyness
needs to be primarily sought at the abstract unit of account.

My argument that analysis of unit of account needs to focus on the
quality of moneyness is not meant to show that there is "real" money
which has "moneyness" that a variety of "quasi-monies" do not have.
Contrary to the position of Ingham, who sees money not issued by the
state as "emaciated," "quasi," "limited-purpose money," or imperfect approximations of the real thing, I do not believe that any medium can serve
as money if it does not have moneyness.[41] The problem Ingham sets up is
really a pseudo-problem. Money (the embodiment of moneyness, the mediating concrete form) is always and everywhere has both qualities (unit
of account and monetary media) simultaneously. Monetary system is always a combination of two sub-systems: one (the money of account)
based on the long-term cycle that seeks to underpin the moneyness of the
monetary media and continuity of the monetary order, the other (media
of account or the phenomenological forms) based on the short-term cycle
that has to do with exchange and interpersonal relationships among individuals with competing or overlapping interests.

Several paragraphs above, I stated that Dodd and Zelizer do not adequately incorporate the role of the unit of account in establishing the moneyness of money in any given monetary space, despite their highlighting
of it as a key property of money. The tone of the discussions that followed

may have given the impression that Zelizer, Dodd, and Hart misunderstand the unit-of-account property of money. Theirs is more of partial understanding than misunderstanding. What has happened is that they focused on one aspect of the dual nature of monies of account. Monies of account have the abstract unit of account (the pure concept of money in Dodd's term or the "Weberian Ideal type" in Zelizer's terminology), which Ingham insists confers moneyness on objects or media. Monies of account also have the quality of establishing connection between quantities and between money and quantities—this is the practical mathematical function of serving as the measure of value. In this sense, it is right for Zelizer and Dodd to argue that different media or forms of money can and do serve as monies of account.

It appears that this partial sense of money (money of account), which enables us to represent values as magnitudes, is deeply entrenched in many scholarly thoughts to the neglect of the quality of "moneyness." Recently, Bruce Carruthers gave a review of the sociological literature on money but regrettably limited his analysis of money as a unit of account to only the connection between monetary valuation and quantitative measurements and to the ability of modern money to induce proliferation of quantitative measurements.[42]

Indeed, deciphering the proper role and place of the *unit of account* in the sociological debate about money is very slippery even for the classical social thinkers. For instance, Simmel who one thought would have had a proper grasp of the subject appears to slip without notice between profound and poor comprehensions of it. In spite of Simmel's profound analysis of money of account, it still suffers from two deficiencies. It lacks a discussion of how the abstract value of money is established and maintained. Simmel also somehow thinks that the abstract value of money depends on the process of dematerialization of money-stuff.[43] This is an error many analysts still make today. The abstract unit of account precedes the concrete medium of exchange and it is not dependent on the abstraction (dematerialization) of monetary media. Economists Tyler Cowen and Randal Kroszner, among many others, argue that "the development of media of account is logically and historically prior to the development of media of exchange."[44]

The unit-of-account property of money appears as the most abstract of the three properties of money under examination in this chapter. And for this reason it is very easy to overlook its social aspect or the social structure that stands behind it.[45] It should not be so. The state is often *one of the crucial sources* of money and the authority that establishes the money of account. In as much as different circuits of exchange can coexist in a given geopolitical space, the kind of money which is usually most readily acceptable in any given monetary space is that produced by the sovereign state or community. The state or political authority has the power to demand payment of taxes in a specified medium. Anything that the state chooses as acceptable in the discharge of its citizens' obligations to it becomes currency.[46] Citizens on their own will accept from one another such item, object, commodity, paper, or token as long as it will enable them to settle their liabilities to the state. Adam Smith recognized this when he wrote that "a prince, who should enact that a certain proportion of his taxes should be paid in a paper money of a certain kind, might thereby give a certain value to this paper money."[47] Similarly Keynes argues that it is the state that decides what thing should answer as money to the current money of account in its domain. The bottom line of this argument, which is normally tagged the Chartalist position,[48] is that credit or debt is the source of money as defined by a sovereign state and the value of such money does not derive from any inherent value within/backing the money. Thus Cambridge University sociologist Ingham argues that money is itself constituted by social relations and "cannot be adequately conceptualized other than as the emergent property of a configuration (or 'structure') of social relations."[49] What Ingham means here must be currency (state-issued currency). It is true that all forms of money, including currency, is constituted by social relations, but it is not true that the qualifying relation is only that of the state.

I stated earlier that the review of the literature on key property of money as a unit of account will be organized around three types of discourse. We have so far discussed the first two types: origin of the money as a unit of account and the distinction between money of account and monetary media. The third type revolves around the debate on the idea that money dissolves social relations. Some classical social thinkers maintained that with money serving as universal measure of values (in its unit-of-account function) qualitative differences were converted into quantitative difference, thus desiccating all social ties.

Classical social thinkers like Karl Marx, Max Weber, and Georg Simmel in different ways interpreted money as "the very essence of our rationalizing modern civilization" and "a tool of rational cost-profit calculations." It is a rational instrument without much "cultural significance" (that is, without much qualitative differentiation, earmarking, personalizing, and non-homogenization), focused only on "arithmetic problems." The general idea is that money and monetization, the twin battering rams of capitalism, have been very successful in transforming "products, relationships and sometimes even emotions into an abstract and objective numerical equivalent"[50] all over the world. Though Marx argued that the objective relations between commodities are the phantasmagoric forms of social relations between people, he still viewed money, a "god among commodities," as the radical, frightful leveler that desiccates all social ties and spaces.[51]

Weber, influenced by Georg Friedrich Knapp's book, *The State Theory of Money*, argued that the rational calculability that money enables in a modern society is based on money of account, the abstract, nominal unit of measure.[52] He regarded money as the arrow head of the rationalization processes in industrial societies. According to Weber, rational calculability, a quintessential feature of all capitalist societies, finds in money "the most abstract" and "'impersonal' element that exists in human life."[53] For Simmel money is "colorless" and it is free from any quality consideration as it is exclusively determined by quantity.[54]

Zelizer and others have argued that this high view of money is not correct. Money is not really *fungible*—not all monies are equal and interchangeable in modern capitalist societies. Different meanings and separate use patterns pertain to different monies. Money carries an interest beyond its quantitative value. In the following section we will examine how the meaning and value of money is socially and culturally constructed and how social structures and personal relations impact the use and interpretation of monetary media. The coexistence of several monetary media in a given monetary space is partly caused by differences in social relations and meanings that people attach to them. The diversity of media has naturally raised the question, which of the media represents the real money?

SECTION 3: THE MULTIPLICITY OF MONETARY MEDIA

One key dispute surrounding the definition of money is this: is there one "real" money and a variety of "quasi-monies," which are imperfect approximations of the real thing? Does there exist a continuum of monies, all real but with different scope? In the last section, I have treated this matter as it relates to the issue of *unit of account*. The conclusion I reached was that it is a pseudo-problem to define real or non-real money on the basis of which monetary medium truly has the unit of account. All monies simultaneously have both qualities of unit of account and medium of exchange and a money does not necessarily have to be denominated in a money of account that is established by the state in order to function as money in its own right. Here I want to enter into a different aspect of the debate: the increasing diversity of monies and what causes it.

The focus on the multiplicity or diversity of money forms is relevant to answering the questions, "what is money" and "what are its key properties" and in offering a correction to the homogenous image of money propagated by both neoclassical economists and classical social thinkers like Marx and Simmel. Against the extraordinarily narrow concept of homogenous money, some scholars, namely Zelizer, have attempted to formulate a more substantial institutional and cultural account of money. They have vigorously put forward the notion of the diverse nature of money, asserting that monetary exchanges are thickly social, cultural, and relational.

Zelizer documents how people *earmark* money, place restrictions on its use to mark social boundaries, create separate spheres of exchange and regulate allocations to create differentiation of homogenous money, affirm cultural distinctions, and elaborate the social meaningfulness of money. In this way, she mounted a vigorous assault against the widespread economistic view of money as absolutely fungible, qualitatively neutral, and devoid of any use value. Her research has shown that money is "neither culturally neutral nor socially anonymous. It may well 'corrupt' values and convert social ties into numbers, but values and social relations reciprocally transmute money by investing it with meaning and social patterns."[55] In directing attention to monetary exchanges as thickly social, cultural, and relational, Zelizer argues that social ties and economic (monetary) transactions repeatedly mingle. In this vein she rejects the idea of "hostile world"[56] and that of "economics-or-nothing reductionism" in economic-sociological analyses.[57]

It is important to note that the sociological interpretation of the diversity of money is not just about earmarking of a particular state-currency which ensures that "not all dollars are the same," it also about alternative currencies to the legal tender in a particular function domain of national money. There are thus two interpretations of the multiplicity of money. "The first interpretation is phenomenological: earmarking renders money meaningful for its users."[58] This interpretation encourages scholars to look at state-issued currency in a different way. Zelizer's work has principally made this interpretation succinct and widespread. She has shown that social relations matter greatly for understanding money's variations. As she puts it:

> All moneys are actually dual: they serve both general and local circuits. . . . Seen from the top, economic transactions connect with broad national symbolic meanings and institutions. Seen from the bottom, however, economic transactions are highly differentiated, personalized, and local, meaningful to particular relations. No contradiction therefore exists between uniformity and diversity: they are simply two different aspects of the same transaction.[59]

The second interpretation is about multiplicity of monetary forms themselves—a diversity that is not marked by social meaning but by distinctions arising from the interplay of state-issued currency and other forms of money (such as e-money, LETS[60] and other alternatives to currency). This diversity is not about variety of forms (media) that circulate in a given monetary domain—for this is not new. Hitherto, the circulation of monetary media has largely depended on the existence of uniform money based on unchanging money of account (official currency). But now both monetary media and monies of account are changing. The emerging new forms of money are "distinguishable from official currency by virtue of the unit of account they are denominated in, not by their material properties as monetary media."[61] They provide an accounting system in which prices, debts and purchasing power are expressed, calculated, and settled.

This second interpretation of money's variation, especially as championed by Dodd suffers a shortcoming. It fails to formally integrate the close interplay between money's variation and the construction of social relations and meaning systems into the analysis. The social basis of money diversity is not properly accounted for. Nonetheless, he has made significant contribution to our understanding of the ongoing process of multiplicity of monies.

Dodd's recent contribution to the literature is to situate this developing diversity in the context of the ongoing homogenization of currencies. The rapid development of variety of the forms of money is seen by him in many places as a direct counterweight to the homogenization of state-issued currencies in many economies. Paradoxically, the ongoing homogenization of currency—for example in the euro zone—is helping to stimulate the increasing diversification of money (both of non state-issued currency monetary media and monies of account). He argues that the prospect of alternative monies becoming successful has been enhanced by the electronic medium through which they are being realized. In the causal trajectories of development he lays out for these currencies, their distinctive status as also monies of account is essential if they are to offset the disadvantages of the large-scale currencies. In addition, their media (electronic or not) are highly relevant to understanding the role they are playing in society and "to how people use and think about money in relation to their own lives and circumstances."[62]

In general, the extant literature on the question, "what is money?" appears to have settled on this point: it is a continuum that runs from generalized forms to limited-purpose money. It rejects the notion that the only "real" consequential money is the state-issued homogenous fungible currency. In the words of one of the leading exponents of this view, money is "a coherent field of variation rather than an invariant, unitary phenomenon."[63] The distinctions between forms of money can no longer be adequately explained by the degree of fungibility. Whether they are real or not can no longer be decided with reference to sovereign political authority either. They are best understood, according to Dodd, in the "light of the distinction between monetary media and monies of account."[64]

Though Dodd draws heavily from her in reaching this conclusion and her own research has been closely associated with the empirical and theoretical investigations of the multiplicity of money, Zelizer rejects his conclusion that distinction between various forms of money can be adequately made in terms of unit of account and monetary media. She argues for a third element: "money's relational differentiation." She insists that money's social element is not trivial as people regularly distinguish forms of money to mark distinct social relations. In her reasoning, any analysis of the key properties of money that ignores the social bases of monetary activity is incomplete. The third property, she argues, exerts significant effect on the first two:

> Which media or unit of account people adopt, when, and how depends on the type of social relations involved. Parent-child, priest-congregant, welfare official-aid recipient, legislator-constituent, courting couple—all these relations sometimes involve monetary transactions, but each calls for a very different combination of media and units of accounts.[65]

We have so far reviewed the discussion of the three-level variation in the properties of money: unit of account, monetary media, and interpersonal transactions. I would like to expand the discussion of social bases of monetary activity and how social relations matter for understanding the sociological category of money by entering into a discussion of the social character of money. The discussions that follow will deepen our understanding of the third property of money by shifting the focus slightly from definition of money to money's role in society. This introduces one of the major themes of chapter 4, "Money as a Social Relation."

SECTION 4: THE SOCIAL CHARACTER OF MONEY

Historically the sociological debate about the role of money has been framed by the question: is money, by introducing uniformity and calculations into every area of society, dissolving all social relations or not? Does the use of homogenous or standardized money presuppose homogenization of social life by money? Marx, Simmel, and Weber appear to answer yes to the question. Today's scholars like Zelizer, Bruce Carruthers, and Milan Zafirovski would answer no, insisting that money is often used to create distinct meaningful social relations. Which group is right?

Parry and Bloch's influential work, *Money and the Morality of Exchange* (1989), provides insight on how to reconcile the views of two groups of scholars, those who argue that neutral and neutralizing money is the ultimate impersonal common denominator and those who argue that money does create meaningful long-term social relations. Parry and Bloch have argued that there are two forms of exchange in any given society: the cycle of short-term exchange is concerned with the transience and the cycle of the long-term is concerned with the reproduction of the social and cosmic order. The short-term sphere is concerned with the reproduction of the viability of the individual, households, or corporations. It is focused more on individual acquisitiveness in short-term frames. This is not exactly the focus of the long-term cycle which is concerned with the reproduction of the whole enduring social order in a time-full manner. It is pertinent to state that the two cycles are essential to each other. The long-term restorative cycle depends on and must negate the short-term transactional cycle which is concerned with individualistic transactions and not with timeless order.[66] Thus Parry and Bloch argue that both schools of thought emphasize the distinctiveness of the two cycles and each is unable to imagine the mechanisms by which they are linked. What the two different discourses and often contradictory representations of money reflect "is the radical divorce between the two cycles, each discourse deriving from the perspective of one side of the dichotomy alone."[67]

Talcott Parsons also offers us a good perspective on the social character of money. Contrary to a good deal of economic scholarship and tradition at the time he wrote, Parsons treats money not as a concrete object, but as a process, a communicative medium. Long before money (monetary media) became increasingly abstract, he forcefully argued that "money is not a physical object, nor a unit of money, e.g. a dollar. Money is a 'symbolic mechanism' and its 'use,' e.g., by 'spending' is a process of communication."[68] For Parsons, money shares deep affinity with other cases of communication in human communities. He regards money as one of the generalized symbolic media of social exchange. All such media share a relationship involving "language," medium of communication, and physical consequences. If any two independent economic agents in a given economy are to influence each other there must be a process through which information is transmitted between them. This is a process through which "physical" media (cash, stones, papers, etc.) containing encoded information is transferred from an agent in one spatial location to another in a different location. This transfer often also induces the transfer of physical products or services from one agent to another.

Although Parsons has been criticized for limiting the symbolism of money to only the economic domain and failing to explore the symbolic meaning of money in other spheres, his analysis of money clearly identifies money as embedded in human relationality and as integrator of functionally differentiated parts of the social system.[69] Parsons, for all his efforts, still has shortcomings because, in analyzing money, he limited himself to viewing money as mere symbolic token and not as value itself, taking for granted the existence of money. He was as functionalist and teleological in explaining money as were the neoclassical economists who also saw money as "neutral."

In order to further deepen our knowledge of the social character of money, let us lift up aspects of Weber's work that bear on the social nature of monetary activity. In his analysis of money as an instrument that produces rational calculability, Weber came upon three ideas that are relevant to understanding the relational nature of money. First, he rejects the mainstream economic notion that prices are only products of the market play of the forces of demand and supply. "Money prices are the product of conflicts of interest and of compromises [that] result from power constellations." Second, money is not a neutral veil, rather it is "primarily a weapon in this struggle ["a struggle of man against man"], and prices are expressions of the struggle; they are instruments of calculations only as estimated quantifications of relative chances in this struggle of interest." Third, Weber argued that inflation and deflation are not mere occurrences but are "always in very complex ways dependent on its [money] scarcity" and on the economic struggle for existence, and the balance of power in the actual processes of production and control of money.[70]

Weber's insight on the effect of power struggle on money has been confirmed by latter-day sociologists such as Wayne Baker and Ingham. Baker, while demonstrating that the power to define and create money is not limited to governments and their central banks, as it is exercised in a network-like organization, shows that power is concentrated in the core of financial structure.[71] His findings revealed that in the United States the most powerful actors play at the core of the structure, while the periphery is where the less powerful actors operate. The types of financial assets used by the actors in the core are considered closest to money. He then argues:

> An economy differentiated into core and periphery structure indicates an unequal distribution of power. The core actors in an economy dominate other actors, control the flow of capital, and wield political power. In contrast, the peripheral actors are in the weak and powerless position.[72]

Ingham has sought to explain the dynamics of interest rates in modern capitalist societies in terms of outcomes of the balance of power struggles between groups. He explains British inflation of the 1970s and the price stability in the 1980s and 1990s in Weberian sociopolitical arguments.[73] Thus he states:

> In capitalism, the pivotal struggle between creditors and debtors is centered on forging the real rate of interest (nominal rate minus inflation rate) that is politically acceptable and economically feasible. On the one hand, too high a

real rate of interest will deter entrepreneurial debtors and inhibit economic dynamism. On the other hand, too low a rate or, more seriously, a negative rate of interest (inflation rate in excess of nominal interest rate) inhibits the advance of money-capital loans. . . . Weber's emphasis on money's status as a weapon in the economic battle directs attention to its political nature. This element is entirely absent from all orthodox economic analysis, which, I would stress, is tacitly endorsed by the other social sciences.[74]

With this insight, we have completed the task we set for ourselves at the beginning of this chapter—that of understanding the key properties of money. At the current level of economic sociology, the debate about definition of money revolves around three key properties: unit of account, monetary media, and interpersonal transactions (the social character of money). The chapter has touched the major authors, problems, and schools of thought. The review was organized around arguments and counter-arguments around these three properties. The conclusion concerning the state of the literature is that there is no one "real money" but a continuum of monies, all real, but with different scope. Money is "a coherent field of variation rather than an invariant, unitary phenomenon."

SECTION 5: CONCLUSION

There are two major shortcomings in the current state of scholarship which I intend now to address. First, there is no proper definition of money which incorporates all the three properties. The empirical work of understanding the forms of money has proceeded to a very advanced stage, but the task of theoretical understanding of money has lagged behind.[75] Where is that inclusive concept of money that can answer the question, "what is money" in the twenty-first century? Indeed, there is no readily acceptable answer. Dodd, after reviewing the state of sociology of money, appears to have thrown up his hands in despair when he says "the problem today is that no single definition of money will suffice on empirical grounds. 'Money,' it appears, is literally disintegrating. The terms of the present debates on money suggest that any attempt to build a coherent theoretical conception of money is bound to fail."[76]

The second shortcoming is this: the sociological literature on money is too steeped in the discourse of money as *matter*, money as a tangible, concrete phenomenon, a quantity or stock (what economists would call the stock concept of money). It offers little or nothing on the analysis of money as a *motion* (the flow concept of money). Economic sociologists have ignored the production and control of money, the flows of money which actually determine who gets what quantity, when, and how. Production and control—motion—precedes social earmarking of money, stock and use, that is, the *matter* of money. Hopefully, things will change soon. Scholars like Carruthers are beginning to focus on flows of money and intertemporal monetary transactions.[77]

Chapter 4 ("Money as a Social Relation") extends the sociological discourse on money. Sociologists have argued that all monetary phenomena are socially contingent. They posit that money is not a neutral, nonsocial substance and that it is influenced everywhere by culture. They have countered the mainstream neoclassical economic perspective that regards money as a given and as nothing more than a lubricant between "real" goods in order to reveal the meaningful social relations among persons or groups in monetary transactions. Nevertheless, even though they have informed us that money is a socially contingent phenomenon, they still have not considered social relations as constitutive of money *itself*.[78] In addition, despite working with some definitions of money they do not provide a general theory of money that specifies the common character of money which allows money's applications to be varied.[79] I will attempt to correct these deficiencies by providing a general theory of what monies have in common, that is, the essential property of "money in general."[80] I will argue that money is *simultaneously a social relation* and a *relational-thing*. As will be shown in the next chapter, this neologism of mine refers to a view of money that incorporates the social relation-view of money and a "thing"-perspective of money.

In sum, economic sociologists display their own version of a shortcoming we observed in the theologies of money. Both sets of studies reveal a neglect of socio-flow perspective of money. The reviews point toward the need for a "money-as-motion" focus, that is, money in structures of flow.

NOTES

1. I would like to acknowledge the assistance and support of economic sociologist Professor Viviana Zelizer of Princeton University in writing this chapter and the next.

2. See for example, Nigel Dodd, "Reinventing Monies in Europe," *Economy and Society* 34, no.4 (November 2005): 558–83; and Viviana Zelizer, "Missing Monies: Comment on Nigel Dodd, 'Reinventing monies in Europe,'" *Economy and Society* 34, no. 4 (November 2005): 584–88.

3. Bruce Carruthers, "The Sociology of Money and Credit," in *The Handbook of Economic Sociology*, 2nd ed., ed. N. J. Smelser and R. Swedberg (Princeton, NJ: Princeton University Press, 2005), 355–78; and Milan Zafirovski, *Exchange, Action, and Social Structure: Elements of Economic Sociology* (Westport, CT: Greenwood Press, 2001), 1–25.

4. Zelizer, "Missing Monies," 584–88; and Carruthers, "The Sociology of Money and Credit," 355–78.

5. Dodd, "Reinventing Monies," 563.

6. K. Hart, *Money in an Unequal World: Keith Hart and his Memory Bank* (New York & London: Texere, 2000), 248. He borrowed this description from Maynard Keynes.

7. Viviana A. Zelizer, "Sociology of Money," in *International Encyclopedia of the Social and Behavioral Sciences* 15 (2001): 1991–94.

8. Neoclassical economics is today the mainstream economics. It developed in the nineteenth century out of classical economics. Classical economists like Karl Marx, Adam Smith, and David Ricardo argued that value (price) depends on cost of production and that the distribution of output or profit to the different social groups or classes depends on the cost of production borne by each group. Neoclassical economists argue that value or price do not necessarily depend on cost but on utility and the influence of demand and supply. They maintain that value is not inherent in the product but on the marginal utility. Thus the marginal utility revolution was born. It is believed that it was the American economist Thorstein Veblen was the first to use the term "neoclassical economists" in recognition of this revolution in thinking. Today "neoclassical economics is what is called a metathory. That is a set of implicit rules or understanding for constructing satisfactory economic theories," E. Roy Weintraub, "Neoclassical Economics," in *The Fortune Encyclopedia of Economics*, ed. David R. Henderson (New York: Warner Books, 1993), 136.

9. See Eugene A. Diulio, *Theory and Problems of Macroeconomic Theory* (New York: McGraw-Hill, 1990): 241. See also Tyler Cowen and Randall Kroszner, *Explorations in the New Monetary Economics* (Cambridge, MA: Blackwell Publishers, 1994), 9; and Frederic S. Mishkin, *The Economics of Money, Banking, and Financial Markets* (Glenview, IL: Scott, Foresman & Co., 1989), 22–26.

10. Paul Samuelson, *Economics*, 9th ed. (New York: McGraw-Hill, 1973), 55.

11. Although it has been accepted for a long time that money came out of barter, it has been recently subjected to scrutiny. The antagonists to the barter-origin theory declare that little evidence exists to support the assertion that barter economies ever existed. See Stephanie Bell, "The Role of the State and the Hierarchy of Money," *Cambridge Journal of Economics* 25 (2001): 149–63, especially pp. 151 and 161. See also the essays collected in this volume, Stephanie A. Bell and Edward J. Nell, eds., *The State, the Market and the Euro: Chartalism versus Metalism in the Theory of Money* (Cheltenham: Edward Elgar, 2003), 1–25, 39–88, 95–97, 104–5,116–17, 130–31, 138–59.

12. A woman who wants to sell her fowl will first have to find someone who likes to buy a fowl (the first coincidence) and that potential buyer will have to offer something she wants (the second coincidence). Monetary exchange eliminates the second coincidence.

13. See Joseph A. Schumpeter, *History of Economic Analysis* (New York: Oxford University Press, 1994 [1954]), 63.

14. This term means that money is non-neutral in the economy; the money supply expands and contracts with the business cycle. Banks would create the financing required to meet the needs of production, and more important, such financing is a precondition for production actually taking place. In this sense, money is not just a veil or symbol of real goods, not something external (exogenous) to the production process, but also internal (endogenous) to it.

15. Schumpeter, *History of Economic Analysis*, 277.

16. Richard H. Thaler, "Mental Accounting Matters," *Journal of Behavioral Decision Making* 12 (1999): 183–206.

17. Geoffrey Ingham, "Money is a Social Relation," in *Critical Realism in Economics: Development and Debate*, ed. Steve Fleetwood (London: Routledge, 1999), 107.

18. Zelizer, "Missing Monies, 587.

19. Dodd, "Reinventing Monies," 562–65.

20. Viviana Zelizer, "Circuits of Commerce," in *Self, Social Structure, and Beliefs: Explorations in Sociology*, ed. C. Williams (Berkeley: University of California Press, 2004), 122–44.

21. Geoffrey Ingham, *The Nature of Money* (Cambridge, MA: Polity Press, 2004), 73.

22. What I am after here are the generalizations about money that hold cross-contextually or inter-culturally. In this sense I am not getting at some "essence" of money, but more, at developing cross-cultural claims about money, working from an analysis of varying context of money usage. See also notes 41 and 80 below.

23. Zelizer in a personal e-mail to me on March 5, 2006, stated that I misunderstand her position here: "You misunderstand one position that I take, which is that multiple media can in fact attach to the 'same' money of account. I do not hold the position that for every transaction and medium, there is a separate money of account." This is not always clear from her writings and this is not how she is interpreted by other scholars.

24. For Hart's work, *Money in an Unequal World*.

25. Dodd, "Reinventing Monies," 572.

26. Dodd, "Reinventing Monies," 564–65, 570–71.

27. Philip Grierson, *The Origins of Money* (London: Athlone Press, 1977), 12.

28. Simmel, *Philosophy of Money*, 177.

29. Keynes, *A Treatise on Money* (London: Macmillan, 1930), 4.

30. Geoffrey Ingham, "Fundamentals of a Theory of Money: Untangling Fine, Lapavitsas and Zelizer," *Economy and Society* 30, no. 3 (2001): 310–11; Ingham, *The Nature of Money*, 90–95; Michael Hudson, "The Credit/Monetarist Debate in Historical Perspective," in *The State, the Market and the Euro*, 38–76; and Michael Hudson, "The Archaeology of Money: Debt Vs. Barter Theories of Money," in *Credit and State Theories of Money*, ed. Randall Wray (Cheltenham: Edward Elgar, 2004), 99–127.

31. Ingham, *The Nature of Money*, 93. Italics in the original.

32. Michael Hudson, "The Credit/Monetarist Debate in Historical Perspective," in *The State, the Market and the Euro: Chartalism versus Metalism in the Theory of Money*, ed. Stephanie A. Bell and Edward J. Nell (Cheltenham, UK: Edward Elgar, 2003), 42.

33. Georg F. Knapp, *The State Theory of Money*, trans. H. E. Batson (London: Routledge & Kegan Paul, 1924), viii, 31–38.

34. Keynes, *A Treatise on Money*, 3–5, 11–15.

35. Grierson, *The Origins of Money*, 16, 19.

36. Ingham, *The Nature of Money*, 47.

37. A. Mitchell Innes, "The Credit Theory of Money," *Banking Law Journal* 31, (January–December 1914): 155.

38. William Stanley Jevons, *Money and the Mechanism of Exchange* (New York: Appleton, 1986); and Carl Menger, "On the Origin of Money," *Economic Journal* 2 (June 1892): 239–55.

39. Tyler Cowen and Randall Kroszner, *Explorations in the New Monetary Economics* (Cambridge, MA.: Blackwell Publishers, 1994), 12; and Ingham, *The Nature of Money*.

40. Ingham, *The Nature of Money*, 25.

41. Ingham, *The Nature of Money*, 12, 187, 198. Moneyness is the quality of an object that makes it an acceptable medium of exchange in a society. The whole debate is about whether an object becomes money or acquires the ability to become money because the "money of account" quality is imposed on or given to it from elsewhere or it is just that it serves as a medium of exchange. Or must the object have both, for it to function as money? See n22 above.

42. Carruthers, "The Sociology of Money and Credit," 358–59.

43. Simmel, *The Philosophy of Money*, 191.

44. Cowen and Kroszner, *Explorations*, 12, see also pp. 17–18.

45. Carruthers, "The Sociology of Money and Credit," 358.

46. "In advanced societies the central government is in a strong position to make certain assets generally acceptable media. By its willingness to accept a designated asset in settlement of taxes and other obligations, the government makes that asset acceptable to any who have such obligations, and in turn to others who have obligations to them, and so on." James Tobin and S. S. Golub, *Money, Credit, and Capital* (New York: Irwin/McGraw Hill, 1998), 27.

47. Adam Smith, *An Inquiry into the Nature and Causes of the Wealth of Nations*, Bantam Classic Edition (New York: Random House, 2003), 419.

48. The Chartalist approach to money emphasizes the role played by the state or political authority in the origin of money and in designating the unit of account and what material exactly answers to it. The opposing school is the Metallist, which emphasizes the market.

49. Ingham, "Money is a Social Relation," 117.

50. Viviana Zelizer, *The Social Meaning of Money: Pin Money, Paychecks, Poor Relief, and Other Currencies* (New York: Basic Books, 1994), 18.

51. See Karl Marx, "The Power of Money in Bourgeois Society," *The Economic and Philosophical Manuscript of 1844* (Moscow: Foreign Language Publishing House, 1956); and *Grundrisse* (New York: Vintage, 1973).

52. Max Weber, *Economy and Society* (Berkeley: University of California Press, 1978), 167–93.

53. Max Weber, "Religious Rejections of the World and their Directions," in *From Max Weber: Essays in Sociology*, ed. H. H. Gerth and C. W. Mills (New York: Oxford University Press, 1958), 323–59, see p. 331 for quote. See also Weber, *Economy and Society*.

54. Simmel, *Philosophy of Money*, 279.

55. Zelizer, *The Social Meaning of Money*, 18.

56. Hostile world: This is the view that economic transactions must be insulated from social ties so that economic inefficiency does not arise or social ties are not polluted by commercial considerations. Nothing-reductionism fails to recognize how intimate and impersonal social relations transform the character and consequences of monetary transactions.

57. See Viviana Zelizer, *The Purchase of Intimacy* (Princeton, NJ: Princeton University Press, 2005); Zelizer, "Circuits within Capitalism," in *The Economic Sociology of Capitalism*, ed. Victor Nee and Richard Swedberg (Princeton, NJ: Princeton University Press, 2005), 289–322; Zelizer, "Sociology of Money," 1991–94; Zelizer, "Payments and Social Ties," *Sociological Forum* 11 (September 1996): 481–95; and Zelizer, *The Social Meaning of Money*.

58. Dodd, "Reinventing monies in Europe," 562.

59. Viviana Zelizer, "Fine Tuning the Zelizer View," *Economy and Society* 29, no.3 (2000): 386.

60. It stands for Local Exchange Trading System. It is a trading network based on and supported by its own self-regulating internal currency within a given limited, local monetary space.

61. Dodd, "Reinventing Monies in Europe," 563.

62. Dodd, "Reinventing Monies in Europe," 564, 570–71.

63. Zelizer, "Missing Monies," 586.

64. Dodd, "Reinventing Monies in Europe," 564, 575n17.

65. Zelizer, "Missing Monies," 587.

66. Jonathan Parry and Maurice Bloch, eds., *Money and the Morality of Exchange* (Cambridge: Cambridge University Press, 1989), 29; Maurice Bloch, *Ritual, History and Power: Selected Papers in Anthropology* (New York: Berg, 1989); and Maurice Bloch and Jonathan Parry, ed., *Death and Regeneration of Life* (Cambridge: Cambridge University Press, 1982).

67. Parry and Bloch, *Money and the Morality of Exchange*, 30.

68. Talcott Parsons, *Structure and Process in Modern Societies* (New York: Free Press, 1960), 274.

69. Talcott Parsons, *Politics and Social Structure* (New York: Free Press, 1969), 360–62, 405–9, 439–72. See also Parsons, *Structure and Process*, 272–75.

70. Weber, *Economy and Society*, 78–80, 107–09, 183.

71. Wayne E. Baker, "What is Money? A Social Structural Interpretation," in *Intercorporate Relations: The Structural Analysis of Business*, ed. Mark S. Mizruchi and Michael Schwartz (New York: Cambridge University Press, 1987), 109–44.

72. Baker, "What is Money?" 118.

73. Ingham, *The Nature of Money*, 155–57, 195–202. See also Geoffrey Ingham, "Class Inequality and the Social Production of Money," in *Renewing Class Analysis*, ed. Rosemary Crompton, Fiona Divine, Mike Savage, and John Scott (Oxford: Blackwell Publishers, 2000), 66–86. It is germane to mention that Charles Goodhart of the London School of Economics and a former central banker at the Bank of England has challenged Ingham's interpretation of the monetary conditions from the 1970s to 1990s in his review of Ingham's book. See C. A. Goodhart, "What is the Essence of Money?" *Cambridge Journal of Economics* 29 (2005): 817–25.

74. Ingham, *The Nature of Money*, 198–99.

75. One exception is Carruthers who made a bold attempt to define money as a "generalized, immediate, and transferable legitimate claims on value." The problem is that he does not relate it to the debates about the properties of money that are raging on in the field. Carruthers, "The Sociology of Money and Credit," 355–56. Ingham is also another exception and sought to formulate an answer in his book *The Nature of Money*.

76. Dodd, "Reinventing Monies in Europe," 571.

77. Carruthers, "The Sociology of Money and Credit," 355–78.

78. The argument is that social relations are by no means secondary, but rather constitutive of money. A notable exception to this neglect is Ingham. See his "The Nature of Money," *Economic Sociology, European Electronic Newsletter* 6, no.1 (October 2004): 18–28.

79. On debate about general theory of money in sociology of money see Ben Fine and Costas Lapavitsas, "Markets and Money in Social Theory: What Role for Economics," *Economy and Society* 29, no. 3 (2000): 357–82; Viviana Zelizer, " Fine Tuning the Zelizer View," *Economy and Society* 29, no. 3 (2000): 383–89; Geoffrey Ingham, "Fundamentals of a Theory of Money," 304–23; and Costas Lapavitsas, "The Social Relations of Money as Universal Equivalent: A Response to Ingham," *Economy and Society* 34, no. 3 (2005): 389–403.

80. What I am after here are the generalizations about money that hold cross-contextually or inter-culturally. In this sense I am not getting at some "essence" of money, but more, at developing cross-cultural claims about money, working from an analysis of varying context of money usage. See n41 above

4

✛

Money as a Social Relation

INTRODUCTION

Many of the works of economic sociologists that I have reviewed in the last chapter claim that social relations significantly influence money. Here, I posit that money *is* a social relation. To clarify our understanding of money as a social relation, I must state what kind or aspect of social relations I see as monetary. This endeavor must start with a definition of social relation such that we can answer the following questions. First, how do we know when we see it? Second, once we identify a social relation, how would we recognize that social relation, or some aspect of it, as money? To what extent and how does money vary as a function of social relations? Our review of the sociological literature on money in the previous chapter has made it clear that these are pivotal questions for the analysis of money. In this chapter I need to propose answers to these questions.

This is not an easy task. How do we understand a phenomenon as protean, amorphous, and slippery as social relation? In this chapter, I will attempt to provide us with an optimal understanding of social relation by moving beyond foundationalist notions of social relation (practice) and overcoming shortcomings of social constructionists' displacement of essentialism. This will be done by recognizing the deeply contextual nature of social relation. This distinctly embedded character of social relation will be fused with an obligation to rediscover the enduring insights of ontology.

Unlike the social-constructionist approach to social analysis, in this essay the acting and self-actualizing subject is not jettisoned, but is reconceptualized and resituated, made performatively present, in the transversally textured space of praxis.[1] This approach calls attention to the transactional character of social relation: social relation is always a complex interaction between the I and *thous* in the public (or private) arena, and between the self and the world. For there to be social relation, there must be personal encounters, the meeting of "power of being" as Paul Tillich would say. It is human beings (persons of flesh and blood) with distinct self-awareness and very specific quests for self-actualization that step into the reality of social relation or practice. The personal interaction is at the heart of social relation (practice).

There must also be the recognition that humans cannot act or encounter one another except through engaging in local contexts and living, developing traditions. Therefore, every social practice or relation makes a dual affirmation: *encounter of beings* and *relations of a communicative praxis*. Together, this means that there is no access to a pure anchor that might serve as a foundation or irreducible ontological reality. Nevertheless, this does not mean that social relation is completely cut adrift from the world or reality and tossed into a linguistic or discursive sea, and thus is not language, discourse, or construction all the way down.

Thus the model or theory of social relation that I seek to formulate in this chapter will explicitly acknowledge the contextuality and constructionist nature of relations (practices). But it will also go on to argue that human self-actualization and affirmation is not only intrinsically connected to the creation and development of social relation (practice), but is indeed an indispensable starting point for any account of established cooperative human behaviors that shape social reality. Social practice or social relation is inseparable from human self-affirmation as linked to social context. In developing this model, I am thinking *with* the social constructionists and pragmatic philosophers while thinking *against* them.

The rest of this chapter will proceed by defining the model and applying it to real-life issues. The discourse will, therefore, proceed in three closely related steps. First, I will define what social relation is. Second, I will then elaborate on this definition to draw out its complexity and richness by looking at the general features of social relations. Finally, I will show how we can recognize aspects of social relations as money and show how money is simultaneously a social relation and a *relational thing*.

It is important to straightaway indicate (or reiterate) how this chapter differs from the last one. In chapter 3, I identified the social character of money (interpersonal transactions) as one of economic sociologists' "key properties of money." The point made there was that money is embedded in social relations. The point I want to make here is that money is not only embedded in social relations, it is created out of social relations. I then go further to make a novel argument that money is not only constituted by social relations, it is simultaneously a social relation and a *relational thing*. I implore the readers (especially those who are not familiar with the current nature of the debates in economic sociology of money) to keep these nuances in view as they go through this chapter.

SECTION 1: A GENERAL DEFINITION OF SOCIAL RELATION

I will attempt to provide a formal definition of social relation by coming at it from two related points of views. I want my definition to provide both social ontological (that is, structural character and processual nature of interactions, the nature and basic structure of social reality) and sociological (the social character of interaction) insights. Ontologically, I will explicate the meaning of social relation by looking at its elements, the static and dynamic elements. The ontological account alone will not fully take into account all the significant facts of human experience in the coming together of two individuals or groups. While ontology gives us the structure and energy in the interactions it is inexact and incomplete as it does not fully account for all the significant claims on life made by social relations. The social relation is not just something which has energy, creativity, and form. Every social relation seeks to draw and retain resources so that the individuals in it can perpetuate themselves into the future. It is in this light that I seek to understand the nature of social relations sociologically. Thus, my definition combines insights from both fields of study. *A social relation is a unity of vitality and form which supports the claims of one life against another either for mutual support or for conflict.*

When any two persons or a given number of persons come together there is vitality (energy[2]) and there is form to the interaction. In the power of its vitality every interaction drives beyond itself toward its *telos*[3] in the ultimate unity of its vitality and form. It unites motion with matter, meaningful structures with creativity. On the side of vitality it includes spiritual, mental, and emotional energy, participation, contents, claims, and self-transcending freedom. On the side of form it includes structures of reality, meaning, rules, and laws, limiting and directing destiny. Relation is the vitality through which form lives, and it is the form which gives structure and meaning to vitality. Any time we look at a relation between two persons we can distinguish between the chaotic creativity of its messiness (its character, frailties, possibilities, freedom, the elements of vitality) and the extensity of its form, between the depth and the boundary (meaning and structure). Without the second element the first element will be all over the map, naked and chaotic, extending to all and everyone, and hence forming no connection to anyone in particular. Without the first element the second element is void, empty. The second element makes the content of the relation distinguishable, definite, and finite; the first makes it full and grounded.[4]

In simple terms, *social relation is a claim on value* (economic and non-economic resources). While the ontological perspective in the definition shows the organic structure and processual character of the reality of the claim (demand) made on one another by parties involved, the sociological aspect elaborates its functionality and meaning. If one were to consider the theological-ethical view of the claim we will be concerned with how conscious, rational reflection on the interaction can or do affect the claim and the subjective aim (*participation* and perpetuation of self into the future) that undergirds the claim. This will not be our concern for now. It is now only incumbent upon us to draw out the general characteristics of social relations as a way of shedding more light on the definition. I will later show that given a certain and predictable changes in these characteristics money as a specific form of social relation, as the conventional instrument or symbol of legitimate claims and the values to which they apply, can emerge.

SECTION 2: GENERAL FEATURES OF SOCIAL RELATIONS

Now what are the general features of social relations? This question is necessary because it would help to clarify the definition I have given above. For our very limited purpose, I will discuss only five of the general features of social relations.[5] First, every social relation serves as a vector between two sets of persons through which resources (matter and energy) move back and forth consciously in order to generate and sustain goods internal to the domain of the flow. It is not every flow of resources between two persons that constitutes a social relation. For instance, energy may flow between a person and a spiritual being but if one of them is not conscious of it one will hesitate to consider it a social relation. Besides, I restrict the use of social relations to between two or more human beings.

There are important terms in the feature just mentioned above. A *relation*, a *vector* of resource flow, is *social* because it is between two or more persons who exchange *resources* (either as *motion* which is energy or intangibles like information, loyalty, and love. Or it is *matter* such as physical materials). An item (of matter or motion) that is transferred derives its value from its relation to the actual and potential actions of the persons in the network. The transfer may be motivated by egoism, altruism, or a kind of Faustian tension between egoism and altruism. In the exchange, matter and motion must be flowing both ways for the persons to be in relation. They both must flow in either direction, and either of them must flow in either direction or either of them must flow in both directions.[6] In addition, the exchange (competitive or non-competitive, zero-sum or non-zero-sum, egoistic or altruistic) are purposed to achieve goods internal to the zone of the transfers flow.

The direction and magnitude (extent of dimension: length, breadth, and thickness) of the vector is defined by norms and rules for which the relating agents hold one another accountable. Social relation is like a vehicle whose limits are the norms and rules and whose content are matter and motion. The flows of matter and motion are generated and allocated and reallocated according to norms of interactions. This flow of motion and matter is undergirded by the ontological drive for *participation*.[7] Person qua person is defined and sustained by participation, the going-out of the centered self to draw resources to sustain life, the self; it is the relations with others that define and uphold identity. Participation cannot be avoided by any living being. No human being is self-referential and self-existing; for *aseity* is not one of the attributes of living souls.

Now the second feature of social relations. Every social relation experiences a tension between fungibility and non-fungibility. The issue is this: can the relations between any two persons be standardized so that many more people can participate in it or it must remain individualized? Take the relationship between a landlord and his tenant. Should the apartment be opened to all or only to the tenant with a certain kind of contract? Consider the difference in the "owner-tenant" relations pertaining to hotel and apartment building. Take coital relationship between a man and woman and you will also notice the tension. On the one hand they can inscribe a set of distinctions into it and render it heterogeneous (that is, socially differentially, highly restricted to the two) or change partners every day. Take another example, that of buyer and seller. They can either settle transactions between them with a value that has a generalized purchasing power or they can use an item that can circulate only between them. This tension, as you can imagine, exists in all relations and as a relation becomes increasingly social and transgresses boundaries the more it moves toward homogeneity and interchangeability (fungibility). One of the major differences between barter and money exchange exactly hinges on this point. While barter is definitely relational, it is hardly social as the non-fungibility of the instrument of exchange severely limits the ability to transgress social boundaries.

The third aspect of relation is trust. Every social relation poses its problem of trust and tries to resolve it in a specific way (embedded relationships or impersonal institutions). Take the surgeon-patient relationship. Does the patient trust the surgeon to do the right thing or not? Either he can rely on the personal knowledge of the surgeon or on the reputation of the hospital. The imperialistic conqueror may or may not trust his subjects to deliver the periodic tributes. The subjects may or may not trust their master to leave them alone after they have delivered the tributes. Do I marry this man or the other and which one of them is more trustworthy?

Generally, individuals have tried to resolve the tension by resorting to personal affiliations and reputations or by explicit contracts and formal institutions. The problem of trust is particularly acute in monetary transactions. The seller either has to trust the buyer and therefore give him credit or she has to demand cash or real goods in exchange.[8] When she decides to take money from him, she does not solve the trust problem but has only shifted it to a different level. She must now trust the state or bank that issues the money. As Ingham puts it:

> [T]he question of trust in money is not a matter of co-traders' *personal* trust, as it is understood in micro-economics' dyadic exchange models. On the contrary, money's significance lies in the fact that it resolves this problem precisely in large anonymous markets where interpersonal trust *cannot* be generated. Money is an *assignable* trust. In the face of real-world radical uncertainty, self-fulfilling long-term trust is rooted in a social world and political legitimacy whereby potentially personally untrustworthy strangers are able to participate in complex multilateral relationships.[9]

Once again, the more trust in a particular relationship is assignable across social boundaries, the more the relation becomes social, societal. In a certain fundamental sense, social relation involves the act of communicating trust across time and space in a given social context. The father-son relation becomes social relations between a prince and his subjects if the typical trust between a father and his son can be generalized and extended to residents in a particular domain. Of course, the citizens may need the apparatus of state to mediate this transformation of relation in the same way as a modern seller relies on credit-rating agencies and state laws to enable her to trust strangers who come into her store and ask for credit. The use of money in modern society makes this point very clear. Money is the bearer and transporter of trust in an economic system. Money is the act of communicating trust over social and temporal gaps. The act or event may be encrusted in hard shells, decked in fine clothes, painted in bright colors or represented by a sequence of ones and zeros as culture, technology, and circumstances demand. Anything can be made money if it is generally agreed to carry the needed trust. For instance, words (spoken or written, or in bytes, or anything that represents a combination of sounds) can be made to bear and transport "promises to pay" (IOUs) over time and space.

Now the fourth feature of social relations. The definition of social relation as claim on value indicates that it has a dimension of obligation.

Whether one realizes it or not, the coming together of two persons and the associated claims and counter claims that pertain to the connection between them harbor this question: is the claim on value freely transferable? Is a claim pertaining to the mother-daughter relation transferable between one woman and her daughter to another mother-daughter dyad? It may not be in certain circumstances, but it is conceivable that a foster home mother can play that role. Often one cannot satisfy one's social obligations to a friend, Paul by transferring to him that owed me by another friend Peter. But there are other relations where my obligations are negotiable and transferable. So another tension of social relation is that between negotiability and non-transferability.

The ability of a particular form of relationship to become a generalized one, transgressing social boundaries and even serving as generalized medium of exchange between spheres of the social depends on negotiability. As both Talcott Parsons and Bruce Carruthers have argued in their various studies of money, "negotiability constitutes a fundamental transformation in relations of obligations."[10] The relationship between a creditor and her debtor took a bold evolutionary step toward money when debts became transferable. According to Carruthers, this ability of an economic agent to satisfy obligations to his creditors by using obligations to himself was a fundamental breakthrough in the evolution of money.

> Negotiability entailed a shift away from direct, concrete relationships between specific individuals and towards abstract relationships between economic roles. With negotiable instruments, the debtor owes whoever holds the instrument, not the person who originally loaned the money. Negotiability dislodges debts from the debtor-creditor dyads that create them, and gives them mobility. A single promissory note can satisfy multiple obligations, and as it circulates, it links transactions and traders in a network.[11]

The origins of credit-money, the form of money used today in all advanced economies are to be found in this type of evolutionary development of detachment and standardization of debts. Let us not forget that the United States operates debt-money, such that every dollar note out there in circulation has a price on its head, so to speak. The Federal Reserves Bank, the central bank of the nation, creates money, "high-power money" by buying government securities from the commercial banks. If the Federal Reserve Board wants to pump in $10 billion dollars into the U.S. economy, it has to buy that amount of government securities from the banks (creating new bank reserves for them) and pay appropriate interest to the commercial banks or their investors. The Fed cannot just create money as the Treasury Department does with its issuance of metal coins which is debt-and-interest free. The reader who is not familiar with modern monetary economics may rightly ask: where do the government securities come from in the first place? The Treasury Department of the United States government sells bonds to borrow from the public in order to supplement tax revenues. The banks buy the debt instruments for its use or for its clients and the government pays periodic interest on the investors. From this you can see that the foundation of the money supply in the United States and in all other modern economies which are not on a commodity standard is debt.

The fifth and final feature of social relation we would consider is "imperialism" or effervescence. Every relation has within it the seed of imperialistic tendency, the teleological impulse to overflow its original social space to include, overlap, or dominate that of another in order to extract (violently or not) resources from others. The father-son relationship becomes king-subjects; the master-slave relationship becomes master-slaves or colonizing power-dependent nations; the barter relation gets widened; the creditor-debtor relationship becomes the basis of a community's monetary system; the local currency becomes imperial vehicular and reserve currency of the world; the 1790s trading between twenty-four brokers under the buttonwood tree outside of 68 Wall Street becomes the giant stock trading machinery called the New York Stock Exchange, and monogamous marriage can become a polygamous one.

As Tillich states "everything real drives beyond itself. It is not satisfied with the form in which it finds itself. It urges towards a more embracing, ultimately to *the* all-embracing form"[12] (italics in the original). Every social relation wants to grow. It tends to overcome both internal and external resistance in a way that transcends its boundaries and draws more external resources into itself. Put differently, it tends toward universality and totality, toward all-inclusiveness of human activities and historical groups. Robert Wright, the American social scientist has explored both the tendency of relations to keep expanding and the growth of social complexity in his book, *NonZero: The Logic of Human Destiny*.[13] He attributes the phenomenon to the relentless search for non-zerosumness in relations, the benefits of interdependence, internal coordination, and cooperation. This very (inherent) process of not leaving anything or person outside its ambit is what I am expressing in the term "imperialism" or effervescence.[14]

Let us not go far off the field with this assertion about the inherent tendency of social relations to totalize. Very often there are countervailing forces that inhibit the move toward totality or all-embracing inclusiveness. There are at once forces moving relations toward fragmentation and integration. The expansionist trend can be checked by the resistance and self-affirmation of others, expansionism of other relations, and other salient considerations. Take racism for example. While racism could be used to support an ever-increasing appropriation of a society's economic and political resources at the expense of an oppressed group, it often does not strive toward embracing the other. The expansion of a specific social groups' interest can also be dangerous for the collective good. Mancur Olson made this point eloquently when he argued that often in stable societies the rise of special-interest lobbies which aspire to draw more and more of an economy's resources to themselves leads to inefficient, sclerotic economic performance.[15] While globalization is totalizing economic and political relations at a worldwide level, the world also appears to be growing more "tribalistic" and factionalizing along ethnic and religious lines.

The preceding discourse in laying out the features of social relations does three things: (1) it indicates to us how to recognize a social relation; (2) it argues that money is a form of social relations; and (3) it has shown what qualitative transformation of the aspects of social relation is needed for money to emerge and what aspects of social relations are monetary. The features of social relation we have discussed in this chapter are not exhaustive but they are sufficient to show that given certain and predictable changes in characteristics of social relation money as a specific form of social relation, as the conventional instrument or symbol of legitimate claims and the values to which they apply, can emerge. In the following section, I will more specifically discuss the emergence of money as a social relations and why I insist that we must define money as social relations.

SECTION 3: MONEY AS A SOCIAL RELATION

In the last section, I gave intimations about how money could emerge from creditor-debtor relationship. Let us now explore this insight further. Here I will examine the specific history of money as a certain type of creditor-debtor social relations that got qualitatively transformed into a general, standardized instrument of exchange. Among other factors, it is based on this evolutionary history of money—money's roots in social relations of debt—and its continued entanglement in debt relations that one argues that money is a social relation. It is quite possible that given a different reading of the history of money and interpretative lenses on the contemporary monetary situation one could arrive at a different understanding of the nature of money. But I intend to demonstrate in this section that the concept of *money as a social relation* is a highly plausible way of comprehending today's money and the concept is indeed very robust for theological analysis of money. I will not hesitate to mention at this juncture that I will undertake to slightly modify the definition of money in order to take into account the phenomenological forms of money (varieties of monetary media).

Now is time to examine the relations between debt and money (capitalist credit-money). Unlike the neoclassical analysis of money we encountered in the last chapter which places the market at the center of money's origin, the debt perspective on money puts states and banks at the center stage. As Ingham states, "capitalist credit-money was produced by a qualitative transformation in the *social relations of the mode of monetary production*. . . . [It] is nothing more than a network of claims backed by banks' and states' promises to pay that are fabricated into a hierarchy of credibility by foreign exchange markets and global credit rating agencies" (emphasis in the original).[16] How did all this happen?

In medieval Italian city-states like Genoa, Florence, and Venice, state and bank debts became accepted as general means of payment. The debts were guaranteed by the states' ability to impose and collect taxes. These credits, "promises to pay" were detached from commodities and were not symbolic reflection of any underlying commodity. These means of payment retained their value not because people expected their convertibility into any metal or commodity. These were just "promises to pay" serving as means of payment, medium of exchange, and depending only on the constitutional legitimacy of the state and institutionalized banking practice. Note that the strength of state theory of money is not that money receives its value from legal tender laws, but from the legal requirement of its citizens to pay taxes; that is, on the state's ability to impose and collect taxes in particular money-stuff (be it commodity, fiat paper, etc.).

We have jumped over some important stages in the evolution of money from debts. Even though capitalist credit-monies were means of payment with no stable relationship to commodities, they did not become currency until debts became *fungible*. To turn to currency, debts and acceptance of "promises to pay" had to be detached from personality, persons, and organizations to become completely transferable.[17] The transformation of the social relations between creditors and debtors, states and their creditors, into money took place gradually and evolved in tandem with the transformation of personal trust into impersonal trust, from accepting IOUs based on person-to-person (limited radius of trust) to an impersonal, generalizable trust anchored on the guarantee of the whole community.

A question suggests itself here: is all money credit-money and what might have served as money before debts became detachable and alienable? When I argue that money is a social relation, I am not limiting the conception to only credit-money which is easy to grasp in an environment of institutionalized banking practice. I also maintain that archaic "commodity forms" of money could not have developed without social relations, and this is in at least two senses. First, every form of money needs a unit of account, abstract measure of value. Once exchange has developed beyond a pure bilateral system into a complex multilateral system of multiple goods there has to be an abstract measure of value which may or may not be embodied in a commodity. And at this stage, that is, the stage which is beyond bilateral dealings between two persons or two sets of good, all exchanges involve a third party. "The pivotal point in the interaction of the two parties recedes from direct line of contact between them, and moves to the relationship which each of them has with the economic community that accepts money."[18] The second sense of money's social relationality concerns the fact that even commodity-money like metallic money is a promise to pay and a claim.

> [M]etallic money is also a promise to pay and . . . it differs from the cheque only with respect to the size of the group which vouches for its being accepted. The common relationship that the owner of money and the seller have to a social group—the claim of the former to a service and the trust of the latter that this claim will be honoured—provides the sociological constellation in which money transactions, as distinct from barter are accomplished.[19]

If Simmel is correct (and I think he is) that all monies are credits, then the question is: are all credits money? Money is not automatically created any time credits, promises/IOUs are generated. A credit only becomes money when the credit is socially accepted as money. Money is simultaneously a credit (asset) and debt (liability). So if a credit (debt) is created between any two economic agents and no third party wants to hold it as an asset it is not money. "Thus, it is more accurate to say that anyone can make promises or offer to go into debt but that the 'problem' is to find someone who is willing to become a creditor (i.e., to hold that "promise to pay" or debt)."[20]

The kind of debts, "promises to pay" which will be most readily accepted in any given monetary space is that made by the sovereign state or community. The state or political authority has the power to demand payment of taxes in a specified medium. Anything that the state chooses as acceptable in the discharge of its citizens' obligations to it becomes currency.[21] Citizens on their own will accept from one another such item, object, commodity, paper, or token as long as it will enable them to settle their liabilities to the state. Adam Smith recognized this when he wrote that "a prince, who should enact that a certain proportion of his taxes should be paid in a paper money of a certain kind, might thereby give a certain value to this paper money."[22] Similarly Keynes argues that it is the state that decides what thing should answer as money to the current money of account in its domain. The bottom line of this argument is that credit or debt is the source of money as defined by a sovereign state and the value of such money does not derive from any inherent value within/backing the money. Thus Ingham argues that money is itself constituted by social relations and "cannot be adequately conceptualized other than as the emergent property of a configuration (or 'structure') of social relations."[23]

What these analyses of the transformation of certain type of credit relations into money glossed over is the origin, nature, and the present dynamics of money in relation to property and property ownership. It is true to say money derived from new types of credit relations, but it is truer to say these credit relations were made possible by the emergence of private property.[24] Ulrich Duchrow and Franz J. Hinkelammert in their recent book, *Property for People, Not for Profit*, provides an analysis of money's origin in connection with the changes in community social relations engendered by the drive to own and accumulate property for profit. They turned to John Locke to argue that money cannot be properly understood apart from property relations which form an integral part of the overall social relations of any society. Their exegesis of John Locke's *The Second Treatise of Government* (1690) shows that the use of money at the early rise of modernity is "itself equated with the right to the accumulation of wealth and increase of property, so that the use of money is not simply a means but a totality of production conditions."[25]

The argument so far lends itself to a quick summary so that we can tentatively capture what has been established so far. Money is a social relation of depersonalized, alienated, exchangeable promises. It is a packaged (monetized) social relation of debt, an institutionalized set of promises between creditors and debtors, guaranteed by a community. The Australian sociologist Jocelyn Pixley in her recent book, *Emotions in Finance*, 2004, puts it this way: "The money in our wallets and purses is part of an abstract chain of social relations of claims and credits, no less organized than plastic card money and bank mortgages."[26]

It is germane to point out at this juncture that the key interest of all of the preceding discourse is *an attempt to locate social relations within money itself rather than seeing social relations as external to money or investigating how money is used to create and mark distinct social relations*. When this last point is taken together with some of the conclusions reached in the last chapter it should be noted that I am trying to make the overall assertion that money is social in two senses. First, it is to acknowledge (as we have done in the last chapter) that monetary transactions are embedded in social relations, to recognize how the monetization process is reshaping social practices or to understand how persons and groups negotiate the intersections of economic processes and social ties. Second, as we are doing in this chapter, is to note that social relations are constitutive of money. It is important to note the overall assertion I am trying to cover by these two points. In the last chapter, I argued that even though economic sociologists have informed us that money is a socially contingent phenomenon, they do not consider social relations as constitutive of money itself. *Here, I am taking the dual stance.*

Let me approach the argument from another perspective which will further establish the social relationality of money—*that of money as a claim*. In 1900 Georg Simmel, seeing money as a form of *sociation*, constituted by the social relation of credit, posits that money is "only a claim upon society" which realization depends upon "the community as a whole or upon the government as its representatives."[27] Simmel's analysis of economic value anticipated the Saussurian structuralist interpretation of value in the twentieth century. In reinterpreting the source of value and meaning of objects, he shifted scholarly focus from referentiality to relationality.[28] He avers:

> the economic value of objects is constituted by their mutual relationship and exchangeability. . . . The philosophical significance of money is that it represents within the practical world the most certain image and the clearest embodiment of the formula of all being, according to which things receive their meaning through each other, and have their being determined by their mutual relations.[29]

One hundred and five years after Simmel's claim theory of money, Bruce G. Carruthers in 2005 followed with this statement: "I define money as *generalized, immediate, and transferable legitimate claims on value*. Money is important because it commands resources. . . . Claims are general only within social communities and spheres of activity. . . . Finally, both claims and values to which they apply are socially constructed. What constitutes value in one society may be valueless in others" (italics in the original).[30]

Once you accept the definition that money is a general claim on value, it follows easily or necessarily that it is a social relation. This point could be elaborated at three levels. First, we have already argued that social relation itself is a claim on value and thus money is only a form of social relations. Second, from another angle it is to note that any general claim on resources within a given society is a social claim—"claims are general only within social communities and spheres of activity." Third, money is advantageous to an individual or any two agents if others use it. Onces exchange transaction developed beyond the two-way arrangement of barter into mediation by money (with its intrinsic social nature as a promise) every exchange became a tripartite transaction. The money that a buyer hands over to a seller in exchange for a product is a claim on the future wealth of society. The piece of paper or metal is accepted by the seller because it will enable her to claim a piece of society's wealth just as the buyer has just done. Pixley adequately captures this promise-of-claim nature of money as supported by third party when she writes:

> In its "claim" dimension, money is not simply bipartisan, imprisoned in a single moment in the space between two people. It is a promise into the future, and as a token of that promise it can only be created between three parties. No one can believe or trust this token or promissory note unless it includes the "community that guarantees the money." . . . It is a three-way relation between the credit and debt relations of the economically active groups and the central power that enforces these promises by unifying and issuing a currency and outlawing counterfeiting.[31]

I will now provide a methodological paradigm which will show how I was able to match social relations with moneyness, and thus lend further credibility to the relational concept of money being developed in this chapter. The matching exercise is a way of recognizing money as a *relational package* and to further support the assertion that money *itself* is a social relation. For this purpose, I will adapt and tweak Viviana Zelizer's *relational work*.[32]   First, is to show what kind of named set of social relationships between economic agents constitute money. Next, it is necessary to define the interactions (transactions) between agents that are within the named set of relationships. Third, we must show the forms, material or virtual media, which are used for reckoning and facilitating transactions within the relations. Fourth, is to show how the boundaries of the relations are marked by a distinctive combination of relations, transactions, and media. The task of tracking and grasping the essence of money is the problem of creating the appropriate match among relations, transactions, media, and boundaries in the vast array of economic exchanges. The most difficult in this matching exercise—and this is where many economists and economic sociologists have failed—is designating the right sort of economic relations which is explicitly and distinctively appropriate for *money*.[33]

I will now embark on the task of tracking and grasping money's distinctive configuration as a social relation by revealing the appropriate match between relations, transactions, media, and boundaries in the vast array of economic exchanges within a geo-political space. Money as we have seen above is a claim upon society; it is simultaneously an asset and a liability, credit and debt. It represents a promise, an IOU. Anyone can create IOUs but such IOUs become money when it is a "two-sided balance sheet operation, where one party agrees to hold the debt of another."[34] How does one identify any IOUs as money? As just indicated above, there are four steps in identifying and matching relations, transactions, media, and boundaries:

First, the kind of named set of relationships between economic agents that becomes money is credit relations. This premier step answers the question posed at the very first paragraph of this chapter: what kind or aspect of social relations in a given community can be considered monetary?

Second, there are specific forms of interactions within the bounds of credit relations that are appropriate for creating and sustaining money or hierarchy of monies in a given monetary space.[35] It is principally the acceptance of a certain kind of "promises to pay" among a plethora of "promises to pay" that transforms a social relation of debt into money form. There is usually a hierarchy of money and the social relation that is packaged as the "decisive" money is the one that is accepted in the discharge of taxes. Money contracts are predominately, if not totally, written in the unit of account in which taxes are settled.

The third step involves showing the forms or media that are used in reckoning and facilitating transactions in the specified set of credit relations. In the United States it is the dollar. The dollar is the "title" or "description" to which all forms and media of money must answer. The dollar is the money of account, but it is not the "money." A certain quantity of gold can answer to it as when the government decided that an ounce of coined gold can answer to $35 of tax liability. Some rectangular shaped green pieces of paper with portraits of dead men, and round silver and copper coins also answer to the same description. As stated by Keynes "if the same thing always answer to the same description, the distinction would have no practical interest. But if the thing can change, whilst the description remains the same, then the distinction can be highly significant."[36] This is to distinguish the phenomenal forms of money from money itself.

Finally, the boundaries of relation are marked by a distinctive combination of credit relations, transactions, and media in the sovereign monetary space of the United States. Since the dollar is a global imperial, reserve, and vehicular currency, this combination has been exported to the rest of the world. The boundaries can also be determined in a very fundamental sense by the social formation within which money is created, distributed, used, and controlled. Credit-monies in capitalist societies are different from those of pre-capitalist social formations due to the kind of social relations that constitute them. As Ingham puts it: "The *differentia specifica* of capitalism is to be found in its particular monetary institutions, in which privately contracted credit relations are routinely 'monetized' by the linkages between the state and its creditors, the central bank and the banking system" (italics in the original).[37]

In developing my concept of money ("money in general"), I have focused only on social relations—relying only on the postfoundationalist aspect of the model of money I intimated I was going to develop at the beginning of this chapter. But money is simultaneously a social relation and a *relational thing*. I purposely postponed any discussion of the second aspect of money (the postconstructionist portion). I now seek to balance the presentation by a discussion of money as a *relational thing*.

SECTION 4: MONEY AS A RELATIONAL THING

In the arguments so far developed, with a high accent put on relationality, the careful reader would have noticed that all social facts have been reduced to relations. My model so far has not explained "why and in what form physical objects are used when monetary transactions are performed."[38] I would like to incorporate the role of things into the social relations of money. My point of departure is the assertion that money is not simply a coin, paper, magnetic traces, or the institutional facts that answer to the money account. It is a "mode of existence," "a way of being. . . . It is a way of *relationship* with the world, with other people, an event of *communion*, and that is why it cannot be realized as the achievement of an *individual*"[39] but only as a *synaxistic*[40] fact. It is a social practice and all social practices are a combination of social relations and *things*.

According to John Searle, every social practice has some "substance," some "brute fact" to it.[41] The soccer game as a social practice has a ball to it; nursing practice has the patients/bodies to it, and money has metal, paper, or computer magnetic traces to it. But it is not right to say the ball is the play or the greenback or magnetic trace is the money. We cannot just speak about the ball or the greenback before speaking about the people who are in relationships, in communion. The relationships or the practices are not something added to the "substance" or rather which follows it. The substance, the physicality, has no "ontological being," apart from the personal relationships, the communion. Being, whether of the ball, coins, or persons no longer exist in itself once incorporated into social practice. It is the relationship that makes any of them "be." It is also true that social practice cannot exist without substance. The ball does have some distinctive being from, say, the soccer match. The metal or paper used as money does have a distinctive being. It is because it has this distinctiveness that it could be used in another context. The soccer player could take the ball and use it in another game, say, volleyball (even though soccer balls and volleyballs are usually different types of balls), or it can be given to children for use in a child's game. A mother in traditional society could give her sick child the imperial British copper penny with a hole at its center, which circulated in colonial Nigeria, as an amulet to ward off evil spirits. In fact what Zelizer has done, as we amply learned in the last chapter, is to show how people are constantly struggling to retrieve distinctiveness from homogeneous, colorless, monetary-exchange communion so as to create distinctive, heterogeneous, colorful, restricted communion. All this is not to deny that it is communion which makes beings "be" but to fully explore the interrelationality between physicality and sociality of practice.[42] The issue is how do we account for the fact that the same ball can be moved from one context to another, without saying it has a certain distinctive being-in-itself, even if its full being is always set by the sociality of its changing contextual settings?

Substance cannot be set apart (but it could be distinguished without being separated) from patterns of human interactions in a social practice. It is precisely this necessary linkage of substance with relations that I am designating as social practice. The substance is not in naked existence, it is not without a social mode of existence. So also the interactions between the humans in a given social practice do not either exist without the complement of substance—the complement (such as ball or the metal coin) is something which permits without controlling the pattern of interactions. The permission, given by the substance (the thing that is co-involved with the relations), is not that of giving the "necessity" of existence or the offering of "necessity" of possibilities to the pattern of human interactions. Rather, the permission given by the complement is that of facilitation. The freedom (in the Niebuhrian sense of it[43]) character of human relationships enables persons to transcend and abolish any such necessity. The expression, "something which permits," signifies that the "mode of existence," that is, the social practice "subsists" as substance. It "stands out" from substance. Social practice is a process of working what is instituted, what is historically given (material and social sedimentation) so as to *con-stitute* it in an event of fresh relationality.[44] We are always taking what is already available to make what is new, to transcend the given in order to reach new forms of sociality, attain fresh levels of unity of form and vitality. Take, for instance, money. Humans and their history (tradition) created money, gave money its being, and it becomes its *true being, its full being,* each time its social practice *con-stitutes* the exchange community as communion. Think about it. Whatever serves as money (whether in its abstract or phenomenal form) "lives" as money and truly does what money does because it is constantly *used* as money and it is thus constantly bringing people together.

Given this dense connection of social practice to substance, how can a particular practice acquire its unique identity? Put differently, is the nature of any social practice determined by the nature of its co-involved thing? If the social practice of soccer has to have a round leather ball, does this immanent physicality serve as its irreducible ontological reality? How does one avoid falling into essentialism when there is a "substance"?

After all, we have argued that magnetic traces, balls, or hard bodies are always involved in the social practices of money, soccer games, or nursing practice. The survival and identity of any social practice is not dependent on any property of the substance. There is just no way to infer how the social practice of soccer game would have evolved and be sustained by the nature of air-filled round leather. In the Nigerian village where I grew up playing soccer, when air-filled balls were not available, as young boys, we used unripe oranges, rubber (latex) balls, tiny stones, clothes wrapped into a bundle or whatever we could improvise to realize the joy and fellowship of soccer games. All this is not to deny that the air-filled, round leather once it is situated in a practice would make a distinctive contribution to the social practice involved. And I tell you, the days when as young boys we got real leather balls to play with, were exhilarating. Social practice is always and everywhere an expression of substance or material used, selected, and worked in human communion.

Once a substance is involved in social practice or when we speak of substance with regard to a social practice we are involved in transforming the idea of substance. To say that social practice makes use of, shapes or works upon a substance, metal, or commodity is to say that substance possesses a relational character. Has the gold coin, sea shell as money medium *ever* existed without its own social practice?[45] The word, "ever" in the sentence is not used temporally but sociologically, ontologically, and logically. It refers not to a time in history of the metal or commodity but to the nature or being of money (monetary media). If money is by nature relational and if it can be signified by a substance (metal, paper, magnetic traces) we can say that inasmuch as that substance signifies the character of being of money that substance (in its monetary role) can only be conceived as relation. In this way of thinking about social practice, it is pointless to talk about social practice in strictly "ontological" or "functional" terms. In view of the relational nature of money, that is, the way of relating between persons, mode of being, social practice of money relates the physical object so profoundly and so existentially to itself that in its *new state* we cannot conceive the object in itself, but only as it "relates to." Existence for both (object and social practice) is not apart from communion, and as Zizioulas argues ontology and function are qualified and determined by communion.[46] This way of thinking is necessary to correct the thinking of sociologists like Ingham who rightly affirm that "money *is* itself a social relation" but neglect to show how monetary objects (media) are physically present in the monetary transactions. My conclusion is that money is simultaneously a social relation and a *relational thing*.

Let me provide some brief summary statements about the difference between (a) money as *social relation* and money as a *relational thing*; and (b) money as embedded in social relations and money as constituted by social relations. *Relational thing* is the identification of a relationship in objects, things, or "brute facts." Put differently, by *relational thing*, I mean an ongoing process between an object used as monetary medium and the social relations that constitute it as money, confers it with moneyness. "Relational" and *thing* are not two separate items; they are like the two sides of a coin. I will make these clearer, in short, clarifying statements that show the logic of the thinking behind the concept of *relational thing*. I am going to combine the kernel of what we have learned about money as social relations in this chapter and the previous one with insights from philosophy and economics on how physical objects or things function in social relationships:

(a) A monetary medium (however dematerialized) exists in relation to the social institutions that confer moneyness on it.

(b) The identification (the setting apart) of a particular object, physical particle is itself relational. An object is brought into certain relationship to serve society as money. Its very existence as money depends on this intentionality of the users, the conscious social agents.

(c) Every existent monetary medium bears such connection or connections as specified above. A physical particle or medium can perform the function of money by virtue of its physical features. But the function is imposed by human beings "only in virtue of a certain form of collective acceptance of the objects as having a certain sort of status. With that status, comes a function, that can only be performed in virtue of the collective acceptance by the community that the object has that status, and that status carries the function with it."[47]

(d) During and after an object is constituted by a particular (detachable and depersonalized) configuration of social relations to become or be counted as monetary medium it still exists within the general, overarching social relations of the community. This is to say, the object is always embedded (situated) in complex social relationships, within the network of personal relations and transactions that make up the society. As Carl Wennerlind puts it: "money does not exist in a vacuum but is part of an elaborate web of dynamic social structural conditions within which people act and interact. As such, money is a social relation in the sense that it mediates the interaction between people [and it is socially contingent]."[48] This is the way to understand what I mean by money being constituted by social relations and being embedded in social relations.

(e) The social relations or the social structures that select an object exist even if they are not or yet recognized by all the users of the monetary medium.

(f) The social relations cannot play their money-constituting role, that of picking out an object to privilege as money, if there is no object, physical particle to define and constitute as money. The social relations cannot become manifest or phenomenological as monetary media without some objects—without some of John Searle's "brute fact" (materialized or dematerialized).

(g) Therefore to become money, social relations would be attached and be "objectified" in something. A set of social relations that bears no relations to something (media) neither exists as money nor is it constitutive of money itself. Let us not forget that all existing forms of money share the dual properties of "unit of account" and medium of exchange."

(h) In sum, money is a *relational thing*—an inseparable unity of purely abstract unit of social relation and materialized or dematerializable thing.

SECTION 5: SUMMARY AND CONCLUSION

On the whole, this chapter has amply shown the social character of money. Money is not only embedded in social relations, it is created out of social relations. There is an advantage to the notion of money as a social relation. It indicates that money always represents what has already been presented. This is all the more so because our definition of social relation is not monetarist, it is rather economic and social. The presentation of the relation in this study is based on the exchange of energy and matter in a social setting. To say that money is a social relation has the advantage of underlining that money "re-presents something which has already been historically and socially presented."[49] Money is a metastructure of the historicosocial structure of society.

From this way of looking at money, we can discern an ambiguity of money. Money is "absolutely tied to the historicosocial presentation and yet also separated from it." The (debt, claim) relations which money *packages*, as we learned from the adaptation of Zelizer's *relational work*, were already constructed by society. Money is historically linked to society. Money, solely capable of representation, cannot package relations whose ruling character or characteristic is absent from the society, as we learned from Duchrow and Hinkelammert's theory of the link between monetizable credit relations and the emergence of private property. It manages, orders, regulates, reinforces, and operates terms of interactions which are already structured by the "whatever" nature of society. On the other hand, because the total relations of society exceed what relations are inscribed into money, because money cannot be identified with the original structure of the society which births it, it is necessarily separate from the society. It is separate because as a "reinforcer" of the nature of a given society, as a coercive apparatus for a given structure of society, it does the structuring of the terms of interactions according to a law which "comes from elsewhere."[50]

The insights we have gained from this chapter, and from the previous one, have at least rendered problematic the use of the *a*social neoclassical economic definition of money as the basis of doing theological analysis of the monetary system. The concept of money ("money *is* itself a social relation") that has been lifted up in these two chapters is better and more adequate for theological-ethical analysis as well as being a more sophisticated and accurate theory of money for many disciplines. In approaching theological and ethical analysis in subsequent portions of this study, it will be important to keep certain points in mind. First, money is rightly seen as a social institution dependent on state structures and coercive powers of taxation. Second, money is a credit or claim and is thus constituted by social relations.[51] The essential property of "money in general" is social relations. Third, money is not just a convenient medium of exchange, "moneyness" is conferred on any item that answers to the money of account. Fourth, money is discursively constructed. There are many objects that can be used as money forms and each of them have an infinite number of attributes and what leads a society to recognize some properties of objects and declare those that possess them as monetary media is not a neutral decision. "The functions of money are socially assigned to *objects*" (italics in the original).[52] The concept of money developed in this chapter incorporates social facts and social relations without neglecting the role of things in the functioning of the monetary system. Fifth, money is simultaneously a social relation and a *relational-thing*. This combination is significant in understanding the social practice of money. Sixth, my concept of money also incorporates Weberian sociological theories to show that prices, inflation, and deflation may be dependent on "class struggle." As we learned in chapter 3, according to Weber, inflation and deflation are not mere occurrences but are "always in very complex ways dependent on its [money] scarcity" and on the economic struggle for existence, and the balance of power in the actual processes of production and control of money. Seventh, a stable money-space rests on the authoritative foundations of sovereign political and social bases. Thus, money is not only an "economic" phenomenon but also a sociopolitical phenomenon. Eighth, money has multiple meanings and different money has different character depending on the social context in which the transaction is done. "Money is neither culturally neutral nor socially anonymous, but values and social relations reciprocally transform money by investing it with meaning and social patterns."[53]

In conclusion, let me point to some topics for further analysis in this study. I wish to state that the economic and sociological foundations necessary for crafting a theology of money cannot be fully set in place without a proper understanding of the dual, ambiguous, and dialectical nature of money. Money relates and separates simultaneously. Money opens up persons, industries, and nations outward to others. It binds persons, corporations, groups, and regions together into communities through its social practice. Money also disconnects. The differences it creates causes systematic crises, discrimination, deprivation, despoliation, separation, and segregation among classes, races, and regions. In chapter 5, this book will undertake a systematic analysis of these issues. I will employ Paul Tillich's concept of the social demonry to analyze money. Chapter 5 will describe money-induced existential ambiguities and tensions of separation and unity in human sociality. It will also trace these ambiguities to the nature of money as a union of contraries: connect: disconnect:: creates: destroys:: embraces: excludes:: local: international. It will as well show the typological-structural tension in the dynamics of money as an exchange medium which drives it toward a trinitarian structure of global trade and payment system and toward its transmutation into a perichoresis of national currencies that anticipates the eschatological gathering of "the whole people of God."

The preceding analyses of money contained in this chapter and the one before it were not extended to dealings between states in the global trade and payment system. What happens when the monetary space of one state expands to include, overlap or dominate that of another such that it is able to extract seigniorage from the other? This is the matter of the relationship and balance of power between strong and weak economies. This is one of the demonic distortions of money as a social relation which we will begin to examine in the next chapter. It is also about the link between money and empire as trading in the foreign exchange market is done through relatively few key, vehicular, and reserve currencies. Global trading was done principally through the pound sterling in the nineteenth century, the dollar, deutsche marks, and yen in the twentieth century, and now through dollar, euro, and the yen. This second set of issues and concerns will be addressed in chapter 6.

What kind of theological resources can be brought to bear on crises and problems in the social practice of money? In chapter 7, I will draw on the practical consequences of the doctrine of the Trinity based on the perichoretic interpretation to show how the global monetary system can be used to create an embracing economic community that brings *unity-in-difference* into perpetual play and justifies no "privileges, and no subjugations and submittances."[54] I am hoping that such a theological reflection can helpfully address the issues we have raised.

NOTES

1. See J. Wentzel van Huyssteen, *The Shaping of Rationality: Toward Interdisciplinarity in Theology and Science* (Grand Rapids, MI: William B. Eerdsmans Co., 1999), 111–77 for a discussion of the postfoundationalist notion of communicative practices informed and imbued with interdisciplinarity and intersecting rationalities or epistemologies. As he puts it on pp. 136–37: "What is at stake in this notion of a transversal rationality is to discover, or reveal, the shared resources of human rationality precisely in our very pluralist, diverse assemblages of beliefs or practices, and then to locate claims of reason in the overlaps of rationality between groups, discourses, or reasoning strategies. . . . In this move the concepts of theory and practices are themselves refigured: theory is here no longer viewed as a system of a priori rules and principles, and practice is liberated from its subordination as a mere application of theory. What now emerges is a third option, the third dimension of *praxis*, which indicates a fusion of thought and action that displays its own discernment, insight, and disclosure, no longer needing a transcendental ego or system of universal rules to swoop down from on high" (italics in the original).

2. Randall Collins, arguing from the perspective of radical microsociology, has shown that human beings are emotional energy seekers in their interactions. He states that in any analysis of social networks we must investigate what opportunities for emotional energy are present and how they are appropriated or maximized. See his *Interaction Ritual Chains* (Princeton, NJ: Princeton University Press, 2004).

3. The word *telos* here is used only to mean the tendency and directedness of interaction to fulfill itself as a relation, becoming a union of vitality and form, giving actuality to that which is potential in interaction; becoming a source of claim of one life against another.

4. The influence of Tillich's thought on my thinking here is obvious.

5. I have partly relied on insights gained from Bruce Carruthers' analysis of supposed differences between money and credit. See his "The Sociology of Money and Credit," in *The Handbook of Economic Sociology*, 2nd ed., ed. N. J. Smelser and R. Swedberg (Princeton, NJ: Princeton University Press, 2005), 355–78.

6. Conceptualize it in this way. In the first scenario, agent A gives motion to agent B and receives matter in return. Agent A also gives matter and receives motion in return. The two-way movement happens on each side at the same time. Each one is a seller, each one is a buyer. In the second case, matter flows one way and motion in the opposite direction. One party only gives one item and the other party takes the other item. In the third case, both agents get motion and matter but not at the same time. Matter is exchanged for motion and motion is exchanged for matter—not simultaneously. This is like the typical market exchange. They are not both seller and buyer at the same time.

7. Relation as we are conceiving it occurs beyond the basic ontological level of self-world (Tillichian sense of the word). It is found at the level of the elements that make up the basic structure of human encounter with the objective world. According to Tillich, these elements are individuality and participation (universality), dynamics and form, and freedom and destiny. In this schema, the elements on the left (e.g., individuality, dynamics) express separation of being, while those

on the right (e.g. participation, form) are for belongingness of being. I understand social relation as situated beyond the power of the self just to be for itself and in the self's character to be part of the world from which it is separated and to which it belongs. *Systematic Theology*, vol. 1, *Reason and Revelation, Being and God* (Chicago: University of Chicago Press, 1951), 176–77. It is a ministructure of manifoldness and that it is rooted in a kind of *eros*, which unites persons to participate in their environment, and also to transcend it, in the quest to produce and reproduce biological and social life.

8. Trust is an emergentist surpervening of promise, the promise to perform. For a definition of emergence see Philip Clayton, *Mind and Emergence: From Quantum to Consciousness* (Oxford: Oxford University Press, 2004), 6, 14–15, 24–25, 49. The supervenience of trust on promise is an example of processual, evolutionary *emergence*. Trust depends on both diachronic and synchronic assessment of the entire relation field as well as a teleological evaluation of the relationality at the point in time when the promise is made and accepted. The dependency on the history and evaluation is neither logical nor metaphysical. Trust is dependent on promise but not reducible to it. It should also be noted that the promise to pay cannot be produced without trust.

9. Geoffrey Ingham, *The Nature of Money* (Cambridge, MA: Polity Press, 2004), 74.

10. Talcott Parsons, *Structure and Process in Modern Societies* (New York: Free Press, 1960); and Carruthers, "The Sociology of Money and Credit," 355–78.

11. Carruthers, "The Sociology of Money and Credit," 370.

12. Paul Tillich, *Love, Power, and Justice* (New York: Oxford University Press, 1960), 54.

13. Robert Wright, *NonZero: The Logic of Human Destiny* (New York: Vintage Books, 2001).

14. It would take us too far afield from our limited purpose here to nuance the meaning of "effervescence" or imperialism here. It suffices, however, to state that one could acknowledge a difference between a more positive "effervescence" and more negative imperialism. There is conceivably a difference between life-enhancing drives found in universality and destructive imperialist drives toward universality and totality.

15. Mancur Olson, *The Rise and Decline of Nations: Economic Growth, Stagflation, and Social Rigidities* (New Haven, CT: Yale University Press, 1982).

16. Geoffrey Ingham, "Fundamentals of a Theory of Money: Untangling Fine, Lapavitsas and Zelizer," *Economy and Society* 30, no. 3 (2001): 311–12.

17. Please refer to the last section on features of social relations to see how this detachment can be socially enacted.

18. Georg Simmel, *The Philosophy of Money*, trans. Tom Bottomore and David Frisby (London: Routledge & Kegan Paul, 1978 [1900]), 177.

19. Simmel, *The Philosophy of Money*, 178. See also pp. 174–79 for the whole argument that metallic money involves credit.

20. See Stephanie Bell, "The Role of the State and the Hierarchy of Money," *Cambridge Journal of Economics* 25, no. 3 (2001): 151.

21. "In advanced societies the central government is in a strong position to make certain assets generally acceptable media. By its willingness to accept a des-

ignated asset in settlement of taxes and other obligations, the government makes that asset acceptable to any who have such obligations, and in turn to others who have obligations to them, and so on." James Tobin and S. S. Golub, *Money, Credit, and Capital*, 27.

22. Adam Smith, *An Inquiry into the Nature and Causes of the Wealth of Nations*, Bantam Classic Edition (New York: Random House, 1776, [2003]), 419.

23. Ingham, "Money is a Social Relation," 117.

24. Ulrich Duchrow and Franz J. Hinkelammert, *Property for People, Not for Profit: Alternatives to the Global Tyranny of Capital* (London: Zed Books, 2004), 6, 186, 191.

25. Duchrow and Hinkelammert, *Property for People*, 63.

26. Jocelyn Pixley, *Emotions in Finance: Distrust and Uncertainty in Global Finance* (Cambridge: Cambridge University Press, 2004), 7.

27. Simmel, *The Philosophy of Money*, 177.

28. In spite of Simmel's profound analysis of money, it still suffers from three deficiencies. It lacks a discussion of how the abstract value of money is established and maintained. Besides, in his relational, subjective interplay of forces and preferences, which establish the value of commodities, money plays only a neutral role, as in the theories of the neoclassical economists. In the autopoietic (self-maintaining and self-referential) functioning of the valuation system, the social structure that stands behind price formation in Max Weber's economic struggle of "man against man" is ignored. Finally, Simmel somehow thinks that the abstract value of money depends on the process of dematerialization of money-stuff (p. 191). This is an error many analysts still make today. The abstract unit of account precedes the concrete medium of exchange and it is not dependent on the abstraction (dematerialization) of money.

29. Simmel, *The Philosophy of Money*, 120, 128–29.

30. Carruthers, "The Sociology of Money and Credit," 355.

31. Pixley, *Emotions in Finance*, 8.

32. Viviana Zelizer, *The Purchase of Intimacy* (Princeton, NJ: Princeton University Press, 2005), 35–38.

33. For example, see Ingham, *The Nature of Money*, 197.

34. See Bell, "State and the Hierarchy of Money," 157.

35. For an explanation of the hierarchy of money see Bell, "State and the Hierarchy of Money," 158–61.

36. John Maynard Keynes, *A Treatise on Money* (London: Macmillan, 1930), 3.

37. Geoffrey Ingham, "Schumpeter and Weber on the Institutions of Capitalism: Solving Swedberg's Puzzle," *Journal of Classical Sociology* 30, no. 3 (2003): 302. For a reply of his criticism of Swedberg, see Richard Swedberg, "Answer to Geoffrey Ingham," *Journal of Classical Sociology* 30, no. 3 (2003): 311–14.

38. Heiner Ganssman, "Book Review: Geoffrey Ingham, 'The Nature of Money,'" *Economic Sociology, European Electronic Newsletter* 6, no. 1 (October 2004): 32.

39. Italics are in the original. I am borrowing Zizioulas' definition of the church and using it for money. I think his idea inspired me to think of money in a certain way. John Zizioulas, *Being and Communion: Studies in Personhood and the Church* (Crestwood, NY: St. Vladimir's Seminary Press, 1985), 15.

40. Synaxis means "gathering or bringing together" in Greek. It is an early church word that is also used for synod, and meeting for worship, especially to celebrate the Eucharist. Simply, it is a mode of sociality.

41. On this point see John R. Searle, "Social Ontology and the Philosophy of Society," *Analyse and Kritik* 20, no. 2 (1998): 147.

42. As Zizioulas argues: "It is communion which makes beings 'be': nothing exists without it, not even God." Zizioulas, *Being and Communion*, 17.

43. See Reinhold Niebuhr, *Nature and Destiny of Man*, vols. 1 and 2 (Upper Saddle River, NJ: Prentice Hall, 1941).

44. I must say once again that the insights about the social practice of money and the language to convey them are coming from John Zizioulas, *Being and Communion*, 22.

45. Please note that I am not talking about gold as a substance per se, but gold coin that is a form of monetary media. So your answer should be no. These media have never existed apart from their social practices. To concede this point is not to posit that the form of each medium has been irrelevant to defining social practice. The nature of the particular medium, its substance, has made some distinctive contribution to the nature of the social practice, even if we admit that the defining and crucial configuration that makes money money or anything what it is, remains fundamentally social. I am trying to guard against a reductionist move, one that would completely reduce substance to sociality so that substance has no contribution at all to the social practice, denying substance its own contribution and partially defining roles.

46. Zizioulas, *Being and Communion*, 226.

47. John R. Searle, "Social Ontology and Political Power," www.law.berkeley.edu/centers/kadish/searle.pdf.

48. Carl Wennerlind, "Money Talks, but What is it Saying? Semiotics of Money and Social Control," *Journal of Economic Issues* 35, no. 3 (September 2001): 557.

49. Alain Badiou, *Being and Event* (London: Continuum, 2006), 106. I have adapted Badiou's reinterpretation of the Marxian notion of the state to inform my interpretation of money here.

50. Badiou, *Being and Event*, 107.

51. See A. Mitchell Innes, "What is Money?" *Banking Law Journal* (1913): 377–408; Innes, "The Credit Theory of Money," *Banking Law Journal* (1914): 151–68.

52. Ganssman: "Book Review: Geoffrey Ingham," 32.

53. Zelizer, *The Social Meaning of Money*, 18.

54. Jürgen Moltmann, *The Coming Of God: Christian Eschatology*, trans. Margaret Kohl (Minneapolis, MN: Fortress Press, 1996), 183.

PART TWO

5

✛

Discerning Distortions in Monetary Relations

INTRODUCTION

In the last chapter I argued that it is hard to draw a distinction between social relations that constitute money and the monetary media. One may be able to make a distinction between them conceptually or in the abstract but the two are inextricably linked. One can pretend to truck and trade only with abstract social relations but the same relations will not do the buyer much good unless the buyer hands over to the seller some phenomenal form (even if it is book entry or computer magnetic trace) of the social relations. The medium (the greenback) is the way that the seller can realize the abstract social relation or the money of account and to exclusively appropriate it if it is to be her possession, private property. Money of account is a mere potential, the reality is the possession of its phenomenal form. A medium is needed to mediate and translate the abstract from the invisible to the visible. Every monetary medium participates in the shared monetary "nature," in moneyness. Moneyness could be expressed in a plurality of modes.

In this chapter, I would like to investigate how monetary relations affect interpersonal relations within human cooperative activities. It examines the ambiguities and distortions in interpersonal relations as a result of money's penetration into the necessary social character of all human existence, into the intersubjective relations that characterize any community. The chapter also looks at how money and monetary phenomena interact with an individual's self actualization, self-determination, transcendence, integration, and participation. Money is paradoxical in its intersection with human intersubjectivity. It simultaneously helps the person to separate from others but it also puts the person in constant social relationship with others. This, again, is money's "dual" or "dialectical" nature. The penetration of money into the interpersonal structural relations of human exclusion and participation is fraught with dangers and oppositions, yet filled with cooperation and opportunities. The analyses here will show in what ways money facilitates or obstructs *participation*, the vital ingredient for human ontological and social self-affirmation.[1] How exactly this is so, is the task of this chapter. It will involve employing Tillich's second root of trinitarian thinking to illuminate tensions, ambiguities, and destructive processes in the sociological character of money. Specifically, I will identify six forms of demonries in the social practice of money in the United States. The various forms of the demonries are traceable in one way or the other to the existence of huge power differentials among economic classes, groups, races, and geographical regions in the United States. It will take us further afield to discuss the dynamics that sustain and propel the various social structures behind the demonries and their associated forms of injustice.

The most appropriate tool for this kind of analysis is Tillich's concept of the social demonry. Demonry is drawn from religious discourse by Tillich and used as a metaphor for identifying vitalist and destructive social practices. This is helpful for identifying distortions at work in money's sociality. Money as a social practice unifies within itself "a formative and a form-destroying element."[2] It is what could be described as a social demonry, a social practice which "consumes" life in order to create life. More precisely, social demonry is a form, a social structure, supra-individual "which supports life, which at the same time contains the force of destruction in such a way that the destructive power is essentially connected with its creative power."[3] It is this dialectic that I investigate in this chapter. The depth of a theological understanding of money is the grasping of this dialectical quality in it. The task of a theology of money is to show how to constrain money from becoming destructive, that is, becoming purely negative, and to indicate how money could be partly relieved of its destructive forces and turned into a more creative force.

Let me now lay out the overall framework of this chapter. There are three sections below. Section 1 further advances the concept of the demonic using a Tillichian methodology. In section 2, I gently lead the reader out of the high and serene world of philosophy to the hurly-burly environment of the marketplace, legal form[4] of money, monetary policies, and *biopower* of money. The immediate goal here is to illustrate the unavoidable and peculiar dialectics of money as a force supporting social reality in modern capitalist society, but also destructive of human sociality. I will attempt to expose the ambiguities which are present in the sociological character of money and show all that are driving it to claim ultimate concern in human affairs. The overall aim is to show that it is virtually impossible to withdraw from the judgment that money is involved in both creative and destructive practices and thus can be referred to, symbolically, as demonic.[5] The final section provides a summary of the main arguments of the chapter.

SECTION 1: MEANING OF SOCIAL DEMONRY

To get purchase on the meaning of the symbol of the demonic we go to the Christian theologian Paul Tillich who "reintroduced" it into modern theological language in the 1930s.[6] Tillich used the term to refer to three forces or tensions that are always embedded in any human or religious phenomenon, process, or being. First, Tillich's main insight, in my opinion, is the recognition that constructive and destructive powers are always imbedded and ambiguously interwoven in every being, person, social group, or historical situation.[7] These powers are the results of the conditions of existential estrangement as beings actualize their potentialities by simultaneously "standing out" (*existere*[8]) and "standing in" in their essential nature.[9]

Second, there is also the drive wherein that which is finite (and not infinite) claims to be infinite. For an example of the finite claiming infinity we can go to 1930s Germany. The Nazi government raised the German state, which is finite, to something of an infinite status, and asked for unconditional demands of commitment. This made the state to be idolatrous. As Tillich put it, "the claim of anything finite to be final in its own right is demonic."[10] When a holy object which points to the divine, and not the holy itself, claims to be the holy it has become demonic. In other terms used by Tillich, a finite being is taking itself as the "ultimate concern."[11]

Third, it refers to the ambiguities that exist in any structural process. The source of life ambiguities, according to Tillich, is traceable to the basic ontological cleavage between subject and object.[12] Humans in this side of eternity are unable in all their cultural functions to transcend subjectivity and objectivity. Their language is not free from this bondage to the subject-object scheme as no language is possible without this subject-object gap. Even human love is not free from its grip. "The separation of the lover and the beloved is the most conspicuous and painful expression of the subject-object cleavage of finitude. The subject of love is never able to penetrate fully into the object of love, and love remains unfilled, and necessarily so, for if it were ever fulfilled it would eliminate the lover as well as the loved."[13]

Note that Tillich's move to identify and situate the demonic in the very essential and existential form of human life and cultural processes, or the subject-object gap, clearly shows that the demonic is not an outside force, where ever it manifests itself, but is rooted in the very character of the being or institution.[14] It lies within its character and drives the being to greatness as well as despair. To him, the demonic is even ensconced in the holy.[15] To say that ambiguities are internal to the existential divide between subject and object should not be construed to mean that the demonic cannot be found in beings that transcend the cleavage between subjectivity and objectivity. Tillich regards the gods which are ultimate concerns to humans as both holy and demonic.[16]

Embedded in any social demonry are the elements of participation and separation, unity, and tension. The demonic, according to Tillich, does not designate antidivine forces in individual and social life. "Demons in mythological vision are divine-antidivine beings. They are not simply negations of the divine but participate in a distorted way in the power and holiness of the divine. The term must be understood against this mythological background."[17] In this sense, demons cut and attach. The activities of the demon, the antidivine are perceived as distinct from the divine, but it is at the same time what attaches them to the divine in a distorted way.[18]

We will soon show that the dialectics of uniting and separating, subjectivity and objectivity is present in the social practice of money. There is an individualization and participation in the depth of the process of social practice. The individual acts to find the fulfillment of her needs but this participation, this stepping into the river, is at the same time an act/practice of fulfillment for all. We cannot separate one from the other. Her fulfillment cannot be separated from the fulfillment of the whole group in which she participates. But also in stepping into the social practice it acts also upon her in co-opting her into its universal fulfillment.

The tension of unity and separation, being and non-being is also at the core of the social practice of money, especially in the attempts of monetary policymakers to sustain the *sociality* inherent in the practice of money. I stated that money unites and separates, excludes and encourages participation. The power to create exclusion or discourage inclusive participation of most people or industry is inherent in the nature of money. Monetary policymakers try to resist non-social practice of money (non-SPM), that is, the quality of money as a social practice by which every person (everything) that participates in SPM is negated.[19] Non-SPM is the negation of SPM within SPM itself. The fact that non-SPM can negate SPM means that non-SPM is not foreign to SPM. This means SPM carries within itself "the destiny not to be." Money connects and money distinguishes and separates. Every SPM—fostering participation and communion—points to an *eros*[20] quality in every interpersonal and intersectoral relation in the economy. I am using *eros*, not in a popular sense, but in a philosophical sense as used by Tillich in his ethics book, *Love, Power and Justice*. In this work, we find the doctrine of *eros* as the power which drives to union with the whole, the greater sociality; it is the uniting form of individual parts and the whole (social) body. It is the structural interdependence, the driving force, the transpersonal impulses in interactions that create communion of social groups.[21]

This quality is fragile and monetary policies can make it to shrink, not grow, and the *eros* quality can thus be successfully resisted. Let me just give four examples of how this might happen—that is, state some of the negative forces within the practice of money that thwarts healthy sociality. First, an incestuous financial circulation of money that is estranged from industrial circulation of money in a sordid orgy of stock market games threatens the integrity of SPM, as opposed to a fully "public" and well-orbed circulation that is implied by well-functioning SPM. Second, huge income inequality and increasing concentration of wealth often cut off or threaten the effective participation of the poor in economic intercourse. It is not inequality which is dangerous and violates justice, but inequality which destroys the disadvantaged instead of working toward their fulfillment. Third, rural-urban disarticulation that creates dual economies within an economy and huge income gaps between urban and rural areas is another negative force that is internal to the SPM. Finally, another internal force that threatens the practice of money is the tendency to use monetary policy for particular self-realization. It is more than likely that the group or class that controls monetary decisions is really "actualizing itself over against the threat of non-being"[22] to itself in the economy. Every social practice, like every civilization, contains forces which threaten to break it down.

It is germane to clarify the relation between ambiguities and demonries. Ambiguities are intrinsic to money as a social practice; the demonic refers to the way a negative destructive element rides along with the positive and productive one in the ambiguity and threatens to destroy or break the configuration down.

Before we close this section and move to the next, it is important to note the wide berth Tillich gives to his notion of the demonic and the role it plays in sustaining justice and injustice in the human world. People's awareness of the power of the demonic provokes calls for justice even as it is also a way of analyzing the complexity of injustice. As Tillich argued in several of his works, the elevation of a being or institution to the level of infinite or ultimate concern will result in the destruction of all other finite beings and institutions around it. To capture the meaning of the demonic in way that elucidates the cryptic Tillichian phrase, "the claim of

anything finite to be final in its own right" cited above, I will press Wolfgang M. Zucker's interpretation of Tillich into service here:

> Tillich's definition of the demonic is all-encompassing. . . . The sense is clear;
> whatever there is, every being thing, every extant is finite and limited. It
> originates from the Ground of all Being, is created and maintained for the
> duration of its time but will eventually have to go and be no more. But as
> Nietzsche said that all that is wants eternity, it resents its finiteness and
> wants finality. It wants to forget its conditional nature and tries to establish
> its own unconditional significance. The order of all being things is tempo-
> rality; their claim to transcend finiteness is therefore a violation of the order
> of being; it is demonic. Thus everything can potentially become demonic,
> the pursuit of any human goal, power or knowledge, art or science, money
> or sex, systems of order and forms of government, love as well as hate. They
> can all become demonic, not because they themselves are evil, but because
> they claim finality.[23]

In noting this tendency in human affairs, Tillich posited that the rise of
that which is not final to finality can and should provoke prophetic criticism before it destroys other finite beings and institutions around it. The
fierce attacks of the Old Testament prophets were induced by a sacra-
mental-priestly system which either elevated the mediums of revelation
and its excellencies into the content of revelation or the conditional to the
unconditional, and even succumbed to religious nationalism.[24] The
prophetic criticism was to bring the priestly system to the judgment of the
divine law in the name of the God of justice. Prophetic criticisms, according to Tillich, force all pretenses of finality which is the source of injustice
to return to its proper place. "The prophets attacked demonic forms of holiness in the name of justice. The Greek philosophers criticized a demonically distorted cult in the name of *Dikē*. In the name of the justice which
God gives, the Reformers destroy a system of sacred things and acts
which has claimed holiness for itself."[25]

From this integral connection between the demonic analysis in all human situations and justice, a major purpose of Tillich's theology stands
out. The demonic analysis is to reveal the areas of human interaction that
have moved too far from the Ground of Being, and have become sources
of injustice and therefore need to be brought under the demands of justice. This is also the focus of this book. We aim to show how ambiguities,
tensions, and destructive processes of modern money as a social practice
could be subjected to the demands of justice. We also aim to show how the
claim of a few finite national currencies to be final in the global monetary
system does not fulfill the principle of justice and they need to be brought
under the demands of justice.

It is now time to turn to concrete sites of operations of money, the social practice of money. In the following section, I will endeavor to translate what we have learned about the theory of the demonic into concrete and specific analyses of the social phenomenon of money. This is only to unearth the tensions and ambiguities ensconced in the sociological character of money.

I need to give a perspective on how the next section fits within the Tillichian trinitarian framework which is the organizing principle for our analyses in this book. In the following section, as indicated above, I will be showing how the *second root of the trinitarian thinking* is useful in illuminating our understanding of money. In chapter 2, I showed, amidst the review of theological writings on money, the application of the third root[26] of the trinitarian thinking to monetary analysis. In chapter 7, I will show how the first root of Tillich's trinitarian thinking can help us to re-imagine the global monetary system. I will argue that the tension between the universal and particular as played out in the global trade and payment system is an underlying principle that can drive particularistic national currencies toward universal and total integration as one global currency (not one or two controlled by national interests). I will also argue that the tension can also define the patterns of interaction between them. According to Tillich, there is a tension between the elements in the idea of God: the dialectics of the need for concreteness (particularity) and absoluteness (ultimacy and universality). The trinitarian principle is what structures the balance between the concrete and absolute drives so that they are united in a living God. He sees trinitarian monotheism as the ultimate realization of this principle. He argues that the Trinitarian God has overcome the typological-structural tension between particularity and universality. The triune God who claims universality and ultimacy, is uncontrolled by local interest, and yet does not lose that God's concreteness. The triune God is absolutely concrete and particular (in Jesus the Christ) and yet is absolutely universal at the same time.[27]

SECTION 2: AMBIGUITIES OF MONEY: SOURCES OF DEMONRIES

Power over the Definition of Money for Monetary Policy

The best starting place for analyzing the ambiguities of money, and hence for understanding money's social demonries, is the influence of social and political powers on the definition of money supply (the estimated amount of money in the economy). Although money is an economy-wide social practice, only very few economic actors have the power to define the money supply and the definition is always a social construction. According to Wayne E. Baker, up until 1960s the Federal Reserve Board (America's central bank) defined money supply as the amount of cash and demand deposits or checks (the so called M1) because these were the primary means of payment.[28] But in the 1960s, rising interest rates on liquid assets, advances in transaction technology which facilitated record-keeping for high-turnover accounts, treasury bills, and other liquid financial instruments became attractive as forms of payment. The proliferation of these new instruments as substitutes of money made it difficult to accurately define money supply. In response to these developments, the Federal Reserve changed the definition of money and came up with new measures of M1 to M5.[29]

Baker's point that the definition of money is situationally specific and it is a social construction provides us with leeway to analyze money as a discourse. As Zelizer argues, and as we have seen, money itself has multiple meanings and different money has different characters depending on the social context in which the transaction is done. Thus, she posits that "money is neither culturally neutral nor socially anonymous, but values and social relations reciprocally transform money by investing it with meaning and social patterns."[30] Indeed, money is discursively constructed. There are many objects used as money and each of them has infinite number of attributes. Thus, what leads the Federal Reserve Board to recognize some properties of objects, and to declare those that possess them to be money, is not a neutral decision. As Lakshman Yapa states in another context, that of the definition of poverty:

> Every object in the world contains an infinite number of attributes whose form depends on the relations between that object and all other related objects. Naturally, the objects of our reflection and conversation can focus only on a few selected attributes; so the form of the object is discursively constructed. *It could not be any other way* (italics in the original).[31]

Baker in consideration of the socially constructed nature of definition of money proceeded to ask: who has the power to construct the definition? He employed block-models (network analysis of social structures) and other forms of advanced mathematics to illustrate that money and its uses in capitalist contexts reflect the structure of the economy, the social structure of the market economy.[32] His findings revealed that in the United States there is a core of the structure where the most powerful actors play and the periphery where the less powerful actors operate. The types of financial assets used by the actors in the core are considered closest to money. He then argues:

An economy differentiated into core and periphery structure indicates an unequal distribution of power. The core actors in an economy dominate other actors, control the flow of capital, and wield political power. In contrast, the peripheral actors are in the weak and powerless position.[33]

The preceding discussion clearly shows the ambiguities of money. Given the nature of the social practice of money, it is supposed to yield power that is immanent and all individuals are to be elements of its articulation. Baker's profound analysis shows, however, that this is not so. It appears that power is not spread evenly in a power network. Part of the ambiguity of money is that Baker's analysis could be read differently—in the sense that power is not exclusively possessed by the state or the Federal Reserve Bank. When it comes to the definition of money there is no great divide between rulers and those ruled. It appears that "power is employed and exercised in a netlike organization"[34]—of banks, investment companies, institutional investors, and the like. Baker's analysis indicates that the power of definition of money is not always imposed from above as it comes from below in a capillary fashion. All this does not distract from recognizing that the power of social construction of money (defining money in terms of what it is and how it is used) is concentrated in the core of the financial structure and any talk about a power network is only substantially limited to the powerful actors at the core.

Zelizer's analysis of commercial circuits can also be used to reach a similar conclusion. The work of Zelizer has shown that there are distinctive kinds of currency within particular circuits of exchange in any given economy. These earmarked monies (currencies in restricted circuits of exchange and culturally specific monies) are tied together by money of account (the official currency) and it relates them and their specific users to one another and to the general monetary system. Ensconced in this connection is the dialectics of interrelation and differentiation. The money of account (the dollar in the case of the United States) relates but culturally specific money separates. The earmarked currencies also indicate differentiation of levels in the capitalist financial markets. The money of account which is matched with non-earmarked currencies (the plain dollar not limited to "restricted circuits of exchange" and to culturally specific uses) form the financial instruments which are open to all but often only accessible to few in the higher echelons of society. But the earmarked monies of the prostitutes, housewives, and poor people's welfare payments are not accessible to all, valuable only in specific circuits of exchange. "These currencies [monies in restricted circuits of exchange] are quite straightforwardly Durkheimian sacred objects, like the shells that circulated in the famous South Sea kula ring . . .; they exist to differentiate the levels of capitalist markets today, from financial instruments accessible only to the highest financial circles, down to the earmarked currencies of poor people's welfare payments."[35]

In sum, the specific ambiguity (the first of the set of six demonries in the social practice of money) we see here is that although money is a technology for an economy-wide social practice, only very few economic agents have the power to define and control its production. This ambiguity could turn into social demonry when the power is used for particular self-realization of a class in society at the expense of the rest of the populace. It would be interesting to spend some effort here to fully examine the connection between the social demonries of money and the structure of power differential in the United States. But, once again, we may have to resist the temptation to engage in this important project to let us principally focus on the nature of the social demonries in the country's monetary system in the light of the second root of the trinitarian thinking.

Biopower of Money as Source of Demonry

The study of the ambiguities of monetary relations is also important from another angle which is intimately linked to the issue of economic growth and development. Monetary policy plays a fundamental social and political role as a necessary aspect of the functioning of *discipline* and control of any society. It creates and maintains social hierarchies by its procedural and ordering (regulative) activity. In this sense, it is a form of *biopower*[36] aimed at producing and reproducing, promoting and regulating all aspects of social life, and at controlling the population.[37] Monetary policy as a whole does not aim to overthrow an existing social order and impose a new order from outside; rather it reproduces and regulates the existing order.

The Federal Reserve or the central bank is given the power to achieve a certain measure of equilibrium in the economy through the power of regulating money. The power to regulate money supply is not done neutrally and blindly. It is dictated by norms. From where do these norms come? They are surely not located on some transcendental plane, or in some other undefiled immanent realm or nature. They arise from specific norms and "the common organization of society and the continuous resolution of the antagonisms that runs throughout it."[38]

Monetary policy does not only create material goods and immaterial products, it also creates and transforms relationships and social life. In this regard monetary policy is at once an economic, political, social, and cultural project. In a modern society (such as the United States) the production of economic goods is always the production of social relationships and ultimately of society itself. Economic production has come to involve, more than ever before, a socialized network of activities based on communications, collaborations, and affective relationships. In this cooperative venture everyone in it is involved in the creation and production of new subjectivities in society which make any economic activity at once a social, cultural, and political force.[39] The economic communication and collaboration that money makes possible is part of the reality of social conditions. Money is never a product of an individual as it can only be created by a social community in communication and collaboration, and thus it is always and everywhere a part of the habits, experience, and practices that serve as the basis of social life.

The central bank in most nations exercises sovereignty over the monetary policy—at least insofar as it is the rule of one (one body, not many) and all other economic actors do not interact on the same plane with it. The central bank is the primary locus of monetary policy, a sovereign standing above the beehive of economic activities, transcendent, supposedly holding at bay the democratic impulses to "unreasonably" open (close) the spigots of money supply. Some commentators have argued for the abolition of this kind of power in the hands of a few unelected men and women. Even if we do not want this sovereignty to be abolished (and I do not), we should subject it to rigorous ethical scrutiny so that central bank's "will to power" is exercised in the interest of widest conception of the common good.

The impact of monetary policy is both productive and negative. For instance, the practice of monetary policies which stimulate investment decisions so as to jumpstart a slumping economy, to encourage production of material goods and immaterial products, and to create new expansive forms of economic life within the existing order itself, is a central example of the productive and creative potential of *biopower*. When, however, monetary policies put minorities like African-Americans in the United States and the poor in dire straits[40] so as to promote higher asset valuation in the financial markets, it is a manifestation of negative and destructive *biopower*. Central banks make conscious choices to promote either full employment or to curb inflation. These choices have differing impacts, depending on whether you are among the poor who need employment most, or whether you are among the bond holders whose assets go up in value because of links between inflation and interest rates.

The Federal Reserve Board in the United States makes monetary policy—setting policies to control the quantity and price of money and credit in the economy. In making their decisions, the members of the Board are focused on efficiency of their policies and the flow of information to economic agents to aid private-sector resource allocation decisions. The governors of the Board do not get into preferences, preference orientation, or welfare matters arising from monetary policies.[41] But the task of monetary policy is much deeper than solving a set of technical problems. Monetary policy has distributional impact.

Recently economists have been looking at monetary policy's differential impact on income groups, poverty, and the labor market. Christina D. Romer and David H. Romer's study identified low inflation and stable aggregate demand as the best way to lower poverty in the United States in the long run. They also showed that a rise in unemployment is associated with a rise in poverty level.[42] While the Romers' study documents the impact of monetary policy on the whole population or the well-being of the poor, Carpenter and Rodgers' study reveals that contractionary monetary policies (increase in the federal funds rate, actions taken by the central bank to hold back "perceived inflationary" growth) affect minorities more negatively and severely than whites in terms of employment-population ratio. The ratio (employment-population mix) declines because of increase in unemployment among minorities—with African-American teenagers bearing the brunt of such decline.[43]

Contractionary monetary policies not only work to increase unemployment in general, they even affect the distribution and type of unemployment. According to Rodgers, "contractionary monetary policy raises the number of unemployed at all segments of the [weeks of unemployment] distribution. However, as a share of the total number of unemployed individuals the increase is greatest among those that have been unemployed 15 weeks or more."[44] In other words, those who can least afford it are the ones who suffer the most.

In terms of the inflation and unemployment debate which is at the core of the philosophy of modern central banking, where do the poor stand? Rebecca Blank and Alan Blinder (a former deputy chairman of the Federal Reserve Board and Princeton University's professor of economics) have argued that the impact of monetary policy on the different demographic groups in the United States is riddled with race, sex group, age, and class conflicts. Nonwhite males are hardest hit by recessions, showing that national macroeconomic policy is "not neutral in spreading the burden of unemployment."[45] Unemployment, not inflation, bears down more heavily on the well-being of poor communities. Blank and Blinder show that a one percentage rise in unemployment depresses the income share of the lowest quintile by 0.13 of a percentage point, whereas a one percentage rise in inflation rate raises their income by 0.03 of a percentage point. They concluded that "unemployment is a regressive tax; inflation is a progressive one. More specifically, high unemployment redistributes income away from the bottom two quintiles and toward the top quintile. Inflation redistributes away from the fourth quintile toward the lowest quintile"[in plain English it means inflation somewhat—at least in the short-run—favors the poor (lowest quintile) and unemployment hurts them in relative terms].[46]

Indeed, the social polarization arising from the monetary policy regime has its counterpart in regional polarization, and to that story we now turn. Monetary policies in the United States have differential impact on regions. The economics textbook's simple view that there is one uniform national effect is simplistic. While professional economists have largely glossed over this matter, ordinary folks, politicians, and playwrights had recognized it for a long time. The William Jennings Bryan free silver campaign of 1896 was a singular vituperance ("You shall not press down upon the brow of labor this crown of thorns, you shall not crucify mankind upon a cross of gold.") against monetary policies that were seen by the South (rural, small businesses, southern and western farmers) as pandering to the crass financial interest of the industrial Northeast (Wall Street, big businesses, and the urban upper class of the east and northeast). The fight was over what metallic standard to be used as currency. Democratic presidential candidate Bryan wanted bi-metallic monetary standard (16 ounces of silver to one ounce of gold). His Republican opponent William McKinley wanted a monometallic gold standard. The Republican won the 1896 election with a vote margin of less than 10 percent. Why were there differences in opinion about the proper monetary standard? According to Milton Friedman, "eighteen ninety-six was itself a year of deep depression, following a number of years of hard times. Unemployment was high and rising; industrial output was low and falling; agricultural prices were low and falling."[47] Understandably, the farmers and small businesses wanted a monetary standard and policy that will inflate the economy as most of them were debtors and falling prices made it more expensive to pay off debts (larger volume of produce or goods was required to meet interest and principal repayments). In general, in a period of unanticipated deflation, creditors gain and debtors lose. The farmers supported by Bryan wanted to reverse things in their favor.

The economist Hugh Rockoff has argued that Frank Baum's *The Wonderful Wizard of Oz* is a fictional account of the silver agitation of the late nineteenth century—it "is not only a child's tale but also a sophisticated commentary on the political and economic debates of the Populist Era." He was able to identify many of the characters, places, and actions in the play with the free-silver movement. The land of Oz is the East, "where the gold standard reigns supreme and in which an ounce (Oz) of gold has almost mystical significance. . . . On a general level the Wicked Witch of the East represents eastern business and financial interests, . . . The silver shoes and the yellow brick road are . . . primary symbols of the two metals."[48]

According to the monetary history of the period, the Wicked Witch of the East won the day and ignored the wishes of the South. But in a remarkable display of political wizardry nearly forty years later, President

Franklin D. Roosevelt deftly swung monetary policy in the way of the South in the midst of the 1930s Depression and deflation. After breaking ranks with the bankers and financiers of the East, desirous of winning the support of southern farmers, and eager to stop the depression, he reflated prices (meaning he pursued inflationary policies). The thinking was that inflated prices would end the Depression and at the same time make it easier for farmers, small businesses, and workers to pay off their debts.[49] Roosevelt played a political game based on common man's idea that regions respond differently to monetary policies.

Gerald Carlino and Robert DeFina studied the impact of monetary policies on the eight Bureau of Economic Analysis (BEA) regions[50] in the United States over 34 quarters and found that there are disparate responses to monetary policies, presenting issues of cross-regional inequality. "We find some evidence that states containing a relatively larger concentration of small firms [fewer than 250 employees] tend to be more responsive to monetary policy shocks than states with smaller concentration of small firms."[51] The states that are most sensitive to monetary shock are in the Great Lakes region (Illinois, Indiana, Michigan, Ohio, Wisconsin) and the least sensitive states are in the Rocky Mountains region (Colorado, Idaho, Montana, Utah, Wyoming). There are certain economic factors that separate these regions from the New England (e.g., Massachusetts) and Mideast (e.g., New York) regions. Differences in industry mix are one of the factors. In places like New York business loans are primarily provided by big banks whose loan portfolios are less sensitive to monetary policy shifts and have relatively fewer number of small firms which depend on bank loans for funding.[52] An unexpected rise in the federal fund rate temporarily lowers real personal income much more in Michigan (2.7 percent) than in New York (0.7176 percent) in one or two quarters immediately following the policy shift. Indeed, owing to the differences in the way monetary policy affects real personal income and output across states and regions one can say that "the cost of disinflation [fighting inflation], for example, is distributed unequally" across states and regions. This suggests that the setting of common monetary policy is not ethically neutral (meaning that monetary policies have distributional consequences that differentially affect economic classes, racial groups, and regions). Similar effects have been found in other countries.[53]

Thus, in sum, the impact of monetary policies is not neutral. Different persons, races, and regions are affected differently by the decisions of the Federal Reserve Board, the central bank of the United States. The Federal Reserve does not make its policies in an ideological vacuum. There is a definite philosophical approach to central banking to which it adheres. Any serious effort to research the ethics of monetary policy will be incomplete if it does not involve an examination of the philosophy of central banking operative among decision makers in a given economy. Our social ethics must go further, then, to understand why central bankers take the decisions that they take, irrespective of their impact on human relations and persons. One needs to dig deep to understand the philosophy of central banking.

The specific ambiguity here is the potential for circulation of money that is estranged from the well-being of the poor and minorities. Monetary policies are generating inequalities which threaten to destroy the underprivileged instead of working toward their self-fulfillment. Yet, there is also the potential to use monetary policy to foster the common good.

Central Banking Practice as Source of Demonry

We can begin by noting that central banks, especially in advanced capitalist economies like the United States and Europe, define their *raison d'e-tre* as managing and preserving the value of their national or community's currency, and not the use of money to create and distribute work and its rewards in the most beneficial or equitable way. In layman's terms preserving the value of money means maintaining price stability by essentially relying on interest rate policy. When a central bank perceives that inflation is a threat it initiates a systemic credit crunch and domestic austerity to raise interest rates to rein in prices. Paul Volcker (a former chairman of the Federal Reserve Board) was once quoted as quipping in a lighthearted mood that "central bankers are brought up pulling legs off of ants."[54] In 1997 one of the Federal Reserve Bank's governors, Laurence H. Meyer, stated that "inflation is caused by too many people working."[55] On the other hand, when the economy is considered to be in recession, central banks try to lower interest rates to encourage investment.

The Federal Reserve Act of 1913 that created the Federal Reserve Board defines its purpose as "to promote effectively goals of maximum employment, stable prices, and moderate long-term interest rates." In the recent decades it has focused almost exclusively on price stability with the belief that sound money is the key to maximizing employment. This preference for price stability, which is often at the cost of employment, is ethically controversial as we shall see below.[56] Even if it is true and uncontroversial that price stability is the key to maximizing employment, what the Federal Reserve and economists regard as maximum employment is not what the average American takes it to be. Economists harbor certain jitteriness about full employment. They theorize that there is a certain level of unemployment necessary to control inflation. They call this the "natural" rate of unemployment, or NAIRU (Non-Accelerating Inflation Rate of Unemployment) and it is said to be in the range of 5 to 6 percent of the workforce. This level of unemployment is considered to be necessary to control inflation. It was the formidable conservative economist, Milton Friedman, who originated the concept of "natural rate" in his 1958 presidential address to the American Economic Association. Thus, as soon as unemployment drops and wages for workers rise, economists, bankers, and central bankers all warn about the damaging effects of wage increases—wages must be kept down to secure the "reserve army of the unemployed."[57] As Christina D. Romer and David H. Romer argue in their assessment of the connection between economic beliefs and performance of monetary policies in the United States, the natural rate framework has emerged as the principle way of thinking about the inflation-unemployment dynamics.[58]

Michael Shuman and others have questioned this philosophy of price stability, especially the whole notion of "natural" rate of unemployment. Shuman argues that if America is really ready to eliminate unemployment and still keep prices stable it could tax corporate managers to redistribute their multiple-figure incomes to workers or make shareholders turn in more of their profits to workers and in either case "wages could go up and product prices could stay even." He states that there is a moral crux to the whole hypothesized linkage between inflation and employment. According to Shuman:

> Inflation, in other words, could be said to reflect not a failure to keep a certain number of people out of work, but a refusal of corporate heads and shareholders to redistribute more fairly the gains from production. A rigorous national anti-inflation policy might better focus on placing upper limits on incomes and profits, rather than lower limits on unemployment. What the popularity of NAIRU theory among economists really demonstrates is a *moral* posture: They would prefer to throw 5 percent of the workforce onto the streets than shrink the rewards to managers and shareholders" (italics in the original).[59]

Whereas, Shuman has approached the morality of the inflation-employment controversy from the perspective of income distribution and plight of unemployment, Henry Liu relates it to modern advanced capitalist societies' evaluation of human worth. The hypothesized inverse relation between inflation and employment and the policymakers' adherence to it reveals that:

> The value of humans is inversely proportional to the value of money. In other words, money exists not to serve the welfare of the people, but rather, people must be sacrificed to serve the stability of money. . . . NAIRU or the natural rate of unemployment would be less obscene if the unemployment were not concentrated on the same group [race] of people. But structural unemployment tends to create a permanent unemployed class, institutionalizing social injustice as a structural aspect of the economy.

The central bank, by adopting the natural rate of unemployment or NAIRU as a component of monetary policy, is condemning 6 percent of the labor force to perpetual involuntary unemployment. It seems self-evident that the population has a natural right not to be forced to be part of this 6 percent of unfortunate souls in the workforce. A natural rate of unemployment flies in the face of U.S. political culture. The "inalienable rights" of *all* people (and not some people) to life, liberty and pursuit of happiness is a concept not compatible with chronic involuntary unemployment caused by government policy, aimed at protecting the value of money at the expense of a particular segment of the working class" (italics in the original).[60]

It is important to mention that often central bankers do not see a conflict between inflation and economic growth, believing that price stability is the key to development. Alan Greenspan, the former chairman[61] of the Federal Reserve Bank, testified in 1995 before the U. S. Congress: "I believe firmly that a key ingredient in achieving the highest possible levels of productivity, real incomes, and living standards is the achievement of price stability."[62] The key point that needs to taken into consideration here is this: there are portions of the American society that do not even benefit in times of prosperity as the various analyses of the distributional impact of monetary policies have indicated.

In sum, we would identify the specific ambiguity here as tension between commitment to flourishing life which the social practice of money is intended to promote and the generation of divisions and divisiveness in society. Money and monetary policies appear to be functioning in complete freedom to the exclusion of the masses and as such works against them.

Before leaving this section, let me try to anticipate and respond beforehand a possible concern professional economists may have regarding the foregoing discussion of the distributional impact of monetary policy and practice of central banking in the United States. Some economists hold the view that that monetary policy's primary focus should be on creating long-run price stability and not impacting the income distribution. Holders of this view argue that issues of distribution are the responsibility of a country's legislative and executive branches.

The distributional consequences of monetary policy as have been shown above strongly suggest that the decision makers need to take into account the impact of their policies on the poor. The foregoing two subsections have clearly shown the importance of developing further research into the ethics of monetary policy owing to the importance of distributional consequences of monetary policy shocks and shifts. More importantly, the arguments and the results of the above analyses indicate that the participation of the poor in the preservation and promotion of the well-being of the community in the United States is severely curtailed by monetary policies. The discussions in these sections have made it clear that monetary policy, justice, and well-being of the poor are not independent events that can go their own separate ways. What happens to money, to the money supply, is closely related to what happens to the well-being of the poor. Money does matter. Ethics of monetary policy do matter also. At the risk of being termed a reductionist, one can argue that it is the most significant economic policy affecting the plight of the poor that is generally ignored by advocates on both the right and the left. This is quite opposite to what happened at the close of the nineteenth century and beginning of the twentieth century when politicians like William Jennings Bryan staked his presidential campaign on monetary issues.

While economists focus on how to solve the technical problems of monetary policy in a detached perspective of human relations, theologians can also contribute to the solution by focusing on the whole network of human relations. Theological ethicists can come up with values that pertain to equity and justice that should inform monetary policy. My hypothesis is that if the Federal Reserve Board were to utilize some canons of equity and justice in its monetary policy the benefit to the society as a whole would be greater than what is currently achievable. An ethical model when combined with the appropriate macroeconomics thinking can maximize economic growth, lessen inequality, and improve the distribution impact of monetary policy and not spark inflation. It promises to move the incidence of monetary policy to a superior *Pareto* outcome.

These two subsections ("Biopower of Money" and "Central Banking Practice") have thus challenged the Federal Reserve Board to rethink how it makes monetary policy. The issues and analyses presented in them have made it obvious that one cannot divorce economic growth policy or monetary policy from distributional policy. On one hand, the Federal Reserve Board needs to develop a focus on distribution, and on the other, fiscal policy needs to be coordinated with monetary policy. Both the president and the Congress (the makers of fiscal policy) need to seriously take into account the decisions of the Board. For instance, when the Fed is raising interest rates to control inflation and consequently raising the unemployment level, it is not the best time for fiscal policymakers to be cutting social services. They need to know that what they do is not independent of the Federal Reserve Board so that they can counter the short- and long-term social impacts of contractionary monetary policy on the poor.

Ambiguities of Participation and Separation as Source of Demonry

There is a more profound ambiguity about money when one examines it in terms of object and subject, self-other which is one important part of every multi-form process. This recognition affords us an opportunity to further clarify the demonic aspects of money. Money as a social practice, in a certain sense, transcends the gap between subjectivity and objectivity. Humans in modern economies cannot deal with money (as a social practice) in detachment. In our participation in the modern economy we oscillate between using the concrete form of money as an object and tools for satisfaction of our purposes and the absoluteness of total surrender and immersion in the social practice of money. In using money, a person becomes an object in the practice of money, a node or wire through which the currents of currency (and of market forces) flow through to other autonomous agents. But as I will argue below, the ambiguities and the cleavage of subject-object still do not totally disappear in the monetary practice because of the subject-object structure of all reality.

Here we see that money as a social practice features a tensive relationship for the persons who participate in it. This is a tension because there is no participation if there is no element of individualization. For separation and participation are bound to each other. We do not even have knowledge of separation unless we have already experienced some unity of intercourse and interdependence of economic life, which is participation. Conversely, we cannot know participation without having experienced separation: for example, a lack of possession of that which enables us to participate in economic life. If one were to remove this wall of separation, social practice of money would cease to be what it is and would become an instrument of domination of one person over the rest of society. It would be like a competitive market which ceases to be competitive and becomes a monopolistic one. In neoclassical economics terms, a monopolist is someone who participates in the market, but has no necessary separation from it so that there is an undifferentiated identity with the whole force field of supply.

This ambiguity (the dialectical relation of separation and participation) is even clearer when the relationship between the concrete (legal form) money and participation are scrutinized. Where there is money there is tension between participation and separation—between money and private economic agents. As a social practice an agent is grasped by it and participates in it. But she can never grasp it. The social practice disappears the very instant she tries to grasp it. Money is always at hand. But she can never say: "It is here, I have caught it! I own it!" Indeed, social practices will cease to be money without separation. She who has money must be separated from the object of her social practice in a certain sense. Otherwise she would possess it and it ceases to be a community's social practice—if she possesses it and becomes its creator she gets undue advantage over everyone else.

In every society the power to issue money is, ideally, put outside the control of individuals and placed under the control of the whole community via its agents, such as a central bank. If any private agent can create her own money and impose it as a socially accepted medium she has a tremendous unfair advantage over all market participants who do not have this power. The woman who can do this will have every incentive to create new money, increase her purchasing power, and "settle" all debts. In this case, she has become an absolute monarch,[63] and anyone who accepts her money is in effect giving her a continuous line of credit, paying tributes and taxes to her in terms of the seigniorage she gets, and her payment for services and goods is ever postponed and there will be no proper settlement of debts. Her participation in the social practice of money, if we even dare to still call it that, has become absoluteness—the validity and the circulation of her money are independent of others in society and her creation of it is not subject to their norms and principles. She now has an absolute point from which she can observe all other participants. All this means her participation is unconditioned. This is not social practice, but a playing God, attaining the status of the Unconditioned One. This is a profound ambiguity as many a participant in the social practice of money under the control of his or her *hubris* ("turning toward one's self as the center of one's self and one's world") and *concupiscence* ("the unlimited desire to draw the whole reality into one's self")[64] would like to transcend the vexing constrain of money by becoming the sole center of money creation. This can only lead the self to a state of disintegration. "The attempt of the finite self to be the center of everything gradually has the effect of its ceasing to be center of anything. Both self and world are threatened."[65] And thus the ambiguity results in, or risks, another social demonry.

The tension (participation versus separation) appears also at another level, that of the business cycle. A business cycle is the up and down (peak and trough) cyclical movements of the total value of goods and services produced in an economy. Reactions to this cycle have always been important in understanding the place money "keeps" in a society. In an uncertain world (that is, in or near the trough where it is no longer worthwhile to produce) entrepreneurs take shelter in liquidity and this flight to liquidity put crisis at the center of economic thinking. Jacques Sapir, a French economist has argued that:

> In a world devoid of uncertainty money would not matter. But money gives every agent in an uncertain world the ability to shelter himself in liquidity. Liquidity in turn allows every agent to defect from the long and continuous chain of interdependence generated by the division of labour. This very possibility of defection introduces a new strategic uncertainty which is at the heart of economic decision-making in money-based economic systems. . . .

Crisis is the permanent horizon of a capitalist economy because either liquidity is too much in demand or it is not wanted at all. The specific uncertainty generated by liquidity pushes economic systems towards under-investment and under-employment.[66]

When social practice of money enables capital-investment participation, that is, engages fully in productive activities, we have economic growth and development. When it induces separation from production (when it defects from "long and continuous chain of interdependence generated by the division of labor") or enters into an incestuous intercourse with itself in an excess orgiastic financialization[67] we have the trough of the business cycle. Out of the sphere of participation (this is when the financial circulation of money engages fully in productive activities) comes increase and development; out of the sphere of separation comes decline and withdrawal. And each is essential for the nature of money. One cannot eliminate the other. Since the use of money is always a risk—there is neither certainty for the entrepreneur that the value embedded in a product can be transmuted into money, nor can money always be changed into value. This is the existential risk (capitalists by occupation have to take in this risk in order to prosper) in the practice of money and to eliminate this risk is to empty it and destroy its creative life. What is needed is the courage to face the risk directly and overcome it.[68]

The dialectics of inclusiveness and separation are also operative at the core of what money is in the modern capitalist economy. In chapter 4 we learned that money is a debt-credit relation and an enhancement of the intensity and extensity of social relations. There we also learned that the foundation of money supply is debt. But in this fact also lies a source of weakening of societal relations. It appears that with money, one can say that where money's strength is, there is also its weakness. Let us examine this strength-weakness combination by examining how interest that is paid on debt actually supports the system.

In the market economy, every producer who intends to stay in business has to cover, at the minimum, his or her cost of capital. Let us say that the risk-free, before-tax interest rate on bonds (only a part of the weighted average cost of capital as cost of equity is ignored in this example) is only 4 percent; it means the profit rate has to be higher than this level for private production to go on. This also means at the minimum the economy has to grow at 4 percent to yield this kind of profit irrespective of any concern, such as that for the environment. The monetary system and the whole mechanics of capitalist production system have this built-in power to grow and grow just to make zero return on invested capital.

Any person who has ever been bothered by "excessive" competition and complained about insufficient cooperation in the U.S. society needs to consider the role of money—not just money or the capitalist system, but interest on debt. Let us not forget that the United States operates debt-money, such that every dollar note out there in circulation has a price on its head, so to speak. The money creation process may not have created competition, but it certainly encourages it and with it a loss in an ethics of cooperation. Everyone who has ever borrowed is compelled by her contract to go out and compete against everybody and earn an interest on the principal. This is how British scholar Bernard Lietaer, a professor of finance and currency trader, explains interest-money's power to heighten competition:

> When the bank created money by providing you with your £100,000 mortgage loan, it creates only the principal when it credits your account. However, it expects you to bring back £200,000 over the next twenty years or so. If you don't, you will lose your house. Your bank does not create the interest; it sends you into the world to battle against everyone else to bring back the second £100,000. Because all other banks do exactly the same thing the system requires that some participants go bankrupt in order to provide you with this £100,000. To put it simply, when you pay back interest on your loan, you are using up someone else's principal.[69]

In summary, the current monetary system obliges citizens to incur debt collectively, and to compete with others in the community just to obtain the means to perform exchange transactions between them. This is not all there is to money interest's impact on the fabric of society. The interest payment generates inequality. This inequality occurs irrespective of the particular monetary policy (contractionary or expansionary) as it is due to the general nature of interest-money—this is not to deny that a central bank's policy of raising interest rates will affect the magnitude of this kind of inequality. Payment of interest is one of the systemic and systematic wealth transfer mechanism siphoning resources from the poor and the middle class to the wealthiest segment of society which owns the bulk of the interest-bearing assets.[70]

The basic ambiguity to keep in mind is this: there are negative and positive forces that are internal to the very social practice of money. Money connects and money separates. When the negative forces become demonic it threatens to break down the whole system.

The Ambiguities of Money as Ultimate Concern

We may take up now a more theological ambiguity with respect to money. How does the ultimate meaning of existence shine through money as a social practice; how does money become a vessel of spiritual content? This is to say, how does money as cultural creation express an ultimate concern, or a transcending meaning in its own "spiritual ground"?[71] Money cannot hide its religious ground. The social practice of a money as a cultural system constitutes an economic culture which is (partly) derived from its surrounding religious ethos. In the depth of money as a social practice something holy and unconditional is implied. Something of religious significance is hidden in it. What is it? If following Tillich, we interpret religion as the "state of ultimate concern" ("the state of being grasped by something unconditional, holy and absolute"),[72] then we need to unveil the dimension of money that gives it meaning, seriousness, depth, and all-determining concern, therefore making it holy, even if this meaning/depth is expressed in secular terms. There are three ways to approach this kind of depth dimension of money as a social practice.

First, we note that the power and significance of being, in modern capitalist society, is present in the productive act. Self-affirmation is primarily sought in courage to be part of the productive process, the creative development of humankind. In the modern capitalist world, money *appears* to be the thing or symbol which gives meaning to all strivings. It is thus an ultimate concern, the spiritual center of value.[73] But as soon a person gains this spiritual center he or she loses it—it can no longer answer the question of the meaning of existence.[74] This is because doubts are raised about money's power to hold the ultimate meaning for life and the belief in work (enterprise) through which money is earned disappears. This loss of meaning is not just related to the traditional alienation from work. Rather, in addition, it is related to the whole lost sense of long-term employment or economic security of wage-centered livelihood due to rising unemployment and widening underemployment. These later two phenomena have increased in the last few decades with the waves of corporate downsizing and dwindling corporate commitment to employees.[75] In this situation, the structure of meaning and order are collapsing or have collapsed. Anxiety is mounting!

The great anxiety is about not being able to be and remain part of the creative development of humankind. One fears being denied self-affirmation in the productive process of history. Why is this fear so threatening for persons in the modern advanced capitalist economy? According to Tillich, "[It is in] the productive act itself in which the power and significance of being is present."[76] The threat of being excluded from participation in this act is felt like a threat to being reduced to nothing, to nonbeing. This threat is expressed in terms of money. Money as return for contribution in the productive process or as payment for appropriating someone else's contribution in the productive act is the spider web within which the modern person lives and spins her thread of economic connectivity. To be threatened with lack of money (due to bankruptcy or erosion of economic support) is to be faced with insecurity or meaninglessness.[77]

Under this circumstance, money in the pocket or in the bank is an indication of "courage to be part" of the creative productive process of history, a symbol of the participation in the "productive act itself in which the power and significance of being is present." Money is an indicator of self-affirmation, of anxiety conquered in the courage to be a part of the productive chain; a reflector of the amount of (economic) nonbeing taken into oneself without the loss of centeredness. Thus, one aspect of "depth" and "ultimate concern" related to money is this struggle with the insecurity and *angst* that money's creative development fosters.

Second, money is not like any other object. It is not thrown alongside others in the cultural space. As that which connects all economic transactions and prevents all productive acts from happening all at once, it is the supporting and transcending center of all economic life. In this sense, money is the "power of being" in every economic activity, that is, in everything that participates in the creative economic life process. Everything is rooted in this creative ground. Therefore, we can find the traces of the ultimate in the social practice of money as a centering and connecting power for all economic life.

Money, or so it appears, is an instrument that creates the forms of personal and social life which does not defer to the Unconditional and the Ultimate. The modern sophisticated economic agent, as source and bearer of culture and religion, genuflects only before the altars of theoretical and practical rationality.[78] Money, as an exemplar of the capitalist epoch and in conjunction with its basic attitude[79] of the age, removes or strives to remove from all spheres of thought and action the idea and form of the Unconditional. Money (a veritable index of economic power and "success") is thus an ultimate concern and demands that all concerns be sacrificed to it. As Tillich puts it:

> It [success, social standing, or economic power] is the god of many people in the highly competitive Western culture and it does what every ultimate concern must do: it demands unconditional surrender to its laws even if the price is the sacrifice of genuine human relations, personal conviction, and creative *eros*. Its threat is social and economic defeat, and its promise—indefinite as all such promises—the fulfillment of one's being (italics in the original).[80]

Thus another aspect of "depth" related to money as a social practice is the "power of being" in every economic activity and it demands unconditional surrender to its laws.

The third way of saying money reveals a hidden quality of the ultimate or universal concern is to see money in terms of fifteenth-century German cardinal of the Catholic Church, Nicholas of Cusa's idea of the "coincidence of opposites." Money's ambiguity lies in being simultaneously good and evil, hate and love, in its reconciling of differences between economic agents. In it there is a coincidence of these opposites. Before relating this notion directly to the Ultimate, we need to state that Tillich's ideas of the demonic as being always ensconced in the holy, as involving both "nearness and distance," and his concept of a *courage to be* that takes in contradictions and threats upon oneself, is in the legacy of Nicholas of Cusa. This is made explicitly clear in the 1948 edition of *Protestant Era*.[81] This paradoxicality that Tillich saw in living beings, Georg Simmel in his *Philosophy of Money* explicitly associated with the notion of God.

> In reality, money in its psychological form, as the absolute means and thus as unifying point of innumerable sequences of purposes, possesses a significant relationship to the notion of God—a relationship that only psychology, which has the privilege of being unable to commit blasphemy, may disclose. The essence of the notion of God is that all diversities and contradictions in the world achieve a unity in him, that he is—according to a beautiful formulation of Nicolas de Cusa—the *coincidentia oppositorium*. Out of this idea, that in him all estrangements and irreconcilables of existence find their unity and equalization, there arises the peace, the security, the all-embracing wealth of feeling that reverberate with the notion of God which we hold.[82]

In sum, the ambiguity here is that money, an instrument human beings created to aid trade and exchange, has become for many people an ultimate concern—a false one for that matter. It demands the total surrender of persons who accept this claim and, increasingly, with such acquiescence, the integrity of community life is surrendered to money's totalizing logic and dynamics. Money has claimed ultimacy in the production and reproduction of economic life.

The Ambiguities of Money's Imperial Tendencies

Money, as an ultimate concern in the capitalist world, has not only transcended multiple barriers and boundaries of human sociality by monetizing (most) human relationships, but it has also driven toward the totality of empire in its transcending of geopolitical economic spaces. The ability of money to transgress national boundaries is not available to all official currencies. Only certain national currencies (such as dollar, euro, and yen) which serve as global vehicular currencies in the international trade and payment system can effectively do this. The ambiguity here is that these national currencies which embody only the soil and concreteness of particular sociopolitical entities, claim universality and absoluteness.[83] They claim universality, especially the dollar, yet they serve only particular national (imperial) interests. In paraphrasing Tillich, I may say that the imperialism of the global vehicular currencies (such as the dollar, euro, yen) which follow from this situation is the basis for all other imperialisms. Monetary imperialism is never the expression of will to power as such. It is a struggle for the absolute victory of a special value system, represented by a national currency or hierarchy of currencies.[84]

Every conquest of the monetization process within and between human societies has the "ambiguity of empire building." The imperial tendency is not only coming from the nature of money as a mere social practice, but also from the vocational consciousness of a group's natural self-affirmation that always trudges along with it. The stronger this passion is, the greater is the tendency of a national currency to be a tool of empire building and global domination.[85]

So far under this rubric of imperial tendencies, I have put forward two principles that give the animus to the imperialistic propensities of major national currencies. They are: (1) the imperialistic outward movement of national currencies is related to the nature of social practice of money, and (2) the vocational consciousness of a nation in the official currency's capacity to transcend national boundaries. I intend to clarify the two ideas with descriptive explanations.

This first idea is related to a characteristic of the texture of social practice—that is, increasing intensity and extensity. "[E]verything real drives beyond itself. It is not satisfied with the form in which it finds itself. It urges towards a more embracing, ultimately to *the* all-embracing form"[86] (italics in the original). Every social practice wants to grow. It tends to overcome both internal and external resistance in a way that transcends its boundaries and draws external resources into itself. Put differently, it tends toward universality and totality, toward all-inclusiveness of human activities and historical groups. This very process of not leaving anything or person outside its ambit "is expressed in the term 'empire.'" As stated earlier, every conquest of the monetization process within and between human societies has the "ambiguity of empire building."

This principle of intensity and extensity also contains a contradictory seed—the ambiguity of growth and destructiveness possibilities. The structure of growth moves toward totalitarian control of all human activities and bonds and this move (by the social practice) contradicts the personal freedom which is necessary for human creativity and differentiation.

This brings us to the second idea. In order for the first idea to work successfully, there must be specific human groups and institutions (specific elements within the very practice) with well-defined interests to keep intact the particular practice in its encounter with other practices. Such groups usually have a kind of vocational consciousness as they strive toward this aim.[87] This particular consciousness is often tied up with other overarching vocational consciousnesses, self-interpretation of a historical group.

SUMMARY AND CONCLUSION

The second Tillichian principle of trinitarian thinking (the application of the concept of life to the Ground-of-Being) has formed the overarching framework for our reflection on the monetary system in this chapter. We have explicated the dialectics of unity and separation in the nature of money and exposed national patterns of "demonic" distortions in monetary relations. We examined the sites of distortions and conflicts in the monetary socioeconomic relations. The conflicts and distortions at these sites indicate that the impact of monetary policy threatens the quality of the moral order. In this it becomes "demonic" and destructively so.

In conclusion, it is important to keep before us the following ambiguities and the demonries they generate. The ambiguities are:

(a) *The ambiguity of money as a social construction.* Though money is a vital aspect of human sociality and a promoter of economy-wide social practice, only few powerful agents in society have the power to define and control its production. There is a lurking danger, if it is not already happening, that the agents would use the power for their self and class self-realization to the detriment of the rest of society.

(b) *The ambiguity of the biopower of money.* Monetary policies which harbor tremendous potentials for fostering the common good have become, in many societies, the generator of inequalities which threaten to destroy the poor instead of improving their well-being.

(c) *The ambiguity of central banking practice.* There is a basic conflict between commitment to flourishing life for all and working against the very masses it is supposed to help.

(d) *The ambiguity of participation and separation.* There are positive and negative forces that are internal to the very social practice of money. Money connects and money separates.

(e) *The ambiguity of money as ultimate concern.* Money has claimed ultimacy not only in the production and reproduction of economic life, but it also generates fears. Money, an instrument created by the human beings, has become, it appears, their own god. Life is subjected to its demand, rather than money being subjected to the requirements of a flourishing communal life.

(f) *The ambiguity of money's imperial tendencies.* The ambiguity here is that few national currencies with very particular and imperial interests, claim absoluteness and universality in the name of their nations and not in the name of justice.

These ambiguities have the potential to generate demonries if they are not addressed. These are some of the negative forces, demonries that can thwart healthy sociality. A financial circulation of money that is separated from industrial circulation of money threatens the integrity of social practice of money. This can eventually hurt the overall production and development in the economy. Huge income inequality and increasing concentration of wealth could become very dangerous and severely limit the effective participation of the poor in the economic intercourse. Rural-urban, poor area-rich area, disarticulation that creates dual economies within an economy and huge income gaps could become the demonry that arises from unchecked ambiguities. There is always the potential that the ruling group, class, or elite could completely hijack the money-policy mechanism to serve its particular self-interest and self-realization. At the international level, if the present use of imperial, monarchical national currencies in the global trade and payment system is not checked, the empire-building tendencies of money will increase with globalization and the "totality of empire" it so eagerly warrants.

In the next chapter, I will empirically examine the patterns of "demonic" distortions and twisting of money at the global level and the inadequacies in the use of imperial currencies in the global monetary system. In other words, I will further explore the ambiguity of money's imperial tendencies. All this is to show how the severe imbalance of power between rich and poor countries in the global trade and payment system inhibits the full participation of developing economies in the ongoing globalization process.

NOTES

1. Participation drives a person beyond herself toward unity in essential and existential forms of being at the self level, community sphere (person-to-person encounter, the social context of the ego-thou encounter), and at the dimension of ultimate being in the transcendental unity of unambiguous life under the impact of the Spiritual Presence. As will be argued in chapter 7, participation is the solution to the social demonry of money that is rooted in ambiguity. See Paul Tillich, *Systematic Theology*, vol. 3, *Life and the Spirit, History and the Kingdom of God* (Chicago: University of Chicago Press, 1965), 30–36; 129, 133–38; 331–32, and 432; Tillich, *The Courage to Be* (New Haven, CT: Yale University Press, 1952), 86–112.

2. Paul Tillich, *The Interpretation of History* (New York: Charles Scribner's Sons, 1936), 80.

3. Tillich, *The Interpretation of History*, 91.

4. This is the concrete, material form money takes in daily transactions. "Nothing in human history has reality without a legal form, as nothing in nature has reality without a natural form." Tillich, *Systematic Theology*, vol. 3, 207.

5. For those who are not familiar with the theological language of Paul Tillich, which I am using here, I need to say that money is not evil and you need to read

the immediate section below to properly understand why I refer, symbolically, to money as demonic.

6. Tillich, *Systematic Theology*, vol. 3, 102–6. The reference to the demonic is everywhere in Tillich's work. In the *Systematic Theology*, vol. 1, *Reason and Revelation, Being and God* (Chicago: University of Chicago Press, 1951), it is found in pp. 116, 133, 134, 140, and 216ff. See also Paul Tillich, *Political Expectation* (New York: Harper & Row, 1971), 50, 66–67.

7. Paul Tillich, *Systematic Theology*, vol. 2, *Existence and the Christ* (Chicago: University of Chicago Press, 1957), 20–25, 40, 60.

8. Creatures stand out of absolute non-being (οὐκ ὀή, *ouk on,*) and relative non-being (μή ´ ὀή ´, *me on*). God, Being-Itself stands only in from one of type of nonbeing (the relative, μή ´ὀή). See Tillich, *Systematic Theology*, vol. 1, 188?89; *Systematic Theology*, vol. 2, 20–21.

9. Tillich, *Systematic Theology*, vol. 2, 20.

10. Tillich, *Systematic Theology*, vol. 1, 134.

11. Tillich, *Systematic Theology*, vol. 1, 12–14, 134, 140, 211–18, 224.

12. Tillich, *Systematic Theology*, vol. 3, 252–65.

13. Tillich, *Systematic Theology*, vol. 3, 253.

14. This move is faithful to the ancient meaning of the word. See Wolfgang M. Zucker, "The Demonic: From Aeschylus to Tillich," *Theology Today* 26 (April 1969): 34–50. "It seems that Tillich throughout his work is fully cognizant of the phenomenology of the demonic as it has developed from Aeschylus through the Romantics, through Goethe, Kierkegaard, and Dostoyevski, to Jaspers. None of their insights is contradicted or neglected. Instead they are built into a theological *summa*, a system that, centered in God as the Ground of all Being, must give account of all that is, including the demonic" (p. 48).

15. Tillich, *Systematic Theology*, vol. 1, 217.

16. He is careful to observe that though these two principles are given in God, the divine ground of being, they never actually do come into disruption. For in Being-Itself, they are always in ecstatic unity. For a discussion of this and especially how Tillich's conception differs from that of Carl Gustav Jung, see Randal B. Bush, *Recent Ideas of Divine Conflict: The Influences of Psychological and Sociological Themes of Conflict upon the Trinitarian Theology of Paul Tillich and Jürgen Moltmann* (San Francisco: Mellen Research University Press, 1991), 71–95, 113–16, especially 92–93.

17. Tillich, *Systematic Theology*, vol. 3, 102.

18. This concept of social demonry, especially its simultaneity of separation and unity, anticipates his view of life and trinitarian relations. Life, according to Tillich, is that which unites subjectivity and objectivity because it is does not pertain to dead object, that is, to the object which is merely an object. The second root of the trinitarian thinking in Tillich's framework involves the application of the concept of life to God. Tillich argues that God must be conceived as life, a living being. For without this principle God would be a "dead identity." See his *Systematic Theology*, vol. 1, 241–42, 269.

19. All this is akin to being and non-being as parsed from Paul Tillich's theology. For a discussion of the relation of being to non-being in Tillichian thought, see Lewis S. Ford, "Tillich's Tergiversations Toward the Power of Being," *Scottish Journal of Theology* 28 (1975): 323–40.

20. Eros is "the drive towards the other, towards an ultimate goal, striving of the person or subject for union with that which it is separated from though it belongs to it." Eros "strives for a union with that which is a bearer of values because of the value it embodies." See Paul Tillich, *Love, Power, and Justice* (New York: Oxford University Press, 1960), 25–30.

21. Tillich, *Love, Power, and Justice*, 30–32, 117.

22. Tillich, *Love, Power, and Justice*, 47.

23. Wolfgang M. Zucker, "The Demonic: From Aeschylus to Tillich," *Theology Today* 26 (April 1969): 48–49.

24. Tillich, *Systematic Theology*, vol. 1, 139–44.

25. Tillich, *Systematic Theology*, vol. 1, 216.

26. I mean the Christological aspect, the logos of the world who gives form, meaning, and structure to its activities and processes, and the principle of *form structuring* productive activities.

27. Tillich, *Systematic Theology*, vol. 1, 16–17, 221–30; *Systematic Theology*, vol. 3, 283–94.

28. Wayne E. Baker, "What is Money? A Social Structural Interpretation," in *Intercorporate Relations: The Structural Analysis of Business*, ed. Mark S. Mizruchi and Michael Schwartz (New York: Cambridge University Press, 1987), 112–13.

29. Baker, "What is Money?" 113–14.

30. Zelizer, *The Social Meaning of Money: Pin money, Paychecks, Poor Relief, and Other Currencies* (New York: Basic Books, 1994), 18.

31. Lakshman Yapa, "Reply: Why Discourse Matters, Materially," *Annals of the Association of American Geographers* 87 no. 4 (1997): 718.

32. Baker, "What is Money?" 114. Note that at the tail end of chapter 4 (in the summary and conclusion) I make the same point philosophically by using French philosopher Alain Badiou's concept of *present* and *represent*.

33. Baker, "What is Money?" 118.

34. Yapa, "What Causes Poverty?: A Postmodern View," *Annals of the Association of American Geographers* 86, no. 4 (1996): 722.

35. Collins, *Interaction Ritual Chains* (Princeton, NJ: Princeton University Press, 2004), 167.

36. Michael Hardt and Antonio Negri, *Empire* (Cambridge, MA: Harvard University Press, 2000), 23–30.

37. Monetary policy is the mobilization of an economy's monetary and financial resources for the preservation, promotion, and ordering of its work. Productive and reproductive work—organization and distribution of rewards thereof—maintains the structure of mutuality of life through which a people shape their lives and cope with their day-to-day problems. Work is therefore a communal moral category which depends for its sustenance and progress not only on the moral web of interpersonal relationships, but also on capacities of persons to participate and on the right relations that are to be maintained among them. The control of the money supply in the economy conditions which work prospers and which work weakens; and so determine "who shall benefit and who shall sacrifice." See Gibson Winter, *Community and Spiritual Transformation: Religion and Politics in a Communal Age* (New York: Crossroad Publishing Co., 1989), 104. Modern central bankers have emaciated this definition, making monetary policy to be only

decisions and actions taken to control the quantity and price of money and credit in an economy. They have basically limited themselves to using only three tools: open market operations, setting of discount rate, and bank reserve requirements, and perhaps a very weak fourth tool, moral suasion. "Using these three tools, the Federal Reserve influences the demand for, and supply of, balances that depository institutions hold at Federal Reserve Banks and in this way alters the FFR [federal fund rate]. The FFR is the interest rate at which depository institutions lend balances at the Federal Reserve to other depository institutions overnight. Changes in the FFR trigger a chain of market events that affect other short-term interest rates, foreign-exchange rates, long-term interest rates, the amount of money and credit, and ultimately, a range of economic variables, including employment, output, and prices of goods and services." Henry C. K. Liu, "More on the US Experience," *Asia Times Online*, November 27, 2002 at http://www.atimes .com/atimes/printN.html.

38. Michael Hardt and Antonio Negri, *Multitude: War and Democracy in the Age of Empire* (New York: Penguin Press, 2004), 156.

39. For a discussion of how modern economic activities create subjectivities see Hardt and Negri, *Multitude*, 66.

40. William M. Rodgers III, "The Impact of Monetary Policy on the Distribution and Type of Unemployment," John J. Heldrich Center for Workforce Development and National Poverty Center, Rutgers: State University of New Jersey, July 2004.

41. This is correct only in a broad and general sense of the way the Fed governors present their discourse framed around narrow technical issues of markets, interest and inflation rate movements, and macroeconomic indicators. Ignoring explicit welfare issues may just be the dominant ideology as interviews and transcripts of Federal Open Market Committee meetings show "awareness of social inequalities and also of evaluative judgments in facing the future" (Jocelyn Pixley, *Emotions in Finance: Distrust and Uncertainty in Global Finance* [Cambridge: Cambridge University Press, 2004], 180; see also pp. 84–86; 102–105). There are often governors that are hawkish and others that are less so. All this notwithstanding, our discussion below, using studies done by professional economists, indicate that the Federal Reserve Board does not score high marks when it comes to distributional impact of its policies on the poor.

42. Christina D. Romer and David H. Romer, "Monetary Policy and the Wellbeing of the Poor," Working Paper No. 6793, National Bureau of Economic Research, November 1998.

43. Seth B. Carpenter and William M. Rodgers III, "The Disparate Labor Market Impacts of Monetary Policy," *Journal of Policy Analysis and Management* 23, no. 4 (2004): 813–30.

44. Rodgers, "The Impact of Monetary Policy," 5.

45. Rebecca M. Blank and Alan S. Blinder, "Macroeconomics, Income Distribution, and Poverty," in *Fighting Poverty: What Works and What Doesn't*, ed. Sheldon H. Danziger and Daniel H. Weinberg (Cambridge, MA: Harvard University Press, 1986), 189–91.

46. Blank and Blinder, "Macroeconomics, Income Distribution, and Poverty," 184.

47. Milton Friedman, *Money Mischief: Episodes in Monetary History* (San Diego: Harcourt Brace & Co., 1994), 107.

48. Hugh Rockoff, "The 'Wizard of Oz' as a Monetary Allegory," *Journal of Political Economy* 98, no. 4 (1990): 739, 745–46. See also See Jack Weatherford, *The History of Money: From Standstone to Cyberspace* (New York: Three Rivers Press, 1997), 175–77.

49. Michael Hudson, *Super Imperialism: The Economic Strategy of American Empire* (London: Pluto Press, 2003), 86.

50. New England, Mideast, Great Lakes, Plains, Southeast, Southwest, Rocky Mountains, and Far West.

51. Gerald Carlino and Robert DeFina, "The Differential Regional Effects of Monetary Policy," *Review of Economics and Statistics* 80, no. 4 (1998): 572.

52. Gerald Carlino and Robert DeFina, "The Differential Regional Effects of Monetary Policy: Evidence from the U.S. States," *Journal of Regional Science* 39, no. 2 (1999): 339–58.

53. Gerald A. Carlino and Robert DeFina, "Monetary Policy and the U.S. States and Regions: Some Implications for the European Monetary Union," National Bureau of Economic Research, Working Paper No. 98–17, July 1998.

54. Liu, "Monetary Theology," 1.

55. Pixley, *Emotions in Finance*, 105.

56. Transcripts of the board's Open Market Committee meetings show that governors of the board are aware of social inequalities and they often agonize over the possible impact of their decisions and actions.

57. Progressive economists regard the theorized link between inflation and unemployment to be not as neat as hypothesized or even falling. See Paul Krugman, *The Age of Diminished Expectations: U. S. Economic Policy in the 1990s* (Cambridge, MA: MIT Press, 1994), 36.

58. Christina D. Romer and David H. Romer, Choosing the Federal Reserve Chair: Lessons from History, Working Paper No. 10161, National Bureau of Economic Research, December 2003.

59. Michael Shuman, *Going Local: Creating Self-Reliant Communities in a Global Age* (New York: Free Press, 1998), 16.

60. Henry C. K. Liu, "More on the US Experience," *Asia Times Online*, November 27, 2002 at http://www.atimes.com/atimes/printN.html.

61. The current chairman is Dr. Benjamin Bernanke, a former economics professor at Princeton University.

62. U. S. Board of Governors of the Federal Reserve System, Federal Reserve Bulletin, April 1995 quoted in Romer and Romer, "Choosing the Federal Reserve Chair," 17.

63. By becoming the sole issuer of money she will even increase the negative effect of the dialectics of demonic money.

64. Tillich defines *hubris* as the elevation of self beyond the limits of finite being; it is self-elevation into the sphere of the divine. *Concupiscence*, he defines, as the unlimited desire to draw the whole of reality into one's self. It is the unlimited character of striving for power, pleasure, sex, knowledge, material wealth, and spiritual values. See Tillich, *Systematic Theology*, vol. 2, 50–53.

65. Tillich, *Systematic Theology*, vol. 2, 62.

66. Jacques Sapir, "Seven Theses for a Theory of Realist Economics; Part 1: Theses 1 to 4," *Post-autistic Economic Review* 21 (September 13, 2003), http://www.bt-internet.com/~pae_news/review/issue/21.htm.

67. There is a positive-creative financialization when the financial circulation of money engages, induces, promotes, and sustains productive industrial activities that forge economic growth and development.

68. Tillich, *The Courage to Be.*

69. Bernard Lietaer, *The Future of Money: A New Way to Create Wealth, Work, and Wiser World* (London: Century, 2001), 51–52.

70. Lietaer, *The Future of Money*, 53–54.

71. Tillich, *The Protestant Era* (Chicago: University of Chicago Press, 1948), xvi–xvii, 57.

72. Tillich, *The Protestant Era*, 59.

73. In a moment, I will make this connection clear.

74. Tillich, *The Courage to Be*, 47.

75. Martin Wolf, *Why Globalization Works* (New Haven, CT: Yale University Press, 2004), 178–79, 238–39, 242–44.

76. Tillich, *The Courage to Be*, 108.

77. One understands that there are many religious types who will say that this fear and anxiety is only featured by those who falsely have made money their ultimate concern. The idea I am putting forward here is that in the modern capitalist economy, money is understandably an ultimate concern, the loss of which generates anxiety.

78. Tillich, *The Protestant Era*, 57.

79. This attitude basically involves two things: a "purely objectifying relationship to the world, to spirit, and to history" and making the highest possible increase of economic welfare as the all-determining and foremost aim of society. See Paul Tillich, *The Protestant Era*, 49, 50.

80. Paul Tillich, *Dynamics of Faith* (New York: Harper & Row, 1957), 3.

81. Tillich, *The Protestant Era*, 303.

82. Simmel, *The Philosophy of Money*, 236.

83. Absoluteness of imperial vehicular money means that validity and circulation are independent of valuing subjects in the foreign economic spaces and are not subject to the norms, principles, truth, and justice of the receiving societies.

84. Tillich, *Systematic Theology*, vol. 1, 214.

85. Tillich, *Systematic Theology*, vol. 3, 339–40.

86. Tillich, *Love, Power, and Justice*, 54.

87. Tillich, *Systematic Theology*, vol. 3, 310–11.

6

+

Money and Empire

INTRODUCTION

In the last chapter I revealed the national pattern of "demonic" distortions in monetary relations, primarily referring to the U.S. economy and society. The national distortions, contortions, and conflicts have their own international counterparts. In this chapter, I want to empirically examine the patterns of "demonic" distortion and twisting of money at the global level, showing how the imbalance of power between rich and poor countries in the global monetary system limits the full participation of developing economies (especially those in Africa) in the ongoing globalization process.

More importantly, I make the argument that globalization is an unfinished business with unfulfilled possibilities. It is unfinished not because it has not yet penetrated into every nook and cranny of the world, but because the currency system that undergirds the global trade and payment system is not globalized. While the production and distribution system of the global economy is tending toward the removal of "centers," the monetary system with powerful national (economic union) currencies is not exactly doing so. The currency system is still nationalized and centered around a few key national currencies. In other words, there is ambiguity of money here—namely, few national currencies that serve as international forms of payment are a source of economic domination and they claim universality in the name of a particular quality of their countries. They have become demonic not only because they, which are particular, are elevated to status of universality; but also because their claims are not

made in the "name of that principle which implies ultimacy and universality—that principle of justice."[1]

With the rising tide of globalization and economic integration, with its
ambiguities and demonries, there is an increasing debate in economic circles about the need for single global currency to replace all national currencies. The dominant thinking is that common currency will increase
trade, integrate economies further, eliminate monetary and exchange
rates as sources of asymmetric shocks and by all this promote stable economic activity and possibly higher growth.[2] Paul Volcker, the former
chairman of the Federal Reserve Bank of the United States, has argued
that *a global economy needs a global currency*. Robert Mundell, the 1999 Noble Prize–winner in economics and whose theory of optimum currency
areas is at the bedrock of the monetary union behind the euro, has similarly called for a world currency as recently as September 2006.[3] African
economists have long called for an international currency that does not
give seigniorage, privileges, and other imperial benefits to the developed
West. John Maynard Keynes with his *Bancor Plan* made a similar call at the
1944 Bretton Woods Conferences that established the World Bank and the
International Monetary Fund.[4]

Empire and money is an intriguing and interesting object of study that
has been neglected in Christian theology.[5] If properly pursued, it could offer brilliant insights into biblical interpretation and directions for Christian response to the changing world, especially with respect to economic
development and globalization.[6] In addition to the benefits for crafting a
proper response to globalization, investigation of empire and money is
necessary for a proper understanding of globalization and for developing
an up-to-date theology of money. For it is the tendency of money to transgress national boundaries and take into its originating countries the national economic spaces of other countries and by this act underpin the
economic globalization process. In spite of these potential contributions to
scholarship, the study of empire and money has been largely neglected in
Christian theology. This chapter aims to correct this imbalance and offers
insights into paradigmatic themes for formulating a theology of money in
the era of empire.

Let me state how I intend to execute my argument in this chapter. I will
focus on an intensive analysis of empire and money in sections 1 and 2 by
engaging in a critical conversation with Michael Hardt and Antonio Negri's *Empire*.[7] Among other endeavors, the sections seek to reveal the relationship between empire, the hierarchical currency system, and social organization of the global financial architecture. In section 3, the chapter
comes to a close with concluding remarks. If one is to formulate a theology of money that incorporates in it issues about empire, one must first
establish that empire exists today. There are many theologians and ethi-

cists, both on the left and on the right, who doubt the existence of empire today. So the question is: does empire exist today?

SECTION 1: DOES EMPIRE EXIST TODAY?

I will start my response with Hardt and Negri's discussion of empire by carefully stating their position in the section titled "No-Center Thesis of Hardt and Negri's *Empire*." In the next subsection, I undertake an "exegesis" of their "no-center" thesis. My conversation with them ends in section 2 where I provide a monetary critique of their "no-center" thesis. The upshot of my argument in this section is that money gives centeredness to empire and their claim that we are now in a world without empire is simply wrong.

My main purpose in this chapter is to present an examination of their book *Empire* through the lens of monetary history and evidence, and to infuse into the discourse of empire and globalization a subaltern perspective. The current post-Bretton Woods global trade and payment system has key, hegemonic currency (currencies) just like the systems of the past, and it is powerful enough to thwart the economic well-being of developing countries.

The manifestations of empire may have changed over the centuries. No doubt there is a long distance between the time when Britain ruled the waves and now when corporate giants dominate the earth, but the "substance" (a summary characterization, the *principle* that gives an identity to the manifestations of a historical process) of empire is still with us. Britain, France, and Portugal were "imperialists" with closed borders and the giant corporations of today are imperial with space that is always open,[8] but there is a commonality to the two sets and we can label that commonality, "substance." Tillich has argued that the category of substance can be specially applied to historical situations.[9] "If a history-creating situation is called a substance, this means that there is a point of identity in its manifestations. . . . Without applying the category of substance to history, either implicitly or explicitly, no historiography would be possible."[10] My contention is that there is a point of identity, a "substance," in all the manifestations of empire. All manifestations somehow have, as their substance, the element of imperial, vehicular and reserve currency in the global trade and payment system.

No-Center Thesis of Hardt and Negri's *Empire*

Hardt and Negri argue in their book *Empire* that the international arena is now characterized by smooth space that is always open; there is no longer a "distinction between inside and outside"; no longer a territorial center of power, it is a "non-place." This "new" international is what is called *Empire* by the authors. *Empire* is "decentered and deterritorialized" and it significantly differs from previous imperialism which was "an extension of the sovereignty of the European nation-states beyond their own boundaries."[11] The upshot of this argument is that this new global logic and structure of rule have led to the demise of boundaries—those between home and factory, between nations, and between inside and outside. Economic activities and attendant power have been decentered and dispersed across national boundaries.

What do Hardt and Negri really mean when they say *Empire* has "no center?" There are eight[12] senses in which they use this scintillating phrase, and they center around the following eight claims:

1. There is no or dramatically attenuated nation-state control over global economic actors as the effectiveness of national juridical structures are weakened.[13]
2. There is no geographic center in terms of metropole and periphery, only a smooth, continuous, uniform space, no distinction between inside and outside.[14]
3. The entire global realm is an open, expanding frontier.[15]
4. A nimbleness of deterritorialized and dispersed informatized production and circulation is accentuated by a market system that is all pervading.[16]
5. Technologies of communication are immanent in the sense of a far-reaching network—no one is outside of its embrace and pervasion.[17]
6. There is now a democratic nature of global activities. Work and production are more cooperatively organized than before.[18]
7. A mobile, hybrid, cooperative labor force is increasingly seen as not a national workforce but as transnational.[19]
8. There exists no deference to authority or constituted power, no transcendental reference. There is a meeting of the absolute democratic power and horizon of immanence.[20]

All these eight claims are intertwined and one can explicate the whole set by starting from any one and going to the others. Or, by even focusing closely on one of them one can get a grasp of the overall thesis—at least that is the way the authors present their work. Yet one finds much ambivalence about the empire in the book *Empire*. There is always an alternation between being a boundless deterritorialized flow and realized located actuality and hierarchies.[21] For instance, Hardt and Negri say empire has no limit and it lacks boundaries on page xix, but on page 58 they say that there is "a virtual center of Empire." If it has no boundaries, how can it have a center? There is something "unrepresentable" about the *multitude* and yet it is conducive to "institutionality" and could become an "order."[22] The postmodern empire and the illimitable *multitude* are presented as not in opposition yet the *multitude's* liberatory actions endow empire with its content as empire reacts to them, and the *multitude* depends on empire.[23] The authors claim that sovereignty and state are undermined and superceded by transnational capital and yet they say corporations need state power to flourish.[24] Empire has come and empire is yet to come, "the coming Empire."[25] They say empire "rules over the entire "civilized" world[26] and once a territory has been organically incorporated into the domain of capitalist production, it can no longer be outside it. But in the now familiar pattern of ambivalence they posited—and rightly so—that sub-Saharan Africa is effectively excluded from capital flows and new technologies.[27] They also averred that the smooth unified global space of empire is also segmented, having a pyramid of global constitution, a real hierarchy with tiers and levels.[28]

These ambivalences, divergent dimensions, and duality that run through the book are very important to keep in focus as we proceed to critique and supplement Hardt and Negri's concept of empire. This ambivalence in the empire discourse, as we shall learn later with global vehicular currencies, may not always interrogate structures of dominance, but often resemble it.[29] These tensions also tell us that reality is full of contradictions and to understand and explain it one must think dialectically.[30] Our task in this chapter is to provide a more realistic picture of global capitalism.

How can one understand what Hardt and Negri are saying in social and sociological terms? Here I will offer an interpretation, which will help to set the stage for my analysis and critique of the authors' main thesis about the "non-center" at work in the current globalizing international arena. Hardt and Negri seek to show that in this new international arena or phase there is no deference to authority in economic intercourse.[31] Capital and market are a self-correcting process which put yesterday's certitudes and any claim of control over them in jeopardy—if not all at once, certainly over time. Hardt and Negri are not only insisting that *Empire* is free-floating, but it is also completely discontinuous with the traditions and practices that preceded it. While Hardt and Negri draw from the traditions and narrative of United States republicanism and the familiar version of this country's exceptionalism, their analyses portray the present as being "a present of rupture"[32] and emphasizes how dramatically different is the relationship between sovereignty and state under *Empire* as opposed to imperialism.[33]

Let me now indicate some of the practices and traditions that they say
have changed with the emergence of *Empire*. Below are their actual words
from the book:[34]

> Along with the global market and global circuits of production has emerged
> a global order, a new logic and structure of rule—in short, a new form of sov-
> ereignty.

> Our basic hypothesis is that sovereignty has taken a new form, composed of
> a series of national and supranational organisms united under a single logic
> of rule. The new global form of sovereignty is what we call Empire.

> Imperialism is over.

> The imperial expansion has nothing to do with imperialism.

> Empire is not a weak echo of modern imperialisms but a fundamentally new
> form of rule.

> Biological differences have been replaced by sociological and cultural signi-
> fiers as the key representative of racial hatred and fear.

One of my goals for writing this chapter is to show that though *Empire*
may not have a foundation, it has a center and this center is the imperial
currency of the United States, the dollar. Insofar as a non-denationalized
imperial currency is still the instrument of default and there is a deference
to it without simultaneously insisting on the defeasibility of all national
currencies in the governance of international economic transactions and
practice, there is no revolutionary discontinuity with previous notions
and forms of imperialism or empire. It is true that transnational capital
and nimble corporations are no longer disposed to bow and scrape before
nation-states and governmental puppeteers as in the past; nonetheless, it
is truer to say they cannot flourish without an imperial currency. The un-
hinged and fluid nature of modern economic transactions can be shown
to have a center without being contained in an authoritative model of
nation-state control.

No economic community can sustain transactions without imposing on
itself a system of keeping track of the flows, entitlements, and transfers
pertaining to the distribution of work and its reward because without this
kind of system there would be no communication—and therefore no exchange of values among members of the community. Each epoch and community has different ways of going about this intertransactional business.
They employ different means, but they must find some ways of doing so.
The activity of value giving and taking is hardly the whole of imperial af-

filiations as a socioeconomic phenomenon, but it is central to it. The empire, indeed, has a center in its payment system and the deference to such.

The job-of-work of this chapter is to highlight this monetary side to empire which Hardt and Negri left out and to show that a fuller knowledge of the role of money in empire will improve our understanding of the logic and dynamics of empire. I would like to start with some philosophical, geographical, and technical (engineering) critiques—all aimed at showing, contrary to Hardt and Negri, that *Empire* has a center.

Philosophical and Technical Exegesis of *Empire*'s "No-Center" Thesis

One of Hardt and Negri's theses or arguments is that empire stands outside of previous traditions of imperialism. They argue that the world of empire is radically different from those before it, that is, it differs from the modernist narrative and tradition of sovereignty and nation-state.[35] At times one gets the sense that being out of tradition means there is no definitive authority to which the current globalization actors owe loyalty and deference. This is in the sense that there is no power or authoritative texts or narratives that supervenes the logic and actions of the globalization process. But this is not the only way to talk about tradition. One can view tradition as a discursive social practice or ongoing narrative.[36] The Western discursive practice on nation-states and sovereignty is more variegated than the uniform and monolithic picture that the authors hang up as a straw man to be shot down. The fact that empire is not governed by tradition in the old sense of being embodied in hierarchical institutions or defined by deference toward authority that defines the good for a people or nation does not mean that empire has stepped outside of tradition or even outside of Western hegemonic tradition over the rest of the world. Hardt and Negri's discourse of empire and the whole of discursive practice on state and sovereignty in which theirs is situated is part of the tradition of Western discursive practice which is only interested in Africa as a marginal existence, as "helpless, agency-less victim," and as the Other whose lived experience does not count for much in formulating universal theories in the ilk of empire and *multitude*.[37]

It is clear to me that sovereign power or imperialist tradition, far from being superannuated, continues to operate in the West's control over Africa's resources (and over other regional economies, especially in Latin America and South Asia) and this is intimately linked to control and domination of the international network of juridical institutions, military organs, governmental police power, industrial technologies, market forms, and payment standards.[38] Theory that ignores the ways in which Western totalizing power and globalized sovereignty subsume African social life and biopolitical forces is a theory that reflects an occidentalist bias.

Besides, if Hardt and Negri had adequately accounted for cultural sources of possibility, existence, and progress of the transnational capital and nimble corporations, they would have found a certain kind of tradition that is at the core of empire and of their own point of view. To paraphrase the ethicist Jeffery Stout, in a narrative that explains how previous traditions have broken down, and then pronounces it disastrous (at least for Western nation-states), "leaves one wondering from what tradition or point of view the verdict could have been reached and how that point of view is to escape the implied condemnation."[39] If Hardt and Negri "did not already occupy an identifiable and defensible normative point of view, the tragic tone of [their] historical narrative and the various evaluations expressed in it is groundless."[40] The tradition from which they were speaking is authentically Western and belongs to the 500-year tradition of Western hegemonic rule of the world.

There is really no conceptual fragmentation in the modernist (Western) tradition and in the eye of the oppressed world; there is no substantive opposition between empire and previous imperialism.[41] As long as the social practices of empire do not liberate people living in Africa, and in other regions of the poorer Global South, and, as long as intellectual discourses such as are in *Empire* overlook the mutual imbrication of Western power and globalization and the mutually constitutive relation of Western economic domination and Third (Majority) World's poverty, Hardt and Negri's *Empire* is a perpetuation of the tradition of Western domination and power over the rest of the world. I will also posit that the use of imperial currencies in global transactions instead of a denationalized currency is very much in the (Western) tradition of the previous imperialism and control and domination of the international arena.

Let us also comment on *Empire*'s thesis of transnational corporations (TNCs) surpassing the jurisdiction and authority of states—for example, "large transnational corporations have effectively surpassed the jurisdiction and authority of nation-states."[42] The anchor of Hardt and Negri's grand theory is that this phenomenon represents a paradigmatic shift that is creating a smooth global space of empire. But for the hapless people in Africa (upon whose situation I will limit my comments), the practice of TNCs functioning as states, ruling as states, and defeating sovereignty is not a new tradition. It is a solid old Western tradition in Africa. Many modern African states started as Western transnational corporations and Westerners' owned firms have continued to maintain inordinate control over sections of territory or resources of Africa.[43]

Just as Africa as a place of lived experience does not feature much in Hardt and Negri's thinking, any specific sense of place is also absent in their grand theory of empire. The book's argument of non-place does not consider the placeness of global cities like New York, London, and Tokyo in instantiating the rhizomatic and fluid embrace of empire over forms of economic and political activities, and in mediating various forms of interactions especially between the *multitude* and capital. Saskia Sassen noting this deficiency in *Empire* wrote:

> The way in which place is constructed in the global city—its strategic character for both the Empire and the multitude, its location on the new cross-border geographies of centrality and marginality—makes it a mediated space. That is to say, it is a space where complex national legal architectures (i.e., the formal institution of citizenship) and global dynamics (global capital, migrations, minoritization) get instantiated. But placeness does not seem to figure in Hardt's and Negri's analysis of political subjectivities: "Having achieved the global level, capitalist development is faced directly with the multitude, without mediation."[44]

Regarding the global cities, it is germane here to mention the nodal role they play in assembling finance capital, concentrating control over vast resources, and sucking up labor, migrants even from rural Africa.[45] They are strategic sites not only for the global economy, but they also stand as imperial concrete *placeness*. We may not be able to properly understand the global economy and deliver ourselves from the false thesis of *Empire* unless we analyze "why key structures of the world economy are *necessarily* situated in cities" (emphasis in the original).[46] Global cities like New York, London, Tokyo, Frankfurt, and Paris are important, according to Sassen, in four ways: "first, as highly concentrated command points in the organization of the world economy; second, as key locations for finance and for specialized service firms, which have replaced manufacturing as the leading economic sectors; third, as sites of production, including the production of innovations, in those leading industries; and fourth, as markets for the products and innovations produced."[47]

Now that we have dispatched philosophical and geographical arguments against the thesis that there is no center, let us pick up what might be called the engineering argument. One of the reasons why Hardt and Negri consider empire as not having a center is because of their metaphor of network. They described today's transnational production and circulation as a network:

> Empire manages hybrid identities, flexible hierarchies, and plural exchanges through modulating networks of command.[48]

> The development of communication networks has organic relationship to the emergence of the new producer. Communication not only expresses but also organizes the movement of globalization. It organizes the movement of multiplying and structuring interconnections through networks.[49]

Today productivity, wealth, and the creation of social surpluses take the form of cooperative interactivity through linguistic, communicational, and affective networks.[50]

What kind of network is *Empire*? They do not tell us and herein lies a problem about their thesis of "no place." There are basically two types of network in the communication engineering and computer world.[51] There is the centralized control network where every machine (*client*) is hooked to a point (central computer, *server*) and this is what is called *master-slave network* or *two-tier architecture*. This is like your local area network (LAN) in the local office where every connection goes through the central point, but it is so fast you do not notice that there is intermediation between your computer and that of your colleague on the same network. The center in this network is not necessarily geographical but only and always logical and the *clients* rely on it for devices and sometimes for processing power. The other network-type is the *peer-to-peer* distributed network in which there is no *master-slave* relationship, like the type telephone companies like Verizon use to distribute and manage calls. It is a full duplex network with no central control; control is in the hands of each peer (node), each node (workstation) has equivalent responsibilities and capabilities, and intelligence in the system is pushed to each peer and end-user. This type of network is highly intelligent, scalable, survivable, and reconfigurable. From these simple descriptions of the types of network one can see what kind of network Hardt (a former engineer and now an associate professor in literature at Duke University) and Negri had in mind when they used the metaphor of network for the empire as a whole. They had *peer-to-peer* network in mind. Their description of empire on page 166 led me to this view: "Empire can only be conceived as a universal republic, a network of powers and counterpowers structured in a boundless and inclusive architecture." In another place, they liken this boundless and inclusive nature of the network to the Internet, naming it as a democratic model. "This democratic model is what is . . . call[ed] a rhizome [the adjectival form of this word is often used to describe *Empire* throughout the book], a nonhierarchical and noncentered network structure."[52]

The question is what fits the evidence of global production and exchange better, client/server or peer-to-peer? I believe that client/server, *two-tier architecture* is the better metaphor; no doubt empire is a network, but it is not a *peer-peer network*. Some dominant nations provide the monetary devices and the processing prowess for economic actors to talk to one another.[53] The imperial, national currencies, the currencies that are used for international transactions, are like the central computer all communications must go through and there is a "fee" paid for this and it is called seigniorage (we will treat this below). While production and distribution may have become globalized smooth non-place, unfortunately, the control of issuance of world means of payment has not become denationalized and deterritorialized. There is certainly no peer-to-peer equality among the currencies of the West and that of African countries like Nigeria, Ghana, and Zimbabwe. Or those of Central America and South East Asian countries.

Empire is not a peer-to-peer network like the Internet.[54] While the electric and electronic impulses that pulsate through the Internet system have no oligarchic rulers over them, not so for the money that courses through the economic world. The authors of *Empire* display not a small misunderstanding of economics. Economics is the study of how human beings produce, distribute, and exchange values via money. Put differently, the subject matter of economics is the study of the creation, distribution (servicing), and liquidation of offer and debt contracts enabled by money. Money is invaluable (but not the sole factor) in understanding any economy and we cannot operationalize any economic interaction (exchange) without money.[55] Economic events live through money.

International currencies like the dollar, yen, and euro allow their issuers to project their geopolitical and economic spaces (including values and interests) into the international geopolitical and economic space such that they include within themselves the spaces of countries which do not have imperial currencies. In an imperial currency regime, a nation is not just a geographical territory, but the sphere of influence of its currency. World currencies like the dollar, yen, and euro "are only [sic] indicators of sovereign geopolitical and economic spaces. They have no other backing than the sovereignties [and wealth] of their respective nations as the whole Western world learned to its cost when the U.S.A abrogated, on August 21st [sic], 1971, the [gold] convertibility of the U.S. dollar."[56] So while the United States may not be increasing its territorial reach as in the old imperialist style, the dollar is doing the totalizing effect and increasing America's "monetary space."[57] From this international-currency perspective, there are well-defined spaces in the global exchange Venn diagram[58] and it is not a centerless non-place. Hardt and Negri fail to realize that imperial currencies like the dollar and euro are the extensions of the sovereignty of nation-states. The distinct national colors of these currencies still mark the imperialist map of the world and have not merged or blended into the "imperial" global rainbow of denationalized world currency. It is not yet *Uhuru*! (It is not yet freedom!).

Apart from matters of seigniorage and national extraversion (extension of territorial reach of national currency), the globalization phenomenon even in one of its best and most lauded manifestations still has a center—it touches ground at some particular quadrant on this *terra firma*. Take the trading in U.S. treasury bonds, which is a good example of a globalization network. This apparently sophisticated, global marketplace characterized by the most technological nimbleness and fluidity has a "specific geography." Permit me to provide a detailed description of this market to show that the ephemeral specter of globalization cannot do without situating and centering its manifest being in spatial actuality. Nigel Thrift and Andrew Leyshon reveal this much in this long quotation:

> At first sight, this [treasury bond market] seems to be a global marketplace. After all, trading takes place 22 hours a day. The trading day begins at 8:30 a.m. local time in Tokyo (7:30 p.m. New York daylight saving time), closing at 4 p.m. (3 a.m. New York), pressing onto London, where it is 8 a.m. At about 12:30 p.m. local time trading passes to New York, where it is 7:30 a.m. Trading continues in New York until 5:30 p.m. But the geography of trading is not that simple. Not surprisingly, given these are U.S. government securities, most of the trading takes place in New York. In 1994, for example, on the average, 94 per cent of all trading volume of U.S. securities occurred in New York, with less than 4 per cent in London and less than 2 per cent in Tokyo. Further, nearly all trading—even overseas—is a response to U.S. events. For instance, market-relevant comments are often made by U.S. government officials during "overseas hours," as is central bank intervention in the market, to coincide with relatively quiet periods. In other words, what seems like a typical global monetary network actually turns out to have a very specific geography which is really quite narrow.[59]

Once again, we have been able to show that empire is not a "non-place."[60] It, indeed, has a center. We have illustrated it by pointing to monetary phenomenon and revealing the subtle relationship between empire and money, a connection Hardt and Negri ignore.

I not only consider the presence and use of imperial, reserve currency in international transactions and concentrated centeredness of monetary trading network as giving the lie to the thesis of "non-place," I also regard the very arrowheads of globalization, the transnational corporations, around which all this fanciful theory about empire swirls as representatives of certain contextualized localities. Globalization is, in a sense, competition among nation-states—the extension of national frontiers by economic means rather than by force. The veritable battle axe in this struggle is the firm, the modern corporation. Competition among nation-states is essentially competition between corporations who represent their countries. Sony is for Japan and Microsoft is for the United States. Push this analysis further and you will realize that competition is mindset versus mindset.[61] Mindset versus mindset is worldview versus worldview. At the bedrock of worldview or ethos is religion.[62] So one way of looking at the empire-center nexus at the level it specifically affects modern economy is to see how worldview or ethics emanating from the corporatized arrow-heads and globalization's pressure on local actors impact the concept and operation of the firm and business ethics in the world. I need not argue that the ethics of the global marketplace is not a democratic mixture of all worldviews. It is also true that the pressure that is put on local ethics in places like South Korea is not coming from Nigeria or Peru. So if the pervading global, imperial business ethics has a point of departure and reference, and do defer to its occidental source of existence, we can argue empire has a center.[63]

SECTION 2: THE IMPERIAL-
MONARCHICAL CURRENCY SYSTEM

In this section of the chapter, I will undertake what for lack of a better word I will call pure monetary critique of *Empire*. It is "pure" because it would solely and precisely focus on money and its global operations to show that (old-fashioned) empire exists and it is not a non-centered, non-place. There are financial centers of gravity in the current global economy. In the previous subsections of this essay, we showed the placeness of empire by taking on technical, geographical, and philosophical issues and revealing their underbelly as monetary stuff with spatial concreteness to it. Here, we will directly investigate plain monetary systems to show that Hardt and Negri did not tell us the whole truth when they posited that empire has no center.

Let us start by offering a simple description of money and proceed to examine the current global trade and payment system. To understand money is to understand empire properly. Money and empire fit hand-in-glove within the time and space compression that increasingly characterizes all socioeconomic life. Money is not just a device that connects decisions across time (spot and forward transactions; past, present, and future dimensions of economic activities). Money also links economic actors across space (here and there). It is this spatio-temporal nature of money which enables any economic agent (e.g. transnational corporations) to transcend spatial and temporal boundaries. This is not the only connection between money and empire. Like empire, money is rooted in social practice, as we have already argued at length. Money is a pure sociopsychological phenomenon deriving its value only from social recognition. Today, the value of money does not depend on any item or commodity backing it.

If it is now clear that the very nature of money is integral to understanding the phenomenon Hardt and Negri have dubbed *empire*, we can now emphasize that the very global payment system by which money is transferred from one economic agent to another is relevant to an adequate understanding of empire and its placeness. Empire is a world accumulation phase of capitalism with sophisticated transnational production and labor systems, but its means of exchange are national currencies rather than any supranational money form. Three key national currencies (U.S. dollar, Europe's euro, and Japan's yen), with dangerous potential for formation of hegemonic spheres of influence, constitute the principal means of exchange in empire. The use of key national currencies as the center of the global payment system violates the global sovereignty of empire in which Hardt and Negri would like us to believe. The currencies are also not in sync with the kind of non-placeness, democratic, deterritorializing, and dispersed tendencies that the authors insist that we must all accept as characteristics of empire.

The use of key national currencies instead of one denationalized currency in the present global trade and payment system violates the principle of credit money. The use of dollar (supported by euro and yen) as the world currency, international unit of value, and means of transfer of value violates the principle that money creation must be placed outside the markets for goods and service—that no participant should have the privilege of seigniorage, make purchases by issuing its money.[64]

Let me give an example to illustrate the point.[65] Two nations are in trade: one (call it Africanus) sells crude oil, and the other (call it Latinus) sells computers. In the absence of a common central bank that creates money for both parties, they will use the barter system, and in this system there is real value for real value exchange. Suppose that nation Latinus can now create its money and impose it as the international medium of exchange, the means of transfer of value, or it simply has now the sole right to issue international money. Country Africanus, if it is still engaged in trade with Latinus, receives mere paper for real goods and services that it sells to Latinus. Africanus's reserve assets depend on the worth of Latinus government's IOUs. Latinus has tremendously increased its purchasing power and can settle all its debts with Africanus without transfer of real value. Eventually, when Africanus buys goods and services from Latinus, the latter simply cancels or erases its own liabilities to Africanus in its accounting books. Now let us ask ourselves which of the two parties has the capability to initiate trade at will? Africanus can expand trade with Latinus only on the vagaries of demand for its goods in Latinus; whereas Latinus with the monopoly privilege to pay with its own currency can buy or increase trade at will and in fact determine the trend of international trade between them. For the fact that Latinus is not under any pressure to fork out real values for its consumption, it can afford the time and luxury for research and development, cultural endeavor, or refinement of military technology.

This is not the whole story. Since Africanus's receipt of national currency of Latinus is not used in its country, its whole reserve has to be managed within the financial system of Latinus. If Africanus needed to borrow money at the international market, it cannot borrow in its own currency. So all borrowing abroad creates a potential lethal *currency mismatch*. The money supply in Africanus is partly determined by Latinus as Africanus exporters convert their earnings in Latinus into local currency. Effectively, the geopolitical and economic spaces of Latinus contain that of Africanus in a way that of Africanus does not. Now we can expand this scenario to include many countries but the basic advantages accruing to Latinus will not change much if it is still the issuer of world money. We might throw in one or two world-currency nations for more complex effects, but there will still be (oligopolistic) advantages for the issuers of vehicular currencies.[66]

Because of this kind of advantage enjoyed by issuers of currency at the domestic level, money creation and proper settlement of debt in the money creation process was placed outside the marketplace and subjected to governmental (neutral body) regulations in all modern economies. As we have seen, this principle is violated in international transactions when certain countries issue the world currencies.

The issuers of world currencies like the United States, Europe, and Japan are not about to have a Pauline "Road-to-Damascus" experience in spite of their democratic pretensions because there are huge advantages to their statuses. First, foreigners who receive dollars, euros, yen for their exports are giving the United States, Europe, and Japan unlimited lines of credit. This is how the economist, Robert Guttman describes it:

> Just as individual buyers or private banks within domestic circulation cannot properly settle their debts by simply issuing their own money, so can no country effectively pay for its excess purchases abroad by issuing and then transferring its own currency to foreign sellers. This is why the country whose currency serves as an internationally accepted medium of exchange has the unique advantage of being able to finance its own imports and capital exports by what amounts to continuous credit supplied by foreigners.[67]

This form of interest-free loans and savings in the United States government's interest payments on its huge debts, due to the foreign governments' holding of reserves in short maturity securities, generates for the United States an income of $11–$15 billion a year.[68] Foreigners just invest the billions of dollars they earned from exporting to America in dollar-denominated securities in the United States. The rest of the world, including the poor countries of Africa and the Caribbean, which keep their reserves in the United States is, indeed, subsidizing the lifestyle of the affluent American people. This is a privilege that the American government guards seriously like a nest egg. For instance, in the 1970s, it struck an agreement with the Saudi Arabian government to conduct OPEC's global oil trade in dollars,[69] thereby forcing almost every country to keep dollars as reserve.[70] International financial imperialism showed a new face and now even occurs among governments themselves. Michael Hudson, distinguished professor of economics at the University of Missouri at Kansas City, succinctly puts it this way:

> Almost without anyone noticing it, . . . central banks have been left with only one asset to hold: U.S. Government bonds. Central banks do not buy stocks, real estate or other tangible assets. When Saudi Arabia and Iran proposed to use their oil dollars to begin buying out American companies after 1972, U.S. officials let it be known that this would be viewed as an act of war. OPEC was told that it could raise oil prices all it wanted, as long as it used the proceeds to buy U.S. Government bonds. That way, Americans could pay for oil in their own currency, not in gold or other "money of the world." Oil exports to the United States, as well as German and Japanese autos and sales of other countries, were bought with paper dollars that could be created *ad infinitim* (italics in the original).[71]

One does not know if OPEC countries are still *truly*[72] respectful of such an agreement forged in the midst of the 1970s crisis, but one thing is clear: members of the cartel have continued to price their commodity in dollars and have consistently recycled their surplus petro-dollars back into the dollar-denominated assets:

> In some respects, the recycling of oil revenues has changed little over the years. According to the BIS [Bank for International Settlements], the share of OPEC deposits denominated in dollars was unchanged at 72 percent and the share held by U.S banks has remained steady over the last 15 years. However, non-OPEC oil exporters have increased their deposits in U.K. banks and the dollar share of these deposits has dropped to 61 percent from 80 percent at year-end 2002.[73]

These are not the only advantages the United States (read all issuers of key currencies) enjoys because of the use of the dollar as the world money. The United States can and indeed does finance its balance of payments by issuing the dollar, its own currency. The United States is free from any external constraint in a way countries like Haiti, Mexico, Argentina, Indonesia, South Korea, and Nigeria are not. The capacity of these other nations to run external deficits is limited by their own foreign exchange reserves. As an issuer of a reserve currency, the United States also enjoys what economists call "external seigniorage."[74] As a banker to the world, U.S. "liabilities are the foreign exchange reserves of other countries which are usually held in short term deposits paying money-market rates. On the asset side we find mostly long-term loans and other capital exports. These typically carry higher rates because of their longer maturity. The profits earned from this yield spread are often referred to as "external seigniorage."[75]

There is still another interest-related benefit (seigniorage) in addition to the two already mentioned. I have noted the savings in government interest payments on its huge debt because of foreign governments' holdings of reserves in short maturity securities. I also referred to external seigniorage which has to do with the spread between liabilities and assets of a reserve currency issuer. The third advantage relates to the benefit of the circulation of raw greenbacks overseas—the benefit from the dollar's penetration into the sovereign monetary (and geographical) spaces of other states. The benefit here is not about the interest-spread or hypothesized reduction of levels of interest rates owing to massive inflows of capital into the United States. This represents interest-free loans on the amount of currency circulating overseas.[76] What do foreigners gain in holding dollars overseas? According to a 2003 report to the Congress by the secretary of treasury: "Foreign dollar holders benefit by acquiring an asset that is liquid, secure, and stable in value, characteristics that are often unavailable in their own country's currency during and after periods of economic and political turmoil."[77]

It is estimated that 55 percent to 60 percent of dollars is circulating abroad. In the 2003 report, the secretary put the actual figure at the end of 2001 at $340 billion to $370 billion of the total $620 billion in circulation.[78] Where is the dollar located outside the United States? It is estimated that 25 percent of the U.S. currency is located in Latin America, 20 percent in Africa and the Middle East, and 15 percent in Asia. The remainder is in Europe and the countries of the former Soviet Union and their neighboring trading partners, such as Turkey.[79]

The value of this external dollar circulation in savings in interest cost (the circulation presumably depresses the general rate of interest in the economy) to the United States is between $14 billion to $16 billion per annum,[80] representing a substantial "windfall to the U.S. taxpayers because of the seigniorage revenues generated by the added currency demand."[81] The report, which was actually drafted by Treasury departmental offices, U. S. Secret Service, and the Federal Reserve System for the secretary of treasury, went further to advise the members of the Congress to regard the dollar as a "valuable export whose quality, or integrity, should be protected."[82]

There may be some readers of this book who may not be familiar with how this huge annual benefit of $14 billion to $16 billion is freely generated for the United States. The report from which I have been quoting gave a lengthy explanation for those of its readers who are not conversant with the economics of this free money. It says:

> Technically, dollars held abroad do not reduce the level of either Treasury borrowing or Treasury interest payments. Rather, by expanding Federal Reserve liabilities (Federal Reserves notes outstanding) and, commensurately, Federal Reserve assets (U.S. government securities), dollars held abroad increase the quantity of Treasury liabilities held by the Federal Reserve and the amount of Treasury interest paid to the Federal Reserve. Since, at the margin, all Federal Reserve earnings are returned to the Treasury, the effect is that the Treasury avoids paying interest on the value of the outstanding debt equal to the Federal Reserve notes held outside the country. For example, in 2001 the Federal Reserve returned $26.1 billion to the Treasury, the bulk of which represented earnings from assets funded by currency issuance. On the basis of our estimate that that one-half to two-thirds of U.S. currency is circulating overseas, the marginal value of external dollar circulation can be estimated at $14 billion to $16 billion.[83]

The extraction of seigniorage by the United States has not been without objection from the rest of the world, including its European allies. Let us recall the French (Europe) complaint[84] in the 1960s (at a time when 80 percent of official exchange reserves of the world was held in dollars) about the extraction of seigniorage by the United States. This was so because the rest of the world had to hold dollars and the United States was busy buying up French (European) factories, companies, and securities or fighting wars with money supplied by the French (Europe and the rest of the world). This was also the time when America openly used its military prowess to force its allies to hold the dollar as their primary reserve currency. "The German objections to holding the overhang of excessive dollars . . . were suppressed by the U.S. counter-threat of troop withdrawal"[85] in the tense context of cold war conflict and a divided Germany.

While in the 1960s and 1970s the complaint and grudges were coming from the European nations; since the 1980s, the exercise of financial muscle has been with the Asian nations. In the 1980s the United States was asking one of its largest trading partners, Japan, to allow the dollar to depreciate—put differently, let the yen appreciate in order to reduce the trade deficit with the Asian nation. This led to the 1985 Plaza Accord. Today, China's yuan is the focus with the massive trade deficits between the two nations which are once again to the advantage of an Asian nation and Washington is nudging China to allow the yuan to appreciate against the dollar.

Let us use the dollar-yuan tango to shed some more light on the operation of the imperial currency system. Many social ethicists and theologians in America are aware of the trade deficit debates between China and the United States and thus I consider it fitting to illuminate the workings of the imperial, key currency system through the lens of these debates. America's current account deficit climbed to $804.9 billion or 6.4 percent of gross domestic product (GDP) in 2005. Among other reasons, the dollar is at the top as the world's key currency because of the willingness of foreign countries like Japan and China to take up $600 billon of America's debt instruments annually. In January 2006 China signaled its intention to diversify its fast-growing reserves away from U.S. treasuries and the dollar.[86] It is estimated that 70 percent of China's reserves are invested in the United States—so it is obvious that a substantial portion of the dollars that "flow out" of the America to pay for imports from China come back as investments in dollar-denominated assets in the United States.

China's foreign exchange reserves, the largest in the world—Japan is now in second place—stands at about $1.4 trillion in the third quarter of 2007, having arisen from $750 billion at the end of 2005. The bulk of these reserves are in U.S. treasury notes. China's trade surplus with the United States (which is an equivalent deficit for the United States) was $202 billon in 2005, which is about 28 percent of the total U.S. trade deficit. Since China uses the dollar as its foreign reserves currency, the following is what China's relations with the United States look like, put bluntly. The United States buys DVDs, sneakers, textiles materials, and other real physical things from China and the Chinese are given papers to hold, which presumably represent future claims on the U.S. wealth; nonetheless, the Chinese hold only papers in the interim and the goods cost the United States virtually nothing. They may take those papers and recycle them into the world economy by buying things like oil, whose prices are denominated in dollars, and whose owners (the Organization of Petroleum Exporting Countries or OPEC) also keep their own reserves in dollar and dollar-denominated assets. The papers just change hands or recycle back into the same or other dollar-denominated assets.

Why are the Chinese not pulling out of the whole deal and immediately demanding real goods, physical things from the United States? First, their foreign exchange reserves stands at about 45 percent of their gross domestic product and any sudden move in the foreign exchange market could hurt them badly. China is in thorny predicament. If it moves quickly to offload its dollar investments, this could trigger a massive sell-off of the dollar and send the value of the dollar, and with it China's investments, plummeting. The rebalancing of the reserves of the People's Bank of China (the country's central bank) could cause similar moves among other central banks in Asia and the rest of the world. These other banks all have huge holdings in U.S. dollars and notes.

It is not only China that is invested heavily in the United States. The dollar-value of foreign-held assets as a share of America's GDP is generally on the increase. It went from 97.0 percent at year-end 2003 to 106.6 percent at year-end 2004, to 99.04 percent at year-end 2005. The actual figures are $10.67 trillion in 2003; $12.52 trillion in 2004, and $12.37 trillion in 2005.[87] Similarly, the use of the American dollar as reserve currency has generally been on the increase recently. The dollar share of global reserves was about 66.5 percent at year-end 2005; 65.9 percent at year-end 2004; 69.2 percent at the end of 2003; 76.0 percent in 2000, and 54.7 percent in 1990.[88] (The euro has benefited from the recent decline in the dollar's share.)[89]

The recent weakening of the dollar in international foreign exchange markets is expected to affect the dollar share of global reserves. Predicting how far the market share is going to decline in the short run is not an easy undertaking as it is related to a set of complex market factors and diplomatic relationships. It, however, suffices to point out some of these factors. With the massive investment in the U.S. economy and the past growth in dollar reserves, the fate of many economies is tied to that of the United States. Often in the past when the United States tried to lower its trade deficit by depreciating the dollar, the Asian central banks purchased U.S. treasuries in order to counter the American move so as to protect and preserve their exports and dollar reserves. Jane D'Arista informs us thus:

> For example, when the Fed lowers interest rates and the dollar depreciates, foreign official institutions amplify the impact of the Fed's purchases of the U.S. Treasuries as they buy dollars to prevent their currencies from appreciating and add to their own holdings of Treasury securities. Conversely, when the Fed tightens by selling Treasuries, foreign official institutions also sell and use the proceeds to buy their own currencies in order to moderate dollar appreciation.[90]

The foreign central banks did this because they wanted to keep the prices of their currencies low, that is, their exchange rates relatively low, so that they could export more to the United States and to the rest of the world in order to increase export revenue and accumulate more reserves. Even as bad as it is staying under the influence of an imperial currency regime, the only way a country can eventually have its currency become the next global imperial reserve currency is to earn more surplus than all other countries, including the current issuer of leading reserve currency. This was how the United States overtook Britain.

The substantial foreign investments in the American economy have gone to support economic growth and helped to force down medium-

and long-term interest rates and benefited both the government and the average citizen by lowering the cost of public and household debt burden. As American economist D'Arista puts it: "Foreign savings have provided substantial support for unprecedented debt growth in the U.S. government and private sector since the 1980s. Any significant withdrawal of that support would produce a credit contraction resulting in losses for borrowers and lenders that would spill over into markets in virtually every part of the world."[91]

The question in the mind of commentators and scholars is how long will America be able to skate on this thin ice? This is exactly how in April 2005 Paul A. Volcker, chairman of the Federal Reserve from 1979 to 1987, described America's predicament:

> The U.S. expansion appears on track. Yet under the placid surface . . . the circumstances seem to me as dangerous and intractable as any I can remember, and I can remember quite a lot. . . . As a nation we are consuming and investing about 6 percent more than we are producing. What holds it together is a massive and growing flow of capital from abroad, running to more than $2 billion every working day, and growing. . . . More recently, we've become more dependent on foreign central banks, particularly China and Japan and elsewhere in East Asia. . . . It's surely helped keep interest rates exceptionally low despite our vanishing savings. . . . The United States is absorbing about 80 percent of the net flow of international capital. And at some point, both central banks and private institutions will have their fill of dollars. We are *skating on increasingly thin ice* (italics added).[92]

How exactly thin is this ice? Economists are divided on this issue. No doubt the dollar's position is precarious but they report about seven factors which make it difficult to say exactly when the ice will crack or when the dollar's position as the premier reserve currency will be effectively challenged.[93] First, the dollar share of the official foreign exchange reserves was until recently on the increase. The dollar share while down from a recent peak of 76 percent in 2000 has made improvement; going from 65.9 percent in 2004 to 66.5 percent in 2005, despite the talk of central banks diversification out of the dollar during this period. Second, central banks generally hold their reserves in short to medium instruments and recently there has been talk to move to a long-term class of assets—especially with surpluses that are not immediately needed for market intervention. Such a move is expected to enhance returns on their overall portfolio. This is a potential move that might just end up benefiting the dollar. The U.S. financial market has more liquidity, depth, and breadth than anywhere else in the world to better absorb the reserves as central banks introduce new classes of assets into their portfolios. The euro is not a viable alternative as of now. This is so because currently the euro is in a distant second place to the dollar—having only about a quarter of the reserves; relative low levels of interest rates in Euroland, and the euro area financial assets market is not as broad and deep as that of the United States. The U.S. economy is still bigger than the economy of the eurozone (12 economies, excluding Denmark, Sweden, and Britain). As Morgan Stanley financial market analyst, Stephen L. Jen sums it:

> As central banks shift from a traditional liquidity management posture to a return-enhancing investment strategy, reserve diversification—simultaneously across currencies and assets—does not necessarily mean USD [U.S. dollar] selling or USD weakness. . . . The U.S. corporate bond market accounts for close to three times the corporate bond market in Euroland, and 3.5 times as big as in Japan. In fact, this market is bigger than the other corporate markets combined. Similarly, the total market cap [market capitalization] of the U.S. equity market is dominant, 2.5–3 times bigger than the markets in Euroland or Japan. Therefore, as central banks diversify across assets, there is greater justification to increase exposure to USD risky asset. . . . Thus, if central banks diversify . . . it is far from clear it will be USD-negative.[94]

Third, history has shown that a premier reserve currency of the world does not easily lose its status. Britain held on to its position long after it had fallen behind in economic power. The United States by 1919 had surpassed the United Kingdom in industrial production and trade surplus and had become the net international creditor. In addition, New York had become the world's financial center. It took two world wars with the devastations they inflicted and gross economic mismanagement to completely knock off the Union Jack from the pedestal.

Fourth, it currently suits the Asian central banks which hold substantial portions of the world reserves not to see further heavy depreciation of the dollar which will mean excessive appreciation of their currencies, a weakening of export strength, and portfolio losses. Fifth, incumbency and network externalities (simply put, that is, the extended beneficial effects for being the current dominant leader) are sources of advantage in the competition for the reserves and savings of the world. Indeed, the dollar has become a fruitful vine that is feeding many ravenous birds and none of them wants the tree to wither just now.

Sixth, Washington continues to use its tremendous clout and influence to ensure that the dollar remains the preeminent reserve currency. For instance, on Monday, February 21, 2005, the South Korean central bank, with the world's fourth largest reserves, announced that it was going to diversify the currencies in its portfolio. This sent ripples through markets and the dollar fell sharply—the biggest daily fall against major currencies in two months. With heavy pressure from Washington the very next day the Korean central bank was pressured to "clarify" its position, saying the desire to diversify the currencies in which it invests did not involve selling the dollar. The faithful friend and ally, Japan, was also at hand to lend support to Washington on Wednesday, February 23. The director of its Ministry of Finance's division of foreign exchange markets, Masatsugu Asakawa, told Reuters that: "We have no plan to change the composition of our currency holdings in the foreign reserves and we are not thinking about expanding our euro holdings."

Seventh, the military strength of the United States is crucial in understanding the resilience of the dollar as the preeminent reserve-currency of the world. In the days when global terrorism and other security are played up, the U.S. military umbrella is valued more than ever before. But as Marshall Auerback argues, this power may be diminishing: "With the country already overstretched by current military operations . . . America's 'big stick' is looking decidedly eviscerated by woodworm."[95]

These advantages, which an imperial-currency nation like the United States enjoys, are often mutually imbricated with domineering military prowess. Indeed, having a credible military capability has always been one of the requirements for a country to maintain its position as the issuer of world's primary reserve currency.[96] Britain emerged as the hegemonic world economy leader with the necessary military might after the Congress of Vienna in 1814–1815 at the end of the Napoleonic war.[97] It was able to impose a new global order based on the sterling standard. On September 21, 1931, Britain suspended the gold backing of the sterling. After fourteen years of chaos with the United States taking up the slack left by Britain, the dollar emerged as the undisputed world currency at the end of the Second World War. Once again it had the relative economic size advantage, expansive financial market, and military might and commitment to back up the world's number one currency, the "almighty dollar." The hegemonic stability provided by the United States gave the prospect of long-term peace to enable entrepreneurs and investors to make long-range decisions.

The unequal distribution of national military umbrellas for currencies severely undercuts the theory of absolute democracy or non-placeness of *empire* that Hardt and Negri are trumpeting. Asset holders and central banks put their assets (reserves) in countries that can best protect them against uncertainty. That special property-protection function is best offered by military might and political stability. Since political stability is usually about the same in key currency nations, military might becomes the most distinguishing factor. This is a throwback to the ancient time of Alexander the Great and Julius Ceasar, when trade and coinage that financed them expanded in tandem with the armies of powerful nations.

The existence of two-tier global payment system (the reserve currencies, such as dollar, euro, and yen, and their allied convertible currencies, on one hand, and the non-reserve, non-convertible currencies, on the other) throws up certain macroeconomic issues, price differentials, and market forms that result in centrifugal pool of resources from the South economies to the Global North. This is how one Nigerian economist, Peter Alexander Egom, describes the foreign exchange market of the Global South and the associated spatial demographics:

> These economies' foreign exchange markets are not level playing economic grounds at all; they are eurocentric [and American] monopolies and oligopolies where everyone seems to demand foreign exchange; everyone seems to want to see Paris and die! So why does everyone in these wretched countries of the global South and of Eastern Europe want to see Paris and die?. . . .
> This is so because the hard currencies are financial convertible and are therefore the global instruments for savings mobilization and distribution. And since no one in his right senses would like to save in an instrument which is only a local money and not an international or global money, we find that the non-convertibility of the soft currencies of the global South and Eastern Europe puts them at a very grave market disadvantage. They must always trade at a heavy discount with the hard currencies of the global North. . . .
> The softness which the eurocentric interest-based regime of central banking imposes on their currencies makes the inhabitants of these unfortunate economies losers in all aspects of their economic lives both at home and abroad. For financial convertibility transforms the so-called hard currencies into "strange attractors" for all the actual and potential savings of these economies. As a result, the human and financial capital, as well as the material resources of these economies, do the Lemming race from their rural areas to the urban areas, and onwards overseas to see Paris and die.[98]

Hardt and Negri waxed eloquently and strong on the rise of a mobile, hybrid, a cooperative labor force that is increasingly seen as not a national workforce but as transnational.[99] If they had analyzed money, especially the United States' dollar as a reserve currency, they would have discovered that the position of the dollar implicates it in the condition of labor in the United States vis-à-vis those of the other countries. The very fact that the United States has the world's reserve currency means that it has to transfer manufacturing jobs offshore and run huge trade deficits. When a country issues the world money, it is saddled with the problem of providing adequate liquidity to the world economy. Foreigners have to accumulate dollars and one very crucial way to do this is to export more to the United States than they import. To allow this the United States must run balance of payment deficits with the rest of the world in order to increase global liquidity and reserves. Encouraging exports into the United States and encouraging investments of U.S. industrial capital abroad are some of the ways of transferring its currencies from its domestic economy into the international circulation.

Based on the preceding analyses of money and the international payment system, we can aver that we do not yet see evidence of Hardt and Negri's *empire*. The world economic system is still in the imperialist economic order. The world economic system as it stands today fulfills the characteristics of an imperial economic order. In my mind there are seven major characteristics of imperial economic order, and they all apply to Hardt and Negri's *empire*:[100]

1. The global economy does not have a global currency as its logical concomitant. The reserve assets of most countries in the world are the U.S. government's IOUs (liabilities), and their worth depends on the worth of the latter;

2. There is a hierarchy of national/imperial currencies with a few serving as reserve currencies. The first-tier currency nations manage the international reserves of their second-tier underlings—savings move from poor countries to rich countries;

3. Centrifugal pattern of control over world's resource use and its related concentration of financial power. The leading countries of the West control the resources of the world and their currencies are "strange attractors" for the savings and resources of the rest of the world. We learned that the foreign exchange reserves of the Global South, for instance, are kept in the banks and financial houses of issuer of global reserve currencies.

4. The imperial financial system discriminates against nations whose currencies are low in the hierarchy in finance and investment. Monetary surpluses are not reticulated (networked) effectively in a non-discriminatory way between surplus-national entities to deficit-national entities. The largest share of capital and investment also goes to the richest group of countries in the system, not the capital-starved and low-labor cost economies;[101]

5. Poor and emerging countries cannot borrow in their own currencies. Nearly 100 percent of debts placed at the international level are done in five currencies: U.S. dollar, euro, yen, pound sterling, and Swiss franc;

6. There is a locus of control over the issuance of international money—meaning the overwhelming percentage of securities for investment capital are floated and raised in the capital markets of a few leading currency-zones. Besides, it is the financial system of an imperial economic entity (and its close allies) that is the motive force in the global exchange and production of economic values; and

7. There are power games going on all the time which show that global control is not evenly distributed and gravitates to certain regions of the earth. The games are played in certain centers with obvious inside

and outside boundaries. The United States, the issuer of world's chief reserve currency, runs a current account deficit with impunity. No poor country can do this. If the United States decides to devalue its currency in order to improve its current account deficits, Asian central banks which have built up huge foreign exchange reserve (which are of course in U.S dollars and government liabilities) immediately go into massive dollar purchases to raise the price of dollar, thus continuing the U.S balance of payments deficit. These games are played by countries which can afford to be in the exclusive, segregated, privileged corner of the international public arena and such games are played from definite localities with repercussions for the rest of the world, especially for Africa which is always outside but looking in through the window as a lad presses his face into the glass pane to view the delicacies in the baker's shop.

Hardt and Negri's *Empire* describes an imperial, reserve, vehicular moneyless world. Their theory of empire neglects imperial money "as the unifying force that integrates otherwise separate and disparate [global trade and payment] activities into a coherent whole capable of reproducing itself in expanding fashion."[102] They have shown an inadequate understanding of what *empire* really is. One also finds this or other types of inadequacy in the understanding of *empire* in works of many theologians and ethicists. An empire does not exist only because it can mobilize and distribute savings or goods and services from far and near by military force, military threat, military umbrella, or political subjugation of other societies, but also by—and often in combination with—the use of its currency's monopoly power to do the same. Empires in general, directly or indirectly, twist and tweak the *space and time contents* of money to their own advantage and to the disadvantage of less-powerful economies under its sway.[103]

If the question of empire is brought into the fundamental framework of international monetary theory, then it is possible to reject the attempts of some ethicists to deny the fact of empire today. The history of empire represents the history of two features of the global trade and payment system and the protest against them. Firstly, the monetary theory of empire holds that whoever controls the production and issue of the medium of exchange in international trade and investment exercises domination (if not control) over the monetary resources of other nations. Powerful nations do not need to politically and militarily conquer and rule territories to dominate the resources of other countries just as today's sophisticated capitalists do not need to turn workers into plantation slaves in order to exploit their labor power. Karl Polanyi in his monumental book, *The Great Transformation*, puts it well when he states that "The Pax Britannica held its sway sometimes by the ominous poise of a heavy ship's cannon, but more frequently it prevailed by the timely pull of a thread in the international monetary network."[104] Secondly, the monetary theory of empire, as we have presented it in this chapter, also holds that every international system of trade and payment, every economic world order, in every era or phase of capital accumulation features a particular configuration for the mobilization of monetary resources. This configuration involves the "loci-of-control over determination and issue of international money" which are in one or two countries. These loci of control act as the monarchs of the world economic order. Look for empire wherever you see a hierarchy of national currencies in any world economic order. Since national currencies are issued by sovereignties and backed by the strength of the sovereignties, the subjugation of one currency to another is the subjugation of one sovereignty to another and the privileging of few monarchical economies. I think so far in this chapter, I have demonstrated that the dollar, euro, and yen are instruments for the mobilization and distribution of savings, resources, services, ideas, space, time, talents, and treasures on a global scale to the advantage of only three economic-currency zones of yore.

SECTION 3: CONCLUSION: AMBIGUITY AND DEMONRY IN THE GLOBAL MONETARY IMPERIUM

In the foregoing sections, I have described and analyzed what exactly and how important the relationship between empire and money is. It shows that money gives centeredness to the empire and its functional existence belies the claim of Hardt and Negri that empire has no center. Part of their thesis of empire is a sharply drawn difference between previous and current postmodern imperialisms. This perception of difference, which I have shown to be false, arises out of an inadequate description and understanding of the function of money in the globalization of production and circulation of products and services.

My trenchant critique of Hardt and Negri's *Empire* has served to bring to the fore the pattern of demonic distortion and twisting at the heart of the global monetary system. The binary and dichotomous logic of imperial vehicular currency system, which puts few national currencies at the top and the plebeian rest of the world currencies at the bottom, hinders the economic development of many countries of the Global South.

The monarchical triumvirate of the dollar, euro, and yen has imposed its particular imperial interests on the global trade and payment system. This coterie of three dominant national currencies claims universality in the name of a particular quality and strength, or in the name of their national economies and their attendant qualities. Their claims are not made in the "name of that principle which implies ultimacy and universality—that principle of justice."[105] These currencies are not independent of their nations, yet they claim absoluteness for themselves. They claim to be adequate for every nation and transaction at the global level, while they only truly fit their particular nations and their particular qualities. They were not created and sustained in the name of principles which are valid for all economies and for the globalizing impulses of the current phase of capitalism. They are not based on a global covenant of justice which is capable of working against a self-absolutizing and consequently demonically distorted monetary system.[106]

I also brought to the fore the ethical tensions between empire and national currencies and between developed, rich countries and the developing, poor countries in the global trade and payment system. I argued that the global monetary system is imperialistic and unethical, and obstructs the full participation of poor and weak economies in it, and in the ongoing globalization process. So how can the system be made receptive to the full participation of the developing countries? How can the global structures and organization of monetary life be nudged toward creating and maintaining an embracing, participation-enhancing economic community that brings *unity-in-difference* into perpetual play and also foster more ethical relationality and justice without stifling its creativity and galvanizing force?

In chapter 7, I will show how the structural tensions in the dynamics and crisis of money could be addressed by re-imagining and outlining a possible ethical alternative to the international monetary system. I will draw on the practical consequences of the trinitarian principles and doctrine of the triune God, based on the perichoretic interpretation, to show how the global monetary system can be used to draw nations more generally into a mutually participative life. This is the point at which I articulate the kind of system of trinitarian principles and relations that is at work in Tillich's model of relations in the triune God. The resulting re-imagined system highlights the importance of relationality in monetary interactions, giving us a perspective on how to redress certain destructive dynamics in today's monetary system. My goal is to point to the possibilities of an alternative global monetary system that can acknowledge and make room for the capabilities of the nations (peoples and economies) who currently do not have sufficient participation in the global monetary system (which is not only ambiguous but often destructive in its creativity) as currently structured.

I will use Tillich's first root of trinitarian thinking to enable me to show how "poly-mediastic" national currencies can become "mono-mediastic," that is, giving way to one global money form. This trinitarian principle is important for looking at the global monetary system. The structural tension in the dynamics of money as an exchange medium in the international monetary system is expressed in two ways: first, particularistic national currencies aspire to transcend their national borders, and second, the present global vehicular currencies (such as the dollar, euro, and yen) are unable to transcend national interests even while they claim ultimacy and universality in the global trade and payment system. The need for a balance between these forces of particular national interests and a global system calls for a trinitarian structure. Following this Tillichian line of reasoning, I will propose that the solution to the tension is a universal currency that can really claim ultimacy and be uncontrolled by local (national) interests without losing the concrete (particular) element in the idea of money. In this way, I seek to transcend the tension between the particular and universal tendencies of all current legal forms of money and imagine an ethical alternative to the today's global monetary system.

NOTES

1. Paul Tillich, *Systematic Theology*, vol. 1, *Reason and Revelation, Being and God* (Chicago: University of Chicago Press, 1951), 227.

2. See Richard N. Cooper, "Proposal for a Common Currency among Rich Democracies," Working Paper No. 27, Oesterreichische National Bank, available at www.oenb.at.

3. Laura Wallace, "Ahead of His Time," *Finance and Development* 43, 3 (September 2006): 4–7.

4. For Paul Volcker's statement see Robert Mundell, "Currency Areas and International Monetary Reforms at the Dawn of a New Century," *Review of International Economics* 9, no.4 (2001): 595–607; Mundell, "A Theory of Optimum Currency Areas," *The American Economic Review* 51, no. 4 (1961): 509–17; Mundell, "The International Monetary System and the Case for a World Currency," Leon Kozminski Academy of Entrepreneurship and Management (WSPiZ) and Tiger Distinguished Lecture Series12, Warsaw (October 23, 2003); Robert Guttmann, *How Credit Shapes the Economy: The United States in a Global System* (Armonk, NY: M. E. Sharpe, 1994); Peter Alexander Egom, *NEPAD and the Common Good* (Lagos, Nigeria: Global Market Forum, 2004); *Globalization at the Crossroads: Capitalism or Communalism* (Lagos, Nigeria: Global Market Associates, 2002); Egom, *Money in the Theory of International Economic Activity: An Inquiry into the Nature and Causes of the Wealth and Poverty of Nations* (Guderup, Denmark: Adione, 1977), and John Maynard Keynes, *The Collected Writings of John Maynard Keynes*, vol. 25, *Activities 1940–1944: Shaping the Post-War World, The Clearing Union*, ed. D. Moggridge (London: Macmillan, 1980).

5. It is important to note that New Testament scholars are making—and have been for a few years now—a vigorous turn toward study of the Gospel using the lens of empire and the politics of empire as the setting for re-interpreting the

gospel. But it appears that they have not taken the economic-coloniality dimension seriously.

6. Jesus Christ might have had an anti-imperial finance stance. He converted Zacchaeus (a chief tax collector of the Roman Empire); Levi, a minor tax official; and possibly many other tax collectors given his relentless witnessing to them (Matt. 9:9–12; Luke 19:1–10). Their conversion attacked the imperial tax-farming system, "the pillars of Roman imperial finances." When he drove out the foreign exchange dealers as recorded in John 2:13–16, he was attacking in a sense the exchange market system that allowed the Roman imperial currency denarius— which represented, as Walter D. Mignolo would say, the coloniality of power, the subalternization of peripheral currencies, and the colonial difference—to project itself into external geopolitical and economic spaces. See Walter D. Mignolo, *Local Histories/Global Designs: Coloniality, Subaltern Knowledges, and Border Thinking* (Princeton, NJ: Princeton University Press, 2000). So the Nigerian unorthodox monetary economist, Luke Peter Egom, avers that it is "plausible for one to hold that Jesus Christ was murdered by imperial Rome simply because" of his attack on the pillars of imperial Roman finances. See Egom (same person as Ashikiwe Adione-Egom), *Globalization at the Crossroads*, xxxi. This statement linking Jesus's death to his anti-imperial financial message should not be construed to mean that this writer devalues the divine and salvific impulses that led him to the cross. Having said this, one needs to note that the divine and salvific are of course related to the financial dimension, and the financial dimension has to also be seen in relation to the the political-social world and context. All these, in fact, in the Hellenistic milieu of Roman occupied Palestine, were much more of a single piece and related than are they are today: the financial-political-divine-salvific. For example, in the Jewish temple (a veritable state system with financial and political, as well as religious ramifications), offerings were made to the Roman Caesar continually. And of course, the Roman Caesar considered himself "savior." See Mark Lewis Taylor: *The Executed God: The Way of the Cross in Lockdown America* (Minneapolis, MN: Fortress Press, 2001), 70–105.

7. Hardt and Negri, *Empire* (Cambridge, MA: Harvard University Press, 2000).

8. Hardt and Negri, *Empire*, xii–xiii, xix, 166–67.

9. Paul Tillich, *Systematic Theology*, vol. 3, *Life and the Spirit, History and the Kingdom of God* (Chicago: University of Chicago Press, 1965), 324–26.

10. Tillich, *Systematic Theology*, vol. 3, 325.

11. Hardt and Negri, *Empire*, xi, xii–xvii, xix, 167–68, 198, 213, 312–17, 332–33, 347, 353.

12. It is conceivable that I missed some of the senses in which the phrase is used throughout the book. But I am sure the ones presented here capture the kernel of their argument.

13. Hardt and Negri, *Empire*, xii, xiv, 50, 213, 306–9, 332–36.

14. Hardt and Negri, *Empire*, xiii–xiv, 187, 190, 332–33.

15. Hardt and Negri, *Empire*, xii.

16. Hardt and Negri, *Empire*, 221, 295, 297–98.

17. Hardt and Negri, *Empire*, xii, 6, 32, 299, 385, 358.

18. Hardt and Negri, *Empire*, 47, 73, 185, 208, 344.

19. Hardt and Negri, *Empire*, 291–94.

20. Hardt and Negri, *Empire*, 47, 75, 185, 202, 309, 344, 373.

21. Hardt and Negri, *Empire*, 150–51, 154, 251, 271, 332–33, 384.

22. Hardt and Negri, *Empire*, 164, 368, and 373 vs. 66, 161, 165, and 410, 400–407.

23. Hardt and Negri, *Empire*, 47, 62, 206–7, 252–53, 261.

24. Hardt and Negri, *Empire*, 307, 308.

25. Hardt and Negri, *Empire*, i and 317 vs. 271 and 384.

26. Hardt and Negri, *Empire*, xiv.

27. Hardt and Negri, *Empire*, 288.

28. Hardt and Negri, *Empire*, 309ff; 336–39.

29. We need to take such ambivalence very seriously as it gives us insights into the deep valence of the work that may not manifest itself at first reading. Hardt and Negri's reactions to America's use of its military power to dominate the world in the wake of 9/11 is very telling in this regard. When confronted with the fact that America's attitude did not jive with their notion that the emergence of *Empire* is drawing major powers into multilateral processes of "global governance," they replied in somewhat surprising manner, as reported by Alex Callinicos: "The responses of Hardt and Negri to the refutation of their theory have been, to say the least, confused. Hardt has argued that 'the captains of the capital in the U.S.' should recognize that the Bush strategy isn't in their interest, and that "there is an alternative to U.S. imperialism: global power can be organized in a decentered form, which Tony Negri and I call 'empire.'" So Empire isn't so much the political form of capitalist globalization as a policy option that enlightened capitalists should embrace. For Negri by contrast, Empire is not an alternative to the Bush war-drive but what explains it: "Preventive war. . . is a constituent strategy of Empire." At stake in the present crisis, according to Negri, are "the forms of hegemony and the relative degrees of power that American and/or European capitalist elites will have in the organization of the new world order." So, in contradiction to what Hardt and Negri argued in their book, Empire involves rival centers of capitalist power after all. Alex Callinicos, *The New Mandarins of American Power* (Cambridge, MA: Polity Press, 2003), 102.

30. This is a quote I heard often from my former college teacher Professor Claude Ake, who is now deceased.

31. One must here once again note the ambivalence in their thought. They also do suggest in their "pyramid of global constitution," where hegemonic powers articulate connections between military, monetary, and cultural biopower on a global level, that there are deference to power and authority in economic matters. See Hardt and Negri, *Empire*, 309–10, 345–48. Hardt and Negri may have suggested notions of monetary dominance in *Empire* in these pages on the global pyramid, but those pages sit awkwardly in relation to their networking, no-center idea.

32. Michel Foucault, "Structuralism and Post-Structuralism: An Interview with Michel Foucault," interview by Gerard Raulet, translated by Jeremy Harding, *Telos* 55 (1983): 206.

33. Hardt and Negri, *Empire*, 172–82.

34. Hardt and Negri, *Empire*, xi, xii, xiv, 166, 146, 191.

35. Hardt and Negri, *Empire*, 304–24.

36. Jeffrey Stout, *Democracy and Tradition* (Princeton, NJ: Princeton University Press, 2004), 135–36.

37. Kevin C. Dunn, "Africa's Ambiguous Relation to Empire and *Empire*," in *Empire's New Clothes: Reading Hardt and Negri*, ed. Paul A. Passavant and Jodi Dean (New York: Routledge, 2004), 143–62, for quote see p. 148.

38. "In the absence of the possibility of power relations to shift, multiply, and contradict one another domination takes over." Quote from p. 245 of Lee Quinby, "Taking the Millennialist Pulse of *Empire's* Multitude: A Genealogical Feminist Diagnosis," in *Empire's New Clothes: Reading Hardt and Negri*, 231–51.

39. Stout, *Democracy*, 121.

40. Stout, *Democracy*, 121. See also Jeffrey Stout, *Ethics after Babel: The Languages of Morals and their Discontents* (Boston: Beacon Press, 1988), 205–07.

41. While there may not be " substantive opposition" between them, there are important distinctions between entities such as colonialism, neocolonialism, and other various forms of domination and such distinctions are important for analysis of empire and developing models of resistance and transformation.

42. Hardt and Negri, *Empire*, 306.

43. Nimi Wariboko, "State-Corporation Relationship: Impact on Management Practice," in *The Transformation of Nigeria: Essays in Honor of Toyin Falola*, ed. Adebayo Oyebade (Trenton, NJ: African World Press, 2002), 295–300, 306–10; and Kevin C. Dunn, "Africa's Ambiguous Relation to Empire and *Empire*," 149–50.

44. Saskia Sassen, "The Repositioning of Citizenship: Emergent Subjects and Spaces for Politics," in *Empire's New Clothes: Reading Hardt and Negri*, 179.

45. In order to understand how the role of African cities, which at the current global stratification of cities, function to attract labor and other local resources and send them off to the world cities see Nimi Wariboko, "Urbanization and Cities in Africa," in *Africa*, vol. 5, *Contemporary Africa*, ed. Toyin Falola (Durham, NC: Carolina Academic Press, 2003), 633–55; and Carole Rakodi, "Global Forces, Urban Change, and Urban Management in Africa," in *The Urban Challenge in Africa: Growth and Management of its Large Cities*, ed. Carole Rakodi (Tokyo: United Nations University Press, 1997), chap. 2.

46. Saskia Sassen, *The Global City* (Princeton, NJ: Princeton University Press, 2001), 4.

47. Sassen, *The Global City*, 3–4.

48. Hardt and Negri, *Empire*, xii–xiii.

49. Hardt and Negri, *Empire*, 32.

50. Hardt and Negri, *Empire*, 294.

51. I am grateful to the communication engineer, Dr. Tunde Odunsaya, of IBM for giving me these descriptions in a telephone conversation on December 12, 2004. I hope I have adequately reflected the true nature of things as he explained them to me.

52. Hardt and Negri, *Empire*, 299.

53. This is something the authors do not deny. See *Empire*, 309–10, 345–48 for the "bomb, money, and ether" connection.

54. Even the Internet is somewhat tiered, since the big companies have their own multimillion dollar created, encrypted private e-mail network.

55. Money is used in the sense that it is a device for preventing every economic event happening all at the same time and space and as a sociopsychological phenomenon without which no exchange can take place.

56. Egom, *Money in the theory of International Economic Activity*, 137. The correct date is August 15, 1971.

57. Below, we will see the U.S. military enforcement of its dollar seigniorage.

58. A Venn diagram is a powerful way to graphically organize data or information. It comes from the mathematics of set theory and it is used to show the logical relationship between different sets of items, things, and so forth.

59. Nigel Thrift and Andrew Leyshon, "Moral geographies of money," in *Nation-States and Money: The Past, Present and Future of National Currencies*, ed. Emily Gilbert and Eric Helleiner (London: Routledge, 1999), 163–64.

60. Nigel Dodd in "Globalisation of Money?: National Sovereignty and the Management of Risk" in *Nation-States and Money* reached a similar conclusion regarding the offshore market: "To describe the offshore market as floating above the national boundaries and threatening them from outside may be theoretically convenient from the perspective of globalisation, but it does not withstand close empirical scrutiny" (189).

61. "Global competition is not just product versus product, company versus company, or trading bloc [read nations] versus trading bloc [read nations]. It is mindset versus mindset." Gary Hamel and C. K. Prahalad, "Strategy as Stretch and Leverage," *Harvard Business Review* (March–April, 1993): 77.

62. "The most profound grasp of ethos always penetrates to questions of religion." Max L. Stackhouse, "Introduction: Foundations and Purposes," in *On Moral Business: Classical and Contemporary Resources for Ethics in Economic Life*," ed. Max L. Stackhouse, Dennis P. McCann, and Shirley J. Roels with Preston N. Williams (Grand Rapids, Mi: William B. Eerdmans Co., 1995), 30.

63. Hardt and Negri may have suggested notions of inequality in *Empire* in their section on global pyramid, but that section sits awkwardly in relation to their networking, no-center idea.

64. Guttman, *How Credit-Money Shapes the Economy*, 63–64.

65. The idea for this illustration came from Egom, *Money in the Theory of International Economic Activity*, 136–46.

66. See Egom, *Money in the Theory of International Economic Activity*, 136–45, for such an analysis; also Guttman, *How Credit-Money Shapes the Economy*, 139–40.

67. Guttman, *How Credit-Money Shapes the Economy*, 139–40.

68. George S. Tavlas, "The Internal Use of Currencies: The U.S. Dollar and the Euro," *Finance and Development* 35, no. 2 (June 1998): 46–49. See also Martin Feldstein, "Stabilize Price, Not the Dollar," *Wall Street Journal*, March 17, 1995, p. A10, who put the figure at $10 billion in 1995. Tavlas quoted the Federal Reserve Board in his paper published in the IMF journal. Please note that this figure is different from external seigniorage, which is about the spread between the yield on liabilities that are mainly central banks' reserves held in short maturities and the returns on assets that are principally long-term loans and other capital exports.

69. This is what U.S. Congressman Ron Paul of Texas said about this on the floor of the House of Representatives on February 15, 2006: "Realizing the world

was embarking on something new and mind boggling, the elite money managers, with a especially strong support from U.S authorities, struck an agreement with OPEC to price oil in U.S. dollars exclusively for all worldwide transactions. This gave the dollar a special place among world currencies and in essence 'backed' the dollar with oil." See http://www.house.gov/paul/congrec2006/cr021506.htm. Also see William Clark, *Petrodollar Warfare: Oil, Iraq and the Future of the Dollar* (Gabriola Island, Canada: New Society, 2005), 19–21.

70. This is how David Spiro explains how all this works. "So long as OPEC oil was priced in U.S. dollars, and so long as OPEC invested the dollars in U.S. government instruments, the U.S. government enjoyed a double loan. The first part of the loan was for oil. The government could print dollars to pay for oil, and the American economy did not have to produce goods and services in exchange for oil until OPEC used the dollars for goods and service [Even when used to buy goods and services the dollars largely still remain in the United States as the new recipients of the printed green papers keep their national reserves in dollars. Nigeria may use its dollar earnings from oil to buy Chinese textiles, but so long as China invests its earnings from Nigeria in U.S. government bonds, the only resource expenditure on the part of the United States since it first bought the oil from the West African country is the efforts it takes for a lowly paid clerk to make the book entry in the computer here in the United States—and of course the cost of printing greenbacks]. Obviously, the strategy could not work if dollars were not a means of exchange for oil. The second part of the loan was from all other economies that had to pay dollars for oil but could not print currency. Those economies had to trade their goods and services for dollars in order to pay OPEC. Again, so long as OPEC held the dollars rather than spending them, the U.S. received a loan. It was, therefore, important to keep OPEC oil priced in dollars at the same time that government officials continued to recruit Arab funds." See David E. Spiro, *"The Hidden Hand of American Hegemony: Petrodollar Recycling and International Markets* (Ithaca, NY: Cornell University Press, 1999), 121–22.

71. Hudson, *Super Imperialism: The Economic Strategy of American Empire* (London: Pluto Press, 2003), 5.

72. It is hard to know for two reasons. First, many analysts believe that the United States is not giving OPEC members room to do as they please. Second, some members of the oil cartel have expressed interest in moving away from the dollar. Congressman Ron Paul has argued that the United States exercises its military muscle to maintain the dollar-oil relationship so that its national currency would remain as the preeminent world currency. According to him, "in November 2000 Saddam Hussein demanded Euros for his oil. His arrogance was a threat to the dollar; his lack of any military might was never a threat. At the first cabinet meeting with the new administration [of Present George Bush] in 2001, as reported by Treasury Secretary Paul O'Neil, the major topic was how we would get rid of Saddam Hussein—though there was no evidence whatsoever he posed a threat to us. . . . Within a short period after the military victory [in 2003], all Iraqi oil sales were carried out in dollars. The Euro was abandoned." (See the *Wall Street Journal* report on Saddam's plan to price his country's oil in euro. Robert Block, "Some Muslim Nations Advocate Dumping the Dollar for the Euro," *Wall Street Journal*, April 15, 2003.) He also linked the coup against President Hugo Chavez in

April 11–12, 2002, which reportedly received assistance from the Central Intelligence Agency, to his threat in 2001 to switch to euro for all its country pricing of oil sales. See http://www.house.gov/paul/congrec2006/cr021506.htm. In June 2004, Iran announced plans to set up a course to trade oil priced in euro. See Terry Macalister, "Iran Takes on West's Control of Oil Trading," *Guardian of the United Kingdom*, http://business.guardian.co.uk/story/0,3604,1239644,00.html.

73. Jane D' Arista, "Another Year Awash in Liquidity," *Capital Flows Monitor* (April 27, 2006): 4.

74. "It was Charles Kindleberger. . . who coined the phrase, 'external seigniorage' for the windfall gains accruing to the government from the yield spread between short-term liabilities and long-term assets. He chose the term carefully to set it apart from the standard (and purely domestic) definition of seigniorage, which refers to revenue gains for the government from an acceleration of inflation made possible by more rapid money creation." See Robert Guttman, *How Credit-Money Shapes the Economy*, 516n15.

75. Guttman, *How Credit-Money Shapes the Economy*, 366.

76. Please note that any money issued by any government earns it interest whether the money circulates only within its sovereign boundaries or not. Money is often considered by economists as a form of debt on which little or no interest is paid by the issuing government (central bank). The government at least earns the difference between the lending and borrowing rates, net of intermediation costs. For a country whose currency is confined to its boundaries the earnings ultimately wash out. According to Canadian economics professor Z. A. Spindler (Department of Economics, Simon Fraser University, Burnaby, Canada), "If a national government's currency is an uncommon currency, that is, a currency mainly traded in that country, then, there are no net seigniorage earnings for the country as a whole. What the government receives in the form of reduced interest cost on public debt by its fiat money is approximately the same interest earnings foregone by the country's residents holding the uncommon [non-imperial] national money. This seldom-recognized accounting reality is apparent only when viewed from a national perspective that consolidates public and private account." See Z. A. Spindler, "Public Choice Perspectives on Monetary Regimes," unpublished paper of January 15, 2004, sent to this writer by the author on December 23, 2004, by e-mail.

77. United States Treasury Department, *The Use and Counterfeiting of United States Currency Abroad*, Part 2, (March 2003), vi.

78. United States Treasury Department, *The Use and Counterfeiting*, v.

79. United States Treasury Department, *The Use and Counterfeiting*, vi.

80. United States Treasury Department, *The Use and Counterfeiting*, 24.

81. United States Treasury Department, *The Use and Counterfeiting*, vi.

82. United States Treasury Department, *The Use and Counterfeiting*, 25.

83. United States Treasury Department, *The Use and Counterfeiting*, 24–25n22.

84. Guttman, *How Credit-Money Shapes the Economy*, 138.

85. Robert Mundell, "Gold Would Serve into the 21st Century," *Wall Street Journal* September 30, 1981, p. 28. See also Michael Hudson, *Super Imperialism*, 35.

86. *Financial Times*, Thursday, January 6, 2006. Talk of China diversifying its reserves away from the dollar was once again in the news in the fourth quarter of 2007 as the dollar continued to slide in the foreign exchange market.

87. Jane D' Arista, "Causes and Consequences of the Buildup in Global Liquidity: Part 2," *Capital Flows Monitor* (October 17, 2005): 2. See also April 27, 2006, p. 1. Another source: U.S Bureau of Economic Analysis.

88. Bank for International Settlements, *Annual Reports*, various issues.

89. The euro is also gaining at the expense of the dollar in the share of international bank lending and investment and international debt securities. See D' Arista, "Causes and Consequences of the Buildup in Global Liquidity: Part 2," *Capital Flows Monitor* (April 27, 2005): 8–10; International Monetary Fund, *Currency Composition of Official Foreign Exchange Reserves (COFER)*, March 2006. Note that IMF admitted that it lacked compositional data on about 33 percent of total reserves. This is so because central banks, mainly in Asia, do not report the composition of their portfolio to the IMF or any other organization.

90. D' Arista, "Causes and Consequences of the Buildup in Global Liquidity: Part 2," 4.

91. D' Arista, "Causes and Consequences of the Buildup in Global Liquidity: Part 2," 4.

92. Paul A. Volcker, "An Economy on Thin Ice," *Washington Post*, April 10, 2005, p. B7.

93. Joachim Felms, "Global: Pondering the Composition of Central Bank Reserves Part 1," *Global Economic Forum*, October 18, 2005, http://www.morganstanley.com/GEFdata/digests/20051018-tue.html; Marshall Auerback, "Last Orders for the U.S. dollars," *Critique* 12, Japan Policy Research Institute, March 2005, http://www.jpri.org/publications/critiques/ critique_XII_2.html; Ramkishen S. Rajan and Jose Kiran, "Will the Greenback Remain the World's Reserves Currency" Unpublished paper, January 2006.

94. Stephen L. Jens, "USD: Is Reserve Diversification Negative for the Dollar?," Global Economic Forum, September 16, 2005, http://www.morganstanley.com/GEFdata/digests/2005916-fri.html.

95. Auerback, "Last Orders for the U.S. dollars."

96. We should not overemphasize the hegemonic role of a military-economic power. Though the hegemonic stability provided by a military and economic power is helpful to the economic and political stability of the world monetary system, it does not in itself guarantee it nor is it absolutely essential to the stable functioning of the international monetary system. Nonetheless, if the events of the 1930s offer any guide we should be wary of a world trade and payment system without an undisputed hegemonic leader. For a scholarly discussion of how the current international system dominated by democratic trading states obviates, or at least reduces, the need for a hegemonic leader see Richard Rosecrance, *The Rise of the Trading States: Commerce and Conquest in the Modern World* (New York: Basic Books, 1986). Giovanni Arrighi makes a different kind of argument regarding the probability of war among the great capitalist nations. He argues that "the kind of world-economic integration via direct investment under U.S. hegemony was less likely to break down in a generalized state of war than the kind of world-economic integration via commodity and financial flows typical of nineteenth century British hegemony." See Arrighi, "Lineages of Empire," in *Historical Materialism* 10, 3 (Summer 2002): 3–16; p. 10 for quote. This argument is actually from his

book, *The Geometry of Imperialism: The Limits of Hobson's Paradigm*, 2nd ed. (London: Verso, 1985), 146–73.

97. Guttman, *How Credit-Money Shapes the Economy*, 358–61.

98. Egom, *Globalization at the Crossroads*, 86, 87, 88.

99. Hardt and Negri, *Empire*, 291–94.

100. I was able to identify these characteristics from many sources, especially from Egom, *Money in the Theory of International Economic Activity*; and Guttman, *How Credit-Money Shapes the Economy*.

101. So Hardt and Negri's assertion that capital goes to "where the price of labor is lowest and where the administrative force to guarantee exploitation is highest" is simply wrong. Yes, it is true that corporations may run to places where they can hire the cheapest labor, but a comprehensive look at the overall distribution of investment capital shows that investors in the advanced countries tend to put more of their capital (direct and portfolio) in advanced economies. We just learned from Paul Volcker, the former chairman of the U.S. central bank, that 80 percent of global capital flows come to the United States.

102. Guttman, *How Credit-Money Shapes the Economy*, 15.

103. In a certain sense, money has two contents: time and space values. The concept of space-and-time values of money draws attention to the mechanics of the intertemporal and interspatial flows of goods and services within and between societies. The time content of money is measured by the *social rate of time preference*, which can be approximated by interest rate or the social discount rate. Time preference is the rate at which society is willing to exchange present consumption for future consumption. The more time value or content a currency contains the better it is. The time value of a currency is inversely related to its average level of interest rate (of relatively safe assets such as treasuries). So the higher the interest rate, the lower the preference for future consumption or stronger the preference for today's consumption and higher the liquidity preference of savers. An economy with a high interest rate, a low time preference rate, usually has the bulk of its investment in the short term as its money is not able to spread investment and development across the time spectrum. In fact, a low time preference rate is not conducive for economic development. The space content of money measures how money is used to spread development across geographic space (urban-rural or regions), social space (which class or income group benefits more from the operating money supply model), spatial arrangement of resources (to what extent are local resources used to meet local needs), and international space (whether savings of other nations are being imported into its national economic space). Geographical space content (spatial concentration of resources) could be measured by the industry centralization and concentration index. Social space could be measured by national distribution of income (wages, profits, dividend, and interest) and asset concentration. Spatial arrangement could be measured by the degree of local value adding in domestic manufacturing industries, the proportion of import or export in the gross domestic product. The international space content of money could be measured by whether the country is net capital export, whether its currency is financially convertible, and the percentage of global reserves managed in its physical locale.

104. Karl Polanyi, *The Great Transformation: The Political and Economic Origins of Our Time* (Boston: Beacon Press Books, 2001), 14.

105. Tillich, *Systematic Theology*, vol. 1, 227.

106. Tillich, *Systematic Theology*, vol. 1, 60, 214, 226–27 for this Tillichian understanding of the meaning of imperialism.

7

✛

A Trinitarian Model of the Global Monetary System

INTRODUCTION

The overall result of the foregoing analyses is the unveiling of the basic existential questions implicit in the social practice of money—essentially showing where the ethical questions are situated in the practice of money. The next logical task is mutually and critically correlating the existential questions with religious response. We need a solution to the ethical problems of money in the global economy; a solution that can properly acknowledge the tensions inherent in the monetary process, foster a fuller and equitable participation of poor countries in the current phase of globalization, preserve the system's vitality, and make the vitality open to the whole of creation without wrecking significant segments of creation (nature in its fullness). The solution I proffer is a single global currency—like the way the European Union has one currency for its member-countries.[1] The world economy, especially those of Africa and other developing countries, will benefit from a global money form. In recent decades, globalization and international economic intercourse have grown with fervency, indicating that the world economy is driving toward universal and total integration. Like Paul Volcker, I think a global economy needs a global currency. This is also the position of Martin Wolf, the celebrated associate editor and chief economic commentator at the *Financial Times*, and the author of *Why Globalization Works*.[2] This study is perhaps the first to make a rigorous, systematic case for a single world currency based on theological and ethical discourse.

In the remainder of this chapter, I will show how the first root of Tillich's trinitarian thinking can help us to re-imagine the global monetary system. I will argue that the tension between the universal and particular as played out in the global trade and payment system is an underlying principle that can drive particularistic national currencies toward universal and total integration as a single global currency (not one or two controlled by national interests) and can also define the patterns of interaction between them. I combine Tillich's notion of trinitarian principles with the perichoretic trinitarian theology of Volf as elaborated in his *After Our Likeness: The Church as an Image of the Trinity*. I found out that—and as the reader will see below—a creative synthesis of the ideas of the two theologians enabled me to develop my arguments about the monetary system and monetary flows (not monetary stock or uses and stewardship of money) better than either of them alone.

I would like to describe a financial way of being in which the eschatological fellowship of the triune God with human beings and with one another is anticipated. Taking full cognizance of the dialectic between "already" and the "not yet," I want to offer suggestions for crafting a new monetary system that considers the social practice of money as not only a repeating proleptic "realization of the eschaton, but at the same time as a movement toward the eschaton."[3] Every economic transaction, every stepping into the social practice of money could and should be seen as an economic *synaxis*[4] that anticipates the eschatological gathering of the whole people of God. If economic development or financial transactions exclude certain persons or groups at the national level or certain economies at the international level, then the social practice of money cannot anticipate the eschatological gathering of all God's people. In this sense, I view every economic exchange or participation as not mere means of acquiring a product or service. It is also a living and concrete expression of a *catholicity* of the social practices of money which is itself a movement toward the eschaton. To specify how all this can be done is the task of the following sections in this chapter. The aim is to fashion a vision of the international monetary system as an image of the triune God.

Let me now outline my procedure. The arguments are divided into four sections. In section 1, I will clarify Tillich's notion of the first root of trinitarian thinking. Without a thorough grounding in the intricacies of this theology it would be difficult for the reader to follow the conceptual moves I am going to make when I adapt the theology to the analysis of money. In section 2, I discuss the typological-structural tension in the dynamics of a few national currencies as an exchange media in the global trade and payment system. It is here that I present my concept of a global money form which I have called *Earth Dollar*. In section 3, I show how we are to think theologically about the relationships between national currencies and the *Earth Dollar* in a manner that is consistent with a perichoretic understanding of the dynamic relations of the triune God. It is in this section that I draw from the nuanced and rigorous social trinitarianism of Yale University systematic theologian Volf to guide me as I chart the terrain of the theological study of monetary flows. Concluding thoughts follow in section 4. I will discuss the potential benefits of the *Earth-dollar* system for the Global South in the next chapter.

SECTION 1: TRINITARIAN THINKING: THE TENSION BETWEEN THE ABSOLUTE AND CONCRETE ELEMENTS

Tillich maintains that there is a tension between the concrete and the ultimate in a human's ultimate concern and in every idea of God.[5] This is the first root of the process of trinitarian thinking. He posits that God must be both concrete and absolute and that the two elements are united. This first root is at the core of Christians' knowledge of God. When they talk about Jesus the Christ as the *Logos*, a question arises about the relationship between the universal *Logos* which is common to all creation and the *logos* of a particular human being. How is Jesus the Christ the perfect concrete manifestation of the ultimate, the absolutely unconditional?

He substantiates his position about the existence of the first principle in every idea of God by examining its presence in forms of polytheism and monotheism.[6] These two forms are relevant for understanding the history of religions in the world. "The concreteness of man's ultimate concern drives him toward polytheistic structures; the reaction of the absolute element against these drives him toward monotheistic structures; and the need for a balance between the concrete and the absolute drives him toward trinitarian structures."[7]

Tillich argues that the tension between the concrete and the universal which is inherent in polytheistic religions is not properly balanced or well integrated. There are three types of polytheism, according to him: universalistic, mythological, and dualistic.[8] In the universalistic variant, it is believed that God or divinity is hidden behind all concrete things and at the same time is manifest through them. They (concrete things) are depicted to be embodiments of a universal, all-pervading sacred power (*mana*). But there is neither full universality (ultimacy) nor full concreteness. The possible resolution of this tension points to trinitarian thinking. In the mythological type of polytheism there are deities with fixed characters and personifications of broad realms of being and value. The tension of concreteness and universality is also manifested in mythological polytheism: the personification of the divine powers is an evidence of the concern for concreteness. The ultimate concern impels the religious imagination to put the mythological gods in hierarchy and one or the other at a particular concrete situation or moment is addressed as ultimate. The third dualist type of polytheism is driven by the concept of the holy and the conflict between divine and demonic holiness such that divinities are basically grouped into two classes. Divine holiness is concentrated in one realm and demonic holiness in another realm. Each class or ultimate is only ultimate in its own realm. It is believed that ultimately the good will embrace itself and its opposite to become the overall ultimate. Tillich concludes his analysis of polytheism by saying that:

> Polytheism could not exist unless it included monotheistic elements. But in all types of polytheism the concrete element in the idea of God prevails over the element of ultimacy. In monotheism the opposite is the case. The divine powers of polytheism are subjected to a highest divine power. However, just as there is no absolute polytheism, so there is no absolute monotheism. The concrete element in the idea of God cannot be destroyed.[9]

There are four types of monotheism: monarchical, mystical, exclusive, and trinitarian.[10] In the first type there is one god that rules over all others and according to Tillich this type lies between polytheism and monotheism. Tillich's description of monarchical monotheism is so telling about, and so analogical to, the current nature of the imperial currency system in the global financial architecture that I will quote him at length here. It shows the relevance of trinitarian thinking both for revealing the existential tensions and questions in the global monetary system and also for addressing its shortcomings. In a monarchical monotheism, Tillich writes:

> The god-monarch rules over the hierarchy of inferior gods and godlike beings. He represents the power and value of the hierarchy. His end would be the end of all those ruled by him. The conflicts between the gods are reduced by his power; he determines the order of values. Therefore, he can easily be identified with the ultimate in being and value. . . . On the other hand, he is not secure against attacks from other divine powers. Like every monarch, he is threatened by revolution or by outside attack.[11]

The concrete side of the god of monarchical monotheism is revealed by his manifold manifestations in form of lower divinities or the procreation of half-gods. The second type of monotheism is mysticism. The idea of God in mysticism is one-sided as the element of ultimacy has swallowed the element of concreteness.[12] In *The Courage to Be*, he states that "mysticism does not take seriously the concrete and the doubt concerning the concrete. It plunges directly into the ground of being and meaning, and leaves the concrete, the world of finite values and meanings, behind."[13]

The third type is exclusive monotheism. Tillich identifies this with the God of Israel. In exclusive monotheism there is the elevation of a concrete god to ultimacy and universality without the loss of his concreteness and without the assertion of a demonic claim.

> The God of Israel is the concrete God who has led his people out of Egypt. . . . At the same time, he claims to be the God who judges the gods of the nations. . . . This God who is concrete and absolute at the same time is a "jealous God;" he cannot tolerate any divine claim besides his own. Of course, such a claim could be what we have called "demonic," the claim of something conditioned to be unconditioned. But this is not true in Israel. Yahweh does not claim universality in the name of a particular quality or in the name of his nation and its particular qualities. His claim is not imperialistic, for it is made in the name of that principle which implies ultimacy and universality—the principle of justice.[14]

Yet like mystical monotheism, Tillich believes, exclusive-monotheism's concept of God is partial as it seeks to eliminate the concrete element in the human experience. The need for the expression of the concrete element in human ultimate concern posits the trinitarian problem. In trinitarian monotheism the ultimate and concrete are united. It is a mistake, Tillich argues, to see trinitarian monotheism as quantitative concept; it is rather a qualitative characterization of God—a way of talking about God as a living being. In trinitarian monotheism, the God who is absolutely transcendent and unapproachable becomes also concrete and present in time and space. He argues that the more the distance between God and human beings increases, the trinitarian problem becomes more urgent and acute as "the concrete element demands its rights."[15] So in cognizance of this tension he writes:

> In the first consideration we have found that the more the ultimacy in our ultimate concern is emphasized, the more the religious need for a concrete manifestation of the divine develops, and that the tension between the absolute and the concrete elements in the idea of God drives toward the establishment of divine figures between God and man. It is the possible conflict between these figures and the ultimacy of the ultimate which motivates the trinitarian symbolism in many religions and which remained effective in the trinitarian discussion of the early church. The danger of falling into the tritheism and the attempts to avoid this danger were rooted in the inner tension between the ultimate and the concrete.[16]

Tillich thinks that the Trinity is the best response to questions implied in human's predicament[17] and his understanding and treatment of major theological and philosophical subjects (such as revelation, epistemology, hermeneutics, ontology, life, and Christology) is inherently trinitarian.[18]

In view of the prevalence of trinitarian framework for the expression of his ideas, his insistence that no being can be separated from the ground of its being, and his belief that every thing in the world is potentially a vehicle through which (trinitarian) revelation can take place, theologian Ronald Bruce Maclennan proposed that an adaptation of Tillich's well-known formula be made. He proposed changing "culture is the form of religion and religion is the substance of culture" to "the world is the form of Trinity, and the Trinity is the substance of the world."[19]

Before I proceed to apply and extend Tillich's trinitarian framework to the global monetary system, I do need to clarify how the notion of Trinity is functioning in this study. The application of Tillich's notion of trinitarian monotheism with a particular perichoretic understanding of the Trinity to the global monetary system is not premised on any notion of *vestigia trinitatis* (vestige of the Trinity in creation).[20] Nor am I making use of the Trinity to project human ideals onto the Godhead or to model God on any ideal of how humans or nations should live together in the twenty-first-century international community.[21] What exactly are you doing?, you may ask me. I will attempt to answer this question in the next section.

SECTION 2: CHARACTER AND NECESSITY OF A SINGLE GLOBAL MONEY

Theological Orientation for Thinking about a Single Global Money

In what follows, I will try to ground the institution of international money theologically by first discussing the typological-structural tension in the dynamics of national currencies as exchange media. This section takes Tillich's typology and structural tension of religions (as found in the various forms of polytheism and monotheism) and applies them to money and the international currency-exchange system.

Let me bring Tillich's crucial thought to the fore. In the idea of God there is a tension between the absolute and the concrete elements. Tillich summarizes the essence of his thesis this way: human beings' need for concreteness in their ultimate concern moves them toward polytheism; but the reaction of the absolute element in the idea of God drives them toward monotheism. The need for balance between two drives is what moves religious systems to trinitarian structure.[22] Now, let us transpose this theological vision into a model for reflecting on international money. The concreteness, particularistic nature of money, drives money toward several national currencies—to *polymediastic*[23] structures and the reaction of its imperialistic element against this drives it toward *monomediastic* structures, as operative in few global vehicular currencies. The need for a balance between these forces calls for trinitarian structures.[24]

Polymediasm is not a quantitative concept but a qualitative one. The existence of multiple currencies is not a quantitative phenomenon, not a plurality of monies, as the concept of money is the same everywhere. It is not the plurality of money *per se* that we are dealing with but a lack of a uniting and transcending single currency,[25] a legal manifestation of money. Each national currency claims ultimacy in the economy of its origin and tries as much as possible to disregard claims made by other national currencies. Nation's central banks and finance ministries often function to do just this. This claim of full concreteness and particularism conflicts with the possible transcending ultimacy of a global currency.

Also, polymediasm cannot survive without the restrictions placed on it by monomediastic elements (in itself and from other currencies). A first restriction from monomediasm comes from the elements of monomediastic ultimacy that struggle with the elements of polymediasm. As we have argued, every national currency embeds a set of logic and dynamic to transcend its borders; but to effectively do this it has to have the production and trade strength in the global marketplace and also contend with other currencies already in the international marketplace or attempting to do so. In a given moment of economic transaction within a national boundary a particular currency is the ultimate, the lord of all economic transactions. The truth is that in another transaction, in which another currency is involved, a different currency might assume the same role.[26]

A second set of restrictions that monomediasm manifests in polymediasm concerns the hierarchical organization in the foreign exchange realm which is daily undertaken by foreign exchange traders in places like New York, Frankfurt, Tokyo, and London. These priests of the economic domain both in the past and now prepare a way for the monarchical type of monomediasm. The world had seen the Spanish dollar, Dutch guilder, British pound of the past, and now the dollar, euro, and yen. These vehicular currencies at one time or the other ruled over the hierarchy of inferior currencies or money-like forms. Like every monarch they are, or were, threatened by attacks from within or outside.

A third kind of restriction from monomediasm is evident if we recall the necessity that all local national currencies are subject to a higher principle—the sum of logic, dynamics, and forces of the international economic scene—before whom they are really powerless in spite of their spirited effort to mediate their local economies and the global one. In this way, their sovereignty, arbitrariness, and claims of ultimacy[27] are limited, and at the same time the path of a global vehicular currency is prepared right before them.

Monomediasm as manifested in vehicular currencies all throughout history has two basic problems. The first problem is that there is an elevation of a particularistic and concrete currency to ultimacy and universality outside its borders without the loss of particularism, the "production ground" (depth) from which it comes and in which it disappears. This type of currency, like the America dollar or the British pound before it, which is concrete and absolute at the same time, is a jealous currency. A monomediastic currency claims there is no other currency beside it. But this claim is not right. Such claims are made in the name of their nations and their particular qualities. Their role and reign in the global marketplace are not independent of their nations and are not in the name of principles which are valid for all nations. They do not imply ultimacy and universality[28]—key principles of justice.[29] The principles of international financial and trade management (principles of domination and perpetuation of elitism) adopted by nations, which in the past and now have issued the self-absolutizing vehicular and reserve currencies, are not valid for all nations.

The second problem with monomediasm is that a monomediastic currency like the dollar rules the rest of the currencies and, as we have clearly seen, determines the order of values in the international marketplace. By this and its imperialistic claims, it tries to collapse and swallow the imperialistic tendencies of all local national currencies so no claim of ultimacy can be made by any other currencies. It transcends or attempts to transcend them all.

The solution to these problems is to have a universal currency that can really claim ultimacy and be uncontrolled by any local interest while maintaining the concrete element in the idea of money; that is, a currency that can participate in national destiny in spite of its power to conquer national imperialisms and interests. It can do this only if as a global currency it transcends the tension between the particularity and universal tendencies of all legal forms of money. This would be money that is absolutely concrete and absolutely universal at the same time. How can a currency be at the same time absolutely concrete and absolutely universal?

> It seems paradoxical if one says that only that which is absolutely concrete can also be absolutely universal and vice versa, but it describes the situation adequately. Something that is merely abstract has a limited universality because it is restricted to the realities from which it is abstracted. Something that is merely particular has a limited concreteness because it must exclude other particular realities in order to maintain itself as concrete. Only that which has the power of representing everything particular is absolutely concrete. And only that which has the power of representing everything abstract is absolutely universal. This leads to a point where absolutely concrete and absolutely universal are identical.[30]

This condition will be met in the area of international currency system by creating a supranational money, which I will call the *Earth Dollar*, which has to meet four crucial conditions. Before laying out these conditions I need to describe the global trade and payment system so the necessity and validity of these conditions will become apparent to all and save this writer from charges of arbitrariness.

The Inadequacy of Global Trade and Payment System Today

In recent times, especially with the Mexican and Asian financial crises, there has been talk about reforming the international system of monetary regime (money creation, credit extension, and management of the trade and payment system). Suggestions ranging from increased surveillance of developing countries by the International Monetary Fund, increasing the capital base of the Bretton Woods Institutions, to global bankruptcy court for countries teetering at the edge of default or in financial distress, have been argued as solutions. All the talks conveniently assume that the global monetary regime is fundamentally sound. The current system, whereby certain key currencies dominate the world trade and payment systems, whereby credit extension is controlled by a few transnational banks of the countries of issue of these currencies, whereby the adjustment burden of the system is not fairly distributed, is prone to instability because of the conflicting national interests and profit motive of banks. If the current international monetary regime was adequate and robust for the present level and sophistication of global trade and capital flows, then the suggestions offered would have merit.

Unfortunately, the adequacy and robustness are not present. More thoroughgoing transformations are necessary. The present global economy characterized by unprecedented global trade and capital movements will require at the minimum four conditions for its efficient, fair, and stable functioning.[31] First, what is needed is an international agreement on world money, its acceptable form, and creation; second, the "regulation" of exchange rates which include, among others, policies for the support of national currencies; third, a fairer system of settlement of debts and payment obligations by nation-states also needs to be put in place. Finally, there is the need for the reorganization of the international credit system and its allocation of resources. This will involve, among others, the stabilization of the relations between creditors and debtors and an institution to act as the lender of last resort. The third and the fourth conditions could be grouped as thus: the requirement of balancing capital flows.

There is nothing new about the four conditions of a stable international monetary regime as spelled out above. They all exist in their basic forms currently. But as they exist and function they are not in congruence with the level and sophistication of the global economic system. The problem is that capitalism is in the global accumulation phase but the means of exchange are still national currencies, instead of supranational money form. This is all the worse because we have three key currencies (dollar, euro, and yen) with the dangerous potentials for the formation of hegemonic spheres of influence. History has clearly shown that the formation of hegemonic spheres leads to war and adversarial relations. In keeping with history and for the sake of sustainable peace, the four conditions as identified above need to be organized to suit the present phase of the capitalist accumulation process.

The changes that will align world money forms to the global capitalist accumulation phase will require at least the fundamental restructuring of the Bretton Woods system. The Bretton Woods system, which established the dollar standard in 1944, is flawed today. An examination of the origin and framework of the Bretton Woods system will make this point clearer. At the end of Second World War, the United States was the undisputed leader of the world. It was, therefore, able to impose its currency as the key, vehicular, and reserve currency of the world. It was not just a matter of negotiation skills that Keynes' Bancor Plan, sponsored by the United Kingdom, was defeated in favor of the plan put forward by Harry Dexter White of the United States Treasury Department. The United States' plan—centered around stabilization scheme, the International Monetary Fund (IMF) and dollar-based gold exchange standard—was imposed on the world because of America's position of absolute dominance. The benign aspect of this domination was that the U.S. was aware of its responsibility as the issuer of world money in terms of satisfying the second, third, and fourth conditions of an international monetary system as identified above.

The United States, like Britain before it and Germany and Japan after it, achieved its position of world economic dominance by running trade surpluses[32] with the rest of the world. The running of trade surpluses and the issuance of world money demand the responsibility of providing liquidity to the world for the purposes of trade and capital movements. The only way the issuer of world money could generate the currencies outflow needed to create the necessary liquidity is to run balance of payment deficits. Since it runs surpluses, it has to have deficits in its capital accounts—that is, encourage massive capital exports. The United States met this requirement by capital exports under the North Atlantic Treaty Organization (NATO) program, the Marshall Plan, forms of official aid, and direct overseas investments by its firms.

General Agreement on Tariffs and Trade (GATT) was established to promote trade and capital flows. The IMF was set up to force adjustment programs and to provide short-term liquidity to countries with balance-of-payment problems. The World Bank provided cheap long-term investment capital. Indeed, the United States did an excellent job of fulfilling almost all the requirements for the functioning of a global monetary regime. Yet the system violated the principle of credit money—it broke the first of our four conditions. The use of the dollar (and later the mark/euro and yen) as the world currency violates the principle that money creation must be placed outside the markets for goods and services—that no participant should have the privilege of seigniorage, making purchases by issuing its own currency.

The current international system is also flawed in another respect, especially when viewed from the angle of global debt crisis or the sudden collapse of national currencies due to flight of "hot money." There are two sides to the global debt crisis or the violent depreciation of the currencies of developing countries. There is the side of credit overextension by private banks. Private bank money creation, as the history of national and international debt crises (and the recent subprime mortgage debacle) has shown, is very prone to credit overextension and subsequent violent contractions. Private multinational banks (and private institutional investors) over-extend credit to nation-states because of profit motive. On the other hand, owing to countries having easy access to credit (e.g., Euroloans and "hot money"), necessary adjustments are delayed until too much debt is loaded on poor, fragile economies. The actions of both parties violate the principle of sound imperial currency-regime management: the issuer of imperial currency should not permit credit overextension, and it should not fail to demand timely adjustment. [33] In the currency-board system operated by Britain from 1912 to 1962, the colonies were not allowed to incur deficits, and their internal money supplies were linked one to one with their external sterling surpluses. The external value of their currencies was linked to the pound sterling. Running deficits meant drawing down on sterling balances and the attendant canceling of an equivalent sum of domestic money. This two-pronged action promoted balance of payment adjustment. Consequently, there was no debt crisis and the currencies of the colonies were as strong as the sterling. While one is not advocating a return to currency-board system, it is pertinent to note that an imperial power must obey the rules of imperial currency management or its should be ready to be a lender of last resort to all, both developed and developing countries.

The second dimension of the debt and currency crises relates to the surplus countries. Countries which run up surpluses in their trade accounts have little or no interest in helping deficit countries to grow out of their problem, and are unwilling to bear their fair share of the burden of global adjustment. Instead of channeling surplus foreign exchange reserves into growth in deficit countries they are fed into investment outlets within the developed world. The overall consequence of all this is uneven development, lack of orderly and timely adjustments and disorderly balance of trade patterns. The debt crises, the monarchical reign of few currencies in the global trade and payment system, and the reaping of seigniorage by a few countries are reflections of the international monetary system of which the so-called saviors like the Bretton Woods Institutions, the dollar, euro, and the yen are an integral part. [34]

Understanding the *Earth Dollar*

What new international monetary system do we propose or imagine? The starting point is with the creation of a supranational money, the *Earth Dollar*, which must satisfy four *requirements*, each of which is a modified form of the previously mentioned *four conditions*. [35] First, the *Earth Dollar* must be created and issued by a central democratic agent outside the marketplace. This agent could be created afresh by consensus of the international community. For now we call this agent, *Earth Central Bank*. It is conceivable that just as the European nations came together, after several false starts and delays and political struggles, to create and organize the European Central Bank, a similar institution may eventually emerge to control the issue of the *Earth Dollar*.

Not only will this first *requirement* ensure that its creation will be free from seigniorage, but also it will ensure that it serves as an effective unit of account. In the current international system all currencies are valued in terms of the key currency, the American dollar. A tautology arises when the dollar is itself valued in terms of other currencies when it is supposed to define them in the first place. *Earth Dollar* will serve as a numeraire so that all national currencies are valued on this basis. The second *requirement* is this: *Earth Dollar* will serve as a simultaneous asset and liability for both issuer and user. Third, the circulation of *Earth Dollar* will be limited to the global payment and settlement system. It will serve all transactions between countries, and national currencies will be limited to circulation within their respective countries. This is the *fourth requirement*: *Earth Dollar* will serve as an international extension of all national currencies. Central banks will keep reserve accounts with the issuing authority, a truly global body to be created. As suggested above, we can call this global authoritythe *Earth Central Bank*. Let me take a brief moment to explain what some of these *requirements* are meant to do.

The second *requirement* (stated above) of the new international system is there to address the need to balance transfers of capital resources. The *Earth Central Bank* will channel reserves of surplus countries to deficit countries to cover reserve deficiencies and finance development projects. Borrowing of deficit countries will be limited to predetermined quotas and once quotas are reached adjustment programs will be required of deficit countries. Free from the profit motive of private banks, the issuing authority is most likely to avoid credit overextension and show more understanding of the needs of deficit countries. It would (should) be able to devise means to make foreign lending counter-cyclical, thus avoiding the pro-cyclical lending pattern of transnational private banks; or at the minimum rediscount notes only in crisis.

The *fourth requirement* is there to inform the determination of exchange rates, fixed but adjustable exchange rates. Currencies will be valued in terms of *Earth Dollar* which acts as the numeraire. The exchange rates will be subject to periodic adjustment to reflect purchasing power differentials and trading imbalances. To spread the burden of adjustment fairly, not only will currencies of chronic deficit countries be depreciated, the *Earth Dollar* prices of currencies of chronic surplus countries have to be raised. Surplus countries will also be required to undertake policy corrections, as advised by the publicly controlled Earth Central Bank[36] which will be created to operate the system of the *Earth Dollar*. Thus, the *Earth Dollar* system will, hopefully, correct the current imbalance of the international monetary system which places most, if not all, of the adjustment burden on deficit, weak, debtor nation-states. The preceding discussion should not be construed to mean that this is all there is to the details of reorganizing the international trade and payment system. *Earth Dollar* and the conditions I have appended to it for proper and equitable functioning of the global monetary system is only meant to stimulate thinking. At the appropriate time one could, with monetary experts and representatives of economies, crank out a full orbed system.

Theologically, how can we conceive the exact relationship between national currencies and *Earth Dollar* as proposed above? Put differently, how can we think of the proposed monetary system in terms of a theological model? What I will be doing shortly is to conceive the global monetary system as a trinitarian model of the global monetary system in an attempt to address the issues and crisis of today's monetary system.

The starting point for this kind of experimental *modeling* is to lay out a nonhierarchical theory of the Trinity. For Christian theologians, one viable approach is to think of the current global set of national currencies as an "ecclesiality" of currencies, conceiving it in the same way as theologians (such as Volf) conceive structures within and between local churches as bearing resemblance to the structure of communality in the Trinity. There are different ecclesiastic structures and the question is which one of them is most appropriate for our limited purpose? I considered the Roman-papal Catholic model but rejected it. Given that one does not posit or assume a world governmental authority, one need not say a national currency receives its "being" or existence from the *Earth Dollar* as local churches receive their "being" from *communio sanctorum* as in Roman Catholic ecclesiology. The local *ecclesia* is a church only from and toward the larger church, the *communio ecclesiarum*.[37] Next, I considered the Eastern Church model and rejected it also because of its understanding of the basic structure of communality in the Trinity in which the local church alone is church but in communion with other churches and the relationship between the universal church and local church is such that "every local church *is* . . . the universal church at a particular place of its concretization."[38] In Orthodox ecclesiology the local churches are considered as concretizations of the universal church. I do not consider the local (national) currencies in the proposed system as concretizations of the *Earth Dollar*. I think that *Earth Dollar* as world money should enjoy (some) precedence before national currencies in the global trade and payment system and not exist only as national currencies, but rather as subject-numeraire existing apart from local currencies. On the whole, my thinking about the *Earth Dollar* is influenced by an explicit trinitarian principle relating to a living God and a certain implicit ecclesiology which is itself shaped by a certain understanding of the Trinity. My *currency-ecclesiology* goes like this: the local church (persons in it and between it and others) has some kind of intraecclesial correspondence to the Trinity. The Trinity is a communion of interdependent divine persons and the relations in it are not monocentric or bipolar but symmetrical.[39] This argument might be transferred to currencies in the international monetary system. The local (national) currency in the system I am proposing would have some kind of intraecclesial correspondence to the *Earth Dollar*. The *Earth Dollar* is "communion" of interdependent national currencies and the relations in it are not monarchical, monocentric, or bipolar. And I need to make this quick point which I will explain more fully below. All national currencies and their values are related to the *Earth Dollar*. It is not the mutual perichoresis of national currencies but rather the value conditioning ("indwelling") of the *Earth Dollar* common to all of them that makes the national economies into a "communion corresponding to the Trinity." Needless for me to state, it is only in a metaphorical sense[40] that we can talk about the gathering of currencies as an ecclesia or expression of the trinitarian communion, and perhaps the metaphor works best for Christians with some experience of "ecclesia," the church, and churches.

The principal way and manner I have so far conceived international money derives from the Tillichian trinitarian principle as applied to money and to the structural dynamics of money as an exchange medium. The next area of discussion is a model of interaction in which both the national economy and world community are given their proper due and in a way that promotes inclusive catholic sociality. The theme of interest to me is the structure (*logic*, the principle of coherence) of the communion at the trinitarian and *financial-polity* levels. While in the preceding discussions I have principally drawn from Paul Tillich's theology, here I will primarily draw from that of Miroslav Volf. Since this is not a work about theories and theologies of the Trinity, I do not intend to go into tedious academic discussions and controversies concerning the doctrine of the Trinity in Christian thought. What I undertake is a more modest task: to transpose into new economic terms and monetary and managerial arguments that which I distill from the perichoretic trinitarian understanding of Volf and a few other contemporary theologians.[41] In this process we can enrich the tradition of extending the features of trinitarian communion to social unities by bringing it into dialogue with organizational models of the international trade and payment system. To this task we now turn.

SECTION 3: THE TRINITY AS A MODEL OF THE INTERNATIONAL FINANCIAL SYSTEM

A Theological Model of Global Money

Theologically, how are we to think about the relationship between the currencies and *Earth Dollar* that is consistent with a perichoretic understanding of the Trinity? In the trinitarian model of international monetary system, each national currency stands in relation not only to other currencies, but is also an economic center of action internal to the other currencies. Contrary to what we have seen in chapter 6 when only the key vehicular and reserve currencies are the economic centers of actions in other currencies, *Earth Dollar* coincides with the communion of all national currencies. This view of global money dispenses entirely with the notion of one numerically identical nature in terms of commodity (gold or silver) or political and economic substance of an imperial currency and instead conceives the unity of global money *perichoretically*. [42]

The task before us now is to show how the relations between the national currencies are to be conceived in trinitarian terms. This is an analogy that cannot be pushed too far because we cannot reasonably conceive of national currencies in strict correspondence to the trinitarian persons. As borrowed from theology, *perichoresis* of currencies refers to the "reciprocal interiority" of the national currencies in the *Earth Dollar* system. To paraphrase Volf, I will say that in every national currency as a subject in the proposed international exchange system, the other currencies also "indwell" it; all values mutually permeate one another. [43] How can this be explained in terms of the mathematics of fixed but adjustable exchange rate?

In the proposed *Earth Dollar* system, the value of national currency is not only about itself, but rather carries within itself the values of the other national currencies. This mutual interiority and catholicity is brought about because the fixed exchange value of a currency would be set with regard to three considerations: (1) the productivity (production and trade volume) of an economy; (2) accounting for the relative positions of other economies; and (3), the exchange rates are subjected to periodic adjustment to reflect purchasing power differentials and trading balances. To spread the burden of adjustment fairly not only would currencies of chronic deficit economies be depreciated, the *Earth Dollar* prices of the currencies of surplus economies would be raised.

There are two possible objections to my conceptualization of the *Earth Dollar* system in terms of the dynamic relations of the triune God. First, someone may argue that rates in today's exchange rate table already impound all information about mutual interiority and the system of exchange value between currencies is also already catholic, so I have not offered anything new with the *Earth Dollar* system. This argument is not correct for three reasons. Number one, today's adjustment burdens and development lags are not borne equally by all currencies—no mutual giving and receiving. The supposed equality[44] (as in my income last year is equal to a certain portion of billionaire Bill Gates' income) is just a mathematical after-product and really does not impound information about equitable burden sharing. I will give some reasons for thinking in this manner.

The dominant, vehicular, imperial currency is always a reference to the whole set of currencies and the set cannot be properly conceived without the unity of referents grounded in the imperial currency or system of imperial currencies. In the imperial system of currency management, the principle of the relationship between the imperial currency and the whole set is derived from a hierarchical doctrine of a center-periphery relation in which the leading currency is dominant. This is far from a symmetrical understanding of exchange relations between national economies. But in the common *Earth Dollar* system a national currency stands in correlation to all—they can all condition the value of the *Earth Dollar* in order that all national economies can grow and share adjustment burden—generating a polycentric structure of exchange rate system.

A second response to this first objection must be made. Even when the American dollar or the euro "indwells," for example, the Nigerian naira, Ghanaian cedi, or Haitian gourde; it does so in an undemocratic way, different from the proposed *Earth Dollar*'s mutual interiority and catholicity. For the interiority is not symmetrically reciprocal. Naira, cedi, gourde are neither internal to the American dollar as subjects, nor subjects of American monetary policies' action in ways similar to how the American dollar-monetary policy is the subject of theirs. America can export its inflation, its adjustment burden, and *bloweth where it listeth, and the naira hearest the sound thereof, but canst not tell whence it cometh, and whither it goeth.* The naira lacks the power of the dollar. Vehicular and reserved currencies (dollar, euro, yen) "indwell" other lesser national currencies like the *naira, cedi, gourde,* whereas the lesser currencies by constraint indwell the value-destroying ambience of the key currencies, not the substance, the core of the key currencies (dominant economies).[45]

Yet, a third response to the first objection is necessary. The mutual interiority in the current global exchange rate system is catholic only in a quantitative sense—that of universality. What I am proposing in the *Earth Dollar* system, in contrast, is a qualitative understanding in that the global trade and payment system is catholic because a greater fullness of *participation* and *justice* is realized within it.[46] This qualitative understanding need not be separated from the catholicity of exchange rate system. The real question, however, is how this fullness of *participation* and *justice* is to be conceived? Fullness of participation and justice in a political economy, as I am thinking of it here, has three aspects. First, there is the opening of the local economy to all citizens and the equipping of all of them to participate equitably in it. Second, fullness of participation and justice demands economies that are opened up to one another. Such opening is necessary so that creative and developmental technologies and ideas are networked to enrich one another. Third, it is germane—especially for Christians, but perhaps also for many others with a sense of international justice—to open up the global monetary system to all nations through a social practice of money that anticipates the eschatological gathering of all God's people. If international financial transactions exclude certain persons at the national level or certain economies at the international level then the social practice of money cannot anticipate the eschatological gathering of all God's people.[47]

Now let us turn to a possible second objection to my transplanting of the trinitarian structures to the global trade and payment system. One can object that the mutual giving and receiving in the monetary system cannot be carried out in the fashion of perichoretic trinity insofar as national currencies are still independent entities or *subjects,* [48] regardless of any level of multilateral agreement between countries. This is the sense that even selfless love between two persons cannot erase the subjectivity of either the beloved thou or the loving self. This objection can stand only if we ignore the character of the *Earth Dollar* global money form. The unity of the plural national currencies is grounded in the interiority of the *Earth Dollar.* All national currencies and their values are related to the *Earth Dollar.* The *Earth Dollar* is the one currency in the many national currencies. It is not the mutual perichoresis of national currencies, but rather the value conditioning ("indwelling") of the *Earth Dollar* common to all of them that makes the national economies into a "communion corresponding to the Trinity."[49] To clarify this point for readers who may not be familiar with nuanced distinctions about perichoresis being made here, I will quote Volf who was similarly led by his application of the notion of the Trinity to the church to make similar fine distinctions. He asked this question: in what does the comparison between divine and human [national] unity consist? His answer, which I quote at length, is this:

> This theological consideration is confirmed exegetically insofar as the statement "as you, Father, are in me and I am in you" is continued not by "may they also be *in one another*," but rather by "may they also be *in us*." Human beings can be in the triune God only insofar as the Son is in them (John 17:23; 14:20); if the Son is in them, then so also is the love with which the Father loves the Son (John 17:26). Because the Son indwells human beings through the Spirit, however, *the unity of the church is grounded in the interiority of the Spirit*—and with the Spirit also in the interiority of the other divine persons—in *Christians*. The Holy Spirit is the "one person *in* many persons." It is not the mutual perichoresis of human beings, but rather the indwelling of the Spirit common to everyone that makes the church into a communion corresponding to the Trinity, a communion in which personhood and sociality are equiprimal. Just as God constitutes human beings through their social and natural relations as independent persons, so also does the Holy Spirit indwelling them constitute them through ecclesial relations as an intimate communion of independent persons. As such they correspond to the unity of the triune God, and as such they are instantiations of the one church (italics in the original). [50]

So the point I am trying to get across is this. What makes for the perichoresis of the national currencies in the *Earth Dollar* system is not the mutuality of the national currencies; rather it is the indwelling of the *Earth Dollar* common to all of them that makes the various national currencies into some sort of communion that may be like unto the Trinity. The *Earth Dollar* constitutes each national currency through its exchange value-relations to it.

Before we proceed further, I need to insert a quick comment here to respond to another possible objection to the use of the Trinity to model the *Earth Dollar*. It is conceivable that someone may still say to me: the Trinity, for all its perichoretic wonder, often still conveys and leaves unchallenged certain patriarchal privilege—Father-Son motif, for example. This objector might go further to suggest that this unchallenged patriarchal metaphor in the trinitarian model could convey something problematic into the model of perichoretic international currency system. In order not to go too far afield, I will give only four responses. First, every metaphor or model, if taken too far, breaks down. This is so because a model or analogy is founded on another familiar phenomenon or institution as its aspiration, and only limited aspects of the familiar are incorporated into the model. [51] Second, models are based on abstraction of relevant features of the prototype—in this case, the Trinity. We have, for our limited purposes here, abstracted the relevant features of the common, non-hierarchical relationality of the dynamics of the triune God to use to reimagine the global monetary system. This is a common practice in model-building, but by no means is error-free. This is how social anthropologist Robin Horton puts it:

> Philosophers of science have often used the molecular (kinetic) theory of gases as an illustration of this feature of model-building. The molecular theory, of course, is based on an analogy with the behavior of fast-moving, spherical balls in various kinds of space. And the philosophers have pointed out that although many important properties of such balls have been incorporated into the definition of a molecule, other important properties such as color and temperature have been omitted.[52]

Though the two responses so far offered might pass muster with philosophers of science and economists, they may not satisfy theologians. So I will attempt to give two theological responses. At the heart of this model and what actually defines the envisioned relationality is the "indwelling property of the *Earth Dollar*." This property is couched in the idiom of the Holy Spirit, the understanding of the Spirit in communal life and development. The Spirit broadens and deepens relationships. A dynamic, cooperative relationship between nations is implied in the pneumatological understanding of the "ecclesiality of currencies." I am hoping that by my pneumatological emphasis, I am pointing to the emergence of "the underivable" as a flourishing of equality, a prevailing of freedom over all forms of the limitations implied in patriarchalism and hierarchicalism, and of the impulses to seek and realize unfulfilled possibilities in relationships. As Tillich once put it: "in the case of spirit, freedom prevails over determination, and the underivably new is created."[53]

I will make the final point by putting my proposal in the context of the work of the Holy Spirit in the proleptic realization of the eschatological gathering of the entire people of God. The creative life-giving and life-completing Spirit is an ecstatic One. It is the Spirit who goes out to draw in all those who are outside, who are beyond the "acceptable" limits. The ecstasy is directed toward the *other*, the one outside to bring him or her into relationship with the divine life.[54] With this in mind, I have proposed an alternative global trade and payment system as an ecstatic instrument for economic communion (*koinonia*) among peoples of the earth, whereby each nation will be caught up with the dynamism of the perichoresis of the "indwelling *Earth Dollar*." This way they will all, hopefully, experience the dynamism and abundance of global economic production. I am pressing forward for an ecstatic global money—ecstatic enough to include the poor nations and to be a pledge (αρρβών, *arrabon*) and foretaste of the eschatological gathering of all God's people.

Economic Orientations for Thinking about a Single Global Money

As it should now be obvious, the exchange rate system under the *Earth Dollar* system is where our "trinitarian theologizing" takes an empirical form, where it touches the ground, so to speak; and as such, it is the point in our theological-ethical reasoning where we should subject the system to economic scrutiny. If this work is not sufficiently *economistic in orientation*,[55] the "public-theology bridge" which it attempts to build across the yawning chasm between church and the public square has no foundation on the side of the public (Wall Street, in this particular case). In addition, if we try to formulate a trinitarian theology of money from some point outside of economics, we cannot authentically advocate for or operate our ideas within any point in the economic system in reference to which we can judge or control our theological understandings of the global financial system. Without a standpoint in economics (orthodox or heterodox) we will be talking only to ourselves and not be able to nudge the system toward the ideals of the church's notion of social justice.

Now the question is this: will our use of a fixed-adjustable exchange rate system pass muster with economists? There are basically two ways to approach this question, but I think only one is viable. Let us begin by presenting the one I consider unviable. We have noted that we need to find a point within economics with which we can test or control our trinitarian conceptions of the global financial system. This can be taken to mean finding some kind of inner coherence of theological ethics of money and economic science that can further serve as a bridge between church and the public square in the task of transforming the global trade and payment system. One place to start is to argue that human beings and nation-states are influenced (or should be influenced) by ethical considerations (such as the Socratic query, "how should one live?," or the Aristotelian question of how do we judge social achievement or "what may foster the good for men?"). Since theological ethics is about influencing behavior, then the task would then be to simply find an ethical "public reason" about ends that are relevant for modern positive economics. This approach, I am afraid, will not bring us to building the bridge because, for most economists working with modern logistic economic models, the issue is obviously not about ultimate ends but about appropriate means to serve assumed, given ends. As Amartya Sen, the Nobel laureate in economic science puts it, among the so-called positive economists there is "the eschewal of deep normative analysis, and the neglect of the influence of ethical consideration in the characterization of actual human behavior."[56] A workable solution would, therefore, be a position that will simultaneously satisfy positive economists and theological ethicists. This is where the fixed exchange rate system comes into consideration. The use of a fixed-adjustable exchange rate has been known to increase economic welfare and reduce volatility of exchange rates[57] and within the framework of the *Earth Dollar* system it can additionally encourage cooperative behavior among nations, thus also promoting the fullness of participation and justice.

If one can show that the *Earth Dollar* system (with its adjustable fixed exchange rate system) can pass muster with economists regardless of our ethical concern for fullness of participation and justice, and also if one can indicate that it has some respectable pedigree in the economics profession, then I would have achieved my target of generating some justification of the proposed system among those who do not care about theological justification. In this regard, I would point to John Maynard Keynes' proposal at the Bretton Woods[58] Conference, New Hampshire, which led to the formation of the World Bank and the IMF in July 1944. This is the more viable approach to the question of how my proposal might pass muster with economists.

When the forty-four allied nations met in the summer of 1944, the purpose was to craft an international economic order and currency cooperation mechanism for the post-Second World War global economy. Keynes, coming from thirty years of experience studying international monetary regimes and working with the British Treasury, posited the idea of an international reserve currency which he called "bancor." It would be managed by a supranational monetary authority, the International Clearing Union (ICU). Under this plan, this currency would serve as both trade currency and unit of account, and values of national currencies under the system would be fixed and linked to *bancor*. The exchange rate could only be adjusted by mutual agreement in recognition of changes in adjustment burdens and prices. With specified limits, deficit countries would be able to draw additional reserves to cover their overdrawn account as in the overdraft or check-covering system in the commercial banking sector. Both surplus and deficit countries whose balances go above or below preset limits were required to take corrective actions. In order to maintain equilibrium, prevent excessive imbalances, and ensure what we have called "mutual indwelling," Keynes planned for countries to pay a graduated range of charges according to levels of excess debits and credits in their *bancor* accounts with the clearing union. Surplus-countries wishing to avoid these charges could lend out their surpluses to deficit-countries. Deficit-countries also would have to devalue their currencies, put some control over capital exports or engage in austerity measures to bring its debit balances down. Keynes envisaged this mechanism as a way of forcing symmetrical adjustment among creditors and debtors.[59]

As you may have already noticed, Keynes' plan puts the accent on almost symmetrical interiority and catholicity. Each national currency was a subject internal to the others. The currencies of the dominant economies could not have the "bloweth-where-they-listeth" features and the currencies of the weaker, smaller, poorer countries were not constrained to indwell the value-destroying ambience of the currencies of the dominant economies.

This system was rejected by the American government, which had initially supported it, when it became obvious that the control of the system by the ICU would have deprived it of what it considered, at the time, the greatest spoils of victory. While Keynes had hoped to establish a truly multilateral system, with no nation in dominant position and deficit or surplus generating nations disciplined alike to equitably distribute the burden of balance of payment adjustment and make room for mutual economic growth and development; the American government argued and got its way with a system whereby all other currencies were tied to a dollar-gold anchor, putting the dollar in an unprecedented monarchical position. No doubt, one of the reasons behind Keynes radical ideas was to protect his beloved weakened Britain (a fallen issuer of global currency) from the dominance of America. He had learned firsthand the huge advantages an issuer of reserve and vehicular currency gained at the expense of the rest of the world. His ideas are still worth considering for the current age. As the economist Guttmann put it: "His radical ideas on money and trade, even though ultimately pushed aside by the Americans in favor of their own proposals at the Bretton Woods Conference in July 1944, have lost none of their relevance. They still deserve close scrutiny."[60]

The dollar-gold link established by the United States began to falter in the 1960s owing to dollar-overhang, more dollar circulating in the international market than what America's gold reserve could cover. Under the Bretton Woods system agreed to by the allied nations under the hegemonic direction of America, the price of the dollar was fixed to a gold value of $35 per ounce and central banks could convert their dollar reserves into gold at this price. But in the 1960s, because of what economists called the "Triffin Dilemma,"[61] the United States was not in a position to meet up with its obligation. As Guttmann put it:

> Due to redemptions and speculation, U.S. gold reserves declined from $22.7 billion in 1951 (equal to 68.3 percent of the non-Communist world's total gold reserves) to $17 billion (43.7 percent) in 1961 and $11.8 billion (29.9 percent) in 1970. During the same period total currency reserves of the capitalist world (except the United States), which were all supposedly convertible with U.S. gold reserves, rose from $13. 8 billion in 1951 to $21.3 billion in 1961 and $49.7 billion in 1970. By the late 1950s U.S. gold reserves no longer sufficed to back all dollars in international circulation.[62]

These problems, and the consequent restlessness of the international community over them, led to the introduction of the Special Drawing Rights (SDRs) in 1969 as a global liquidity device and substitute for dollar and gold. This money, inchoate as it was, was the first supranational money in the world. It was also the first international money that was backed by nothing—there was no underlying asset and it was not convertible into any hard assets.[63] Finally, international money had become a pure relationality—all that matters now is general acceptance. The IMF, which ran the system, also used a basket-of-currency valuation system which yielded more stable exchange rates between currencies. The system was not allowed to fulfill its potential partly because of the interest of the United States not to make the SDRs attractive to the point of becoming a threat to the reserve-currency status of the dollar and the other interest of surplus nations like Germany and Japan.[64]

Economist Jane D'Arista, a leading progressive thinker and longtime observer of the American economy and international monetary system, has offered a similar (to Keynes') proposal also aimed at encouraging increased participation of developing countries in the international monetary system and straightening out distorted credit flows in both national and international markets. Her plan is also geared toward helping to phase out the current system in which the default choice of reserve holdings is largely restricted to financial assets issued in a few countries whose wealth support the strength of their currencies. She also draws from Keynes' Bretton Woods proposal. As she puts it:

> While Keynes' plan was designed for a very different world, the basic structure in his concept—an international clearing agency (ICA)—could be updated to serve as the international platform for a new global payments system that encompasses more egalitarian objectives and fosters more balanced outcomes. The new ICA would clear transactions denominated in member-nations own currencies and adjust the ownership of reserves by crediting and debiting members clearing account, using a trade-weighted basket of currencies to value the international reserve assets [this is similar to my *Earth Dollar* concept]. [65]

Another move toward a common currency is the euro which was introduced in 1998 and has eliminated the maddening congeries of European national currencies in preference of one currency and has encouraged economies that are opened to each other. It took the Western European countries thirty years to go from multiplicity of national currencies to a common currency, the euro. The process required a major investment of political capital on the part of the countries involved.[66] The movement to a single currency embodied some of the ideas of reciprocity and mutual interiority we have highlighted in the *Earth Dollar* system.[67] The summary description of movement and cooperation that led up to euro by two of UNCTAD's (United Nations Conference on Trade and Development) economists is apt. Yulmaz Akyüz and Heiner Flassbeck wrote that:

> In the process leading up to a common currency, . . . both anchoring and anchor countries shared the common objective of achieving monetary convergence and internal and external stability for their currencies. The system was also designed to reduce one-way bets, which might have been encouraged by inflation and interest rate differentials, by establishing bands around the so-called "parity grids." It established obligations for *symmetric interventions* as well as unlimited short-term credit facilities among central banks designed to maintain bilateral exchange rates within the band. It also *made available to member countries various types of external payments support to enable ERM participants both to keep their currencies within prescribed fluctuation limit* and to cope with circumstances that might threaten orderly conditions in the market for a member country's currency. In addition, it stipulated concrete procedures for realignment of the bands. Furthermore, European integration allowed special arrangements in the ERM for the less advanced countries—Greece, Ireland, Portugal and Spain—including the provision of considerable fiscal compensation, which did much to enable them to achieve monetary and fiscal convergence and meet the EMU stability criteria" (italics added).[68]

Given the history of the movement toward the euro and other existential realities of the global capitalist system, one actually thinks that the path to one truly stateless, world money appears narrow, and the probability of securing agreement for it among all the economies of the world appears slim. All this should not make us lose hope. The logic and dynamics of contemporary capitalism and globalization which is driving towards pure immanence, the decentering of production and distribution, the sheer dynamics of money which leads it to cross national boundaries, and the prospects of economies (even in Africa) to move toward regional common currency and common market, make one think that the full working of the *telos* of capitalism will (may) lead to truly global currency without subordination and without supremacy, but perichoretic sociality. There is a time coming when "relationality and mutuality" will be at the heart of the global trade and payment system. According to monetary economist Guttmann, "such a money form is, in my opinion, the logical step in the evolution of contemporary capitalism, a distinct possibility as we complete our transition to a global accumulation regime."[69] I believe this point will be reached not only because of the economic trend identified in the preceding statements, but also because of political struggles, part of which will be persistent resistance to empire. Invisible and visible hands, as well as hands from the Global South clenched to hands from the Global North, have to work together to bring this vision to reality.

With the above analysis of development of world money—Keynes' Bancor Plan, the SDRs issued by the IMF, the Euro just to mention a few[70]—one can argue that our concept of *Earth Dollar* developed in this chapter can meet and indeed appears to have met the standard of mutual intelligibility or mutually critical correlation. It is sufficiently economistic in orientation to bridge the chasm between the church's concern for social justice and the global trade and payment system's interest in efficiency and vitality. The "mystery" of the global financial system is not regarded in this work as apophatic to theological inquiry. We have tried to formulate a trinitarian theology of money that could be inside economic science, but it should not be construed to mean that the economic analysis or the convergence between the trinitarian model of money and certain major views about the global financial system exhausts the theology of money. This is so, among other reasons, because the theology of money is always an attempt to offer a partial answer to the implicit question or questions that arise from the privilege, pain, and ambiguities of the monetary situation in any given era. I have consciously used the phrase "partial answer" to indicate that the answer provided by any theological system is not absolute, but fragmentary and anticipatory and it has to always give "ontological primacy to the future." [71] Volf is right when he argues that as the Christian theologian relativizes her own statements out of the realization that she is not pronouncing "theological judgments from the seat of the Final Judge," she must always be "ready to hear the voice of the Spirit of God in moral discourse of non-Christians (without forgetting, however, to apply a 'hermeneutic of suspicion' here too). Christian moral discourse is exclusive in the sense that it is based on the concept of new creation ushered by Christ, but it is also inclusive in the sense that it respects other traditions and is ready to learn from them because it is ready to hear from them also the voice of the Spirit of Christ." [72]

In addition, the theology of money needs to function as a critical partner in the contemporary economic discourses about money, intersection of money and development, and reforms concerning the global financial architecture. In this partnership, the task of the church is to show how the Spirit can break into "finite forms and drive them beyond themselves" [73] and thereby facilitate transformation of the social practice of money "toward ever-greater correspondence with the coming new creation." [74] As Jeffrey Stout has argued, arguments on the behalf of the whole public community should be accepted as legitimate and considered even if they proceed from religious or theological assumptions (here, trinitarian ones) that many in the public (here, say, economists) might not and need not embrace even if they accept some of the conclusions from religious and theological starting points.[75]

Indeed, theology of money also goes beyond the trinitarian model—which is just one theological perspective we have developed to enable fruitful dogmatic reflection on money. In so doing, we have provided ethical theological reflection on money within a type of theological framework that engages broad reflection on the nature and consequences of social practices with human capability development, nonhuman environment, and with God's eschatological purposes for creation. Theology of money's main task is to provide a *theological-ethical framework* for understanding money as a social practice and to bring into awareness the ethical principles that can inform efforts to assess and restructure the monetary system, the role of money in human development, and the economic development of countries in the still-open future.

SECTION 4: CONCLUSION

The theology that informs this chapter, and indeed has informed the entire book, is principally Tillich's notion of trinitarian principles. The ethics is in the ideological critique of the contemporary global monetary system which exposes the values and the hegemonic domination of the system that are threatening the moral order of the international community. The critique also reveals the ways the monarchical currency regime hinders participation in global monetary system and the economic progress of developing economies. I round off the ethics discourse with a re-imagination of an alternative to today's global monetary system. The envisioned system is geared to increase the participation of poor, developing countries and to subject the current global financial architecture to the demands of justice. This theological-ethical study was carried out in a continuous correlation with sociology, philosophy, and economics. In so doing, this book has presented an interconnected and interrelated way of reading, interpreting, evaluating, and envisioning the contemporary monetary situation.

NOTES

1. There is a slight difference between my proposal and the present structuring of the euro. In the euro, particularity is lost in favor of universality. My proposal balances universality with particularity. There is yet another area of difference. Speaking more accurately, *Earth Dollar* is not a single currency for the world as Euro is for the parts of Europe in the European Union, but it is a *numeraire* for in-

ternational, cross-border transactions. National currencies are alive but limited to circulating only within their own borders. At best *Earth Dollar* is only a preliminary stage toward the goal of a single global currency.

2. Martin Wolf, "We Need a Global Currency," *Financial Times* (August 3, 2004) http://search.ft.com/ftArticle?queryText=We+Need+a+Global+Currency&y=10 &aje=true&x=19&id=040803008394&ct=0. This is how he summed up his argument for a single global currency: "A world in which borrowing abroad is hugely dangerous for most relatively poor countries is undesirable. A world that compels the anchor currency country [the United States] to run huge current account deficits looks unstable. We should seek to lift these constraints. The simplest way to do so would be to add a global currency to a global economy. For emerging market economies, at least, this would be a huge boon."

3. Miroslav Volf, *After Our Likeness: The Church as the Image of the Trinity* (Grand Rapids, MI: William B. Eerdmans Co., 1998), 100.

4. *Synaxis* means "gathering or bringing together" in Greek. It is an early church word that is also used for synod and meeting for worship, especially to celebrate the Eucharist. Simply, it is a mode of sociality.

5. Paul Tillich, *Systematic Theology*, vol. 1, *Reason and Revelation, Being and God* (Chicago: University of Chicago Press, 1951), 224.

6. Tillich, *Systematic Theology*, vol. 1, 220–29.

7. Tillich, *Systematic Theology*, vol. 1, 221.

8. Tillich, *Systematic Theology*, vol. 1, 222–25.

9. Tillich, *Systematic Theology*, vol. 1, 225.

10. Tillich, *Systematic Theology*, vol. 1, 225–29.

11. Tillich, *Systematic Theology*, vol. 1, 225–26.

12. Tillich, *Systematic Theology*, vol. 1, 226.

13. Tillich, *The Courage to Be* (New Haven, CT: Yale University Press, 1952), 186. It is germane to note that this view of concreteness is qualified in another place. He also writes: "Yet even the most radical negation of the concrete element in the idea of God is not able to suppress the quest for concreteness. Mystical monotheism does not exclude divine powers in which the ultimate embodies itself temporally. And, once admitted, the gods can regain their lost significance, especially for people who are unable to grasp the ultimate in its purity and abstraction from everything concrete." See Tillich, *Systematic Theology*, vol. 1, 226.

14. Tillich, *Systematic Theology*, vol. 1, 227.

15. Tillich, *Systematic Theology*, vol. 1, 229.

16. Paul Tillich, *Systematic Theology*, vol. 3, *Life and the Spirit, History and the Kingdom of God* (Chicago: University of Chicago Press, 1965), 283–84.

17. Tillich, *Systematic Theology*, vol. 3, 285.

18. For a thorough study of this see Ronald Bruce Maclennan, "The Doctrine of the Trinity in the Theology of Paul Tillich," unpublished PhD dissertation (Chicago: Lutheran School of Theology, 1991), 435.

19. Maclennan, "The Doctrine of the Trinity in the Theology of Paul Tillich," 435. Maclennan maintains that for Tillich, the *analogia entis* is an *analogia trinitatis*. See pp. 452–63 of same text.

20. Karl Barth was right when he waxed eloquently against the idea that we can find traces of the Trinity in the creaturely world. See his *Church Dogmatics*, ed. G. W. Bromiley and T. F. Torrance (Edinburgh: T. & T. Clark, 1936), 1.1:389–99.

21. For a critique of the social theories of the Trinity see, Karen Kilby, "Perichoresis and Projection: Problems with the Doctrines of the Trinity," *New Blackfriars* 81, no. 956 (October 2000): 432–45.

22. Tillich, *Systematic Theology*, vol. 1, 221.

23. This is a word I made up to replace Tillich's "polytheistic." Money is a medium of exchange. "Mediastic" is formed from media or mediation.

24. Compare with Tillich, *Systematic Theology*, vol. 1, 221.

25. The euro in replacing all the multiple currencies of member-nations has become a uniting and transcending single currency for all member-nations of the European Union. It unites the former currencies into one and in so doing transcends each of them.

26. Of course, you are not going to notice this if you are living in monomediastic currency zone like the dollar or euro sphere.

27. Tillich uses the term *ultimacy* in a specific way. I am using it in this context to refer to the tendency of national currencies to assume the position of the key vehicular and reserve currency of the world. In chapter 6, I pointed to the imperialistic and expansionist tendencies of particular national currencies to become the global currency of choice for all international transactions.

28. Tillich links the idea and ideal of justice to ultimacy and universality. Justice has an overarching character and never ceases to be a demand for the self-fulfillment and self-affirmation of all persons and groups—the fulfillment of humanity in all individuals (universality). It is also a demand to destroy any claim of a particular person, institution, group or nation to be directly identified with the absolute (the ultimacy principle). It sets as its goal over all tensions among nations or groups, the overarching concept of humanity. Every claim arising from the power of origin is to be transformed and subjected to unconditional demands of justice and cleansed of its demonic powers of claiming ultimacy. Tillich, *The Socialist Decision*, trans. Franklin Sherman (New York: Harper & Row, [1933] 1977), 140–42, 151. See also Tillich, *Systematic Theology*, vol. 3, 143–44, 358. In another place, he writes: "Justice is the aim of all cultural actions which are directed toward the transformation of society . . . the fulfillment of the inner aim of all social groups and their mutual relations." Humanity is "the fulfillment of man's inner aim with respect to himself and his personal relations." For these quotes (from p. 67) and for discussions on these concepts see Tillich, *Systematic Theology*, vol. 3, 67–68, 75, 79–86, and 143.

29. Tillich, *Systematic Theology*, vol. 1, 227.

30. Tillich, *Systematic Theology*, vol. 1, 16–17.

31. I owe a heavy debt to Guttmann, *How Credit-Money Shapes the Economy* (Armonk, NY: M. E. Sharpe, 1994). This book helped shape my ideas about the international monetary system.

32. This means it earned more in exports than it spent on imports. China is doing the same today.

33. Wolf, *Why Globalization Works*, 278–304.

34. For a provocative analysis on the discourse and practice of development and on imperial intervention in the society and culture of poor countries in the guise of economic development, see Arturo Escobar, *Encountering Development: The Making and Unmaking of the Third World* (Princeton, NJ: Princeton University Press, 1995).

35. See Guttmann, *How Credit-Money Shapes the Economy*, 427–52.

36. By "publicly controlled," I do not mean as controlled by the public in stock market parlance. By this I mean that it is to be controlled by various "publics" as represented by their countries. I am not naïve to think that power will be equally shared by all nations. I hope that a working arrangement would be crafted as the Europeans have done with the European Central Bank or the American states with the Federal Reserve Board.

37. Volf, *After Our Likeness*, 29–72.

38. Volf, *After Our Likeness*, 201 (emphasis in the original). For a fuller discussion see pp. 73–123.

39. This is the basic position of Volf in *After Our Likeness*.

40. It is germane to mention that this analogy has to be handled with care as we cannot reasonably conceive of national currencies in strict correspondence to the trinitarian persons. Every theological model, as theologian Sallie McFague states, is always a judgment of similarity and difference between two worlds or thoughts. It is shot through with the tension of the "is and is not." See Sallie McFague, *Metaphorical Theology: Models of God in Religious Language* (Philadelphia: Fortress University Press, 1982), 51–65.

41. Volf, *After Our Likeness*, 24.

42. See Leonardo Boff, "The Liberating Design of God," in *Mysterium Liberationis: Fundamental Concepts of Liberation Theology*, ed. Ignacio Ellacuria and Jon Sobrino (Maryknoll, NY: Orbis Books, 1993), 397–400. See also Todd H. Speidell, "A Trinitarian Ontology of Persons in Society," *Scottish Journal of Theology* 47 (1994): 283–300.

43. Volf, *After Our Likeness*, 209.

44. For instance, one America dollar is equal to 140 naira (currency of Nigeria), and this can be read off in the exchange table. This kind of mathematical equality is available for all currencies in the world and hence the system can be considered catholic. But what kind of equality is this?

45. See Miroslav Volf, *After Our Likeness*, 211, for a comparison of the divine interiority in the Trinity to one-sided personal interiority of Holy Spirit and human beings. The distinctions I have made between the interiority in the current exchange rate system and the *Earth Dollar* exchange rate system are inspired by his comparison.

46. Participation and justice are inextricably linked—especially in a work like this which is a kind of "prophetic proclamation about what constitutes the good life." According to Volf, justice can be described as "the ordering of the social relations which secures for each person life with dignity and integration into community." Volf, "The Church as a Prophetic Community and a Sign of Hope," *European Journal* 2, no. 1 (1993): 22.

47. The theology of money in a globalizing world that I am developing in this work not only crafts a framework that raises questions about the absence of uni-

versal humanity and justice in the national and international monetary systems, but it is also designed to show how the global trade and payment system can participate in the striving toward the Kingdom of God, that is, "life is just relationship." For this view of the Kingdom of God, see Ulrich Duchrow and Frank J. Hinkelammert, *Property for People, Not for Profit* (London: Zed Books, 2004), 26.

48. Please do not fail to notice the implicit argument here about subjects. It has to be understood in comparison with the persons of the triune God. This objection points to the fact that the hypothetical questioner does not conceive of the persons of the Trinity as independent subjects as human beings are subjects. The hypothetical questioner is thinking that the Trinity is not tritheism—the Godhead is not three separate beings or gods forming a triad.

49. Volf, *After Our Likeness*, 213.

50. Volf, *After Our Likeness*, 212–13.

51. Robin Horton, *Patterns of Thoughts in Africa and the West: Essays on Magic, Religion, and Science* (Cambridge: Cambridge University Press, 1993), 215.

52. Horton, *Patterns of Thoughts*, 215.

53. Tillich, *Systematic Theology*, vol. 3, 324.

54. Denis Edwards, *The God of Evolution: A Trinitarian Theology* (New York: Paulist Press, 1999), 95–96.

55. By not being sufficiently economistic I mean only having a theological model/theory that has, at best, only some hidden inscrutable and unexplained economic theory in it and not a proper explication, explanation, and justification derived from economic science.

56. Amartya Sen, *On Ethics and Economics* (Malden, MA: Blackwell, 1988), 7.

57. Arguing against a free floating exchange rate system, Yulmaz Akyüz and Heiner Flassbeck have this to say, "Quite apart from how appropriate such a regime [free floating regime] might be, for a number of reasons it is particularly unsuitable for developing countries and transition economies, as well as for smaller industrial countries. Compared to the major industrial economies, developing and emerging-market economies are much more dependent on foreign trade, which is typically invoiced in foreign currencies. On the average, the share of international trade in their domestic production is twice as large as in the United States, the EU or Japan, so that the impact of exchange rate movements on their domestic economic conditions—including prices, production and employment—is much greater. Moreover, these economies have higher net external indebtedness, a larger proportion of which is denominated in foreign currencies. Consequently, sharp changes in their exchange rate tend to generate debt servicing difficulties, and liquidity and solvency problems. In sharp contrast, a country such as the United States can borrow in its currency, therefore effectively passing the exchange rate risk onto creditors." Akyüz and Flassbeck, "Exchange Rate Regimes and the Scope for Regional Cooperation," in *Reforming the Global Financial Architecture: Issues and Proposals*, eds. Akyüz and Flassbeck (Penang, Malaysia: Third World Network, 2002), 89.

58. Seven hundred delegates from forty-four countries met at a resort hotel at the foot of the mountain called Mount Deception. "Rather than naming their agreement after the [ominously named] mountain on which it was signed, they chose to name it Bretton Woods, after the mailing address of the hotel where they

stayed." See Jack Weatherford, *The History of Money: From Sandstone to Cyberspace* (New York: Three Rivers Press, 1997), 183–84.

59. See John Maynard Keynes, *The Collected Writings of John Maynard Keynes*, vol. 25, *Activities 1940–1944: Shaping the Post-War World, The Clearing Union*, ed. D. Moggridge (London: Macmillan, 1980), chap. 1.

60. Guttmann, *How Credit-Money Shapes the Economy*, 387.

61. When a country issues the world money it is saddled with the "problem" of providing adequate liquidity to the world economy. To do this it must run balance of payment (BOP) deficits with the rest of the world. Without running deficit BOP accounts of capital flows and trade, it cannot transfer its currencies from its domestic economy into international circulation. Since a country becomes issuer of world money because of its hegemonic dominance of world trade (running trade surpluses) it must be a net exporter of capital in order to create the required BOP deficits. To stimulate and sustain growing and expanding world trade the issuer of world money has the responsibility to increase liquidity, create increasing reserves for others. But the hegemonic power can meet the increasing need for liquidity by sustaining larger payment deficits. The problem is that increasing balance of payment deficits creates doubts in the minds of foreigners about the quality of the world money. These doubts could lead to diversification into other currencies and to devaluation (depreciation). Should the issuer return to BOP surplus, global liquidity will be reduced and consequently world trade will decline. This is the dilemma of a reserve currency as stated by the Belgian economist Robert Triffin. See Guttmann, *How Credit-Money Shapes the Economy*, 139–40.

62. Guttmann, *How Credit-Money Shapes the Economy*, 138.

63. Guttmann, *How Credit-Money Shapes the Economy*, 391–92.

64. Guttmann, *How Credit-Money Shapes the Economy*, 393–95.

65. Jane D' Arista, "Causes and Consequences of the Buildup in Global Liquidity: Part 2," 7. There is a slight difference between my ideas and Arista's. I argue for a single global currency but she is advocating for a system whereby all currencies are used in cross-border as well as domestic transactions. See her "Reforming the Privatized International Monetary and Financial Architecture," *Financial Markets and Society* (November 1999): 1–22.

66. The history of the evolutionary process is worth retelling here briefly. "The first major political initiative for a European monetary union was taken in 1969 with the adoption of the Werner Report, which proposed: for the first stage, a reduction of the fluctuation margins between the currencies of the member states of the Community; for the second stage, the achievement of complete freedom of capital movements, with integration of financial markets; and for the final state an irrevocable fixing of exchange rates between the currencies. In its first effort at creating a zone of currency stability, the EEC attempted in 1971 to fix European parities closer to each other than to the dollar, but with some flexibility ("the snake"). The "snake" rapidly died with the collapse of the dollar-based Bretton Woods system, but was reborn in 1972 as the "snake in the tunnel," a system which narrowed the fluctuation margin between the Community currencies (the snake) in relation to those operating between these currencies and the dollar (the tunnel). During the currency turmoil that accompanied the 1973 oil crisis, this arrangement could not function well, leading to various exits and floating, until the

establishment of the EMS in 1979." (Akyüz and Flassbeck, "Exchange Rate Regimes and the Scope for Regional Cooperation," 97.

67. There is a slight difference between my proposal and the present structuring of the euro. In the euro, particularity is lost in favor of universality. My proposal balances universality with particularity. There is yet another area of difference. Speaking more accurately, *Earth Dollar* is not a single currency for the world as the euro is for the parts of Europe in the European Union, but it is a *numeraire* for international, cross-border transactions. National currencies are alive but limited to circulating only within their own borders. At best, *Earth Dollar* is only a preliminary stage toward the goal of a single global currency.

68. Akyüz and Flassbeck, "Exchange Rate Regimes," 98.

69. Guttmann, *How Credit-Money Shapes the Economy*, 427.

70. I have not treated the thoughts of Robert Mundell, who received the Nobel Prize in economics in 1999, here even though he advocates for a global currency and fixed exchange rate system—literally for one big optimum currency area. He argues for gold as the anchor of such a global monetary system. (He rejects a fiat world currency because, according to him, without first establishing a security area, the use of a world currency backed by one or more precious metals is the best.) I consider the use of gold (or some improved version of the international gold standard) as problematic in this era, to say the least. Besides, the use of gold as the anchor in my system would imply a different, and frankly, a very troublesome conception of the nature of the triune God. It would bring in the notion of common identical *substance* and monarchical, undemocratic ideas into my minimal theory of relations (*logic*) in the Trinity instead of conceiving the unity of the Godhead as a perichoretic communion. For arguments against the "substance" view of the Trinitarian Godhead see Leonardo Boff, "The Liberating Design of God," in *Mysterium Liberations: Fundamental Concepts of Liberation Theology*, ed. Ignacio Ellacuria and Jon Sobrino (Maryknoll, NY: Orbis Books, 1993), 397–400. See also Todd H. Speidell, "A Trinitarian Ontology of Persons in Society," *Scottish Journal of Theology*, 47 (1994): 283–300. In the Islamic world, the former prime minister of Malaysia (1981–2003), Dr. Mahathir bin Mohamad, also proposed in 2001 a 100 percent gold-backed currency (named *Islamic gold dinar*) for trade among Muslim nations. He believed this would reduce dependence on the U.S. dollar as a reserve currency and also free the Islamic economies from using a debt-backed currency in international transactions. Islamic laws prohibit charging interest on debts.

71. See Wolfhart Pannenberg, "The God of Hope," *Basic Questions in Theology* (London: SCM Press, 1971), 234–49.

72. Miroslav Volf, *Work in the Spirit: Toward theology of Work* (Eugene, OR: Wipf & Stock, 1991), 81.

73. Tillich, *Systematic Theology*, vol. 3, 187.

74. Volf, *Work in the Spirit*, 83.

75. Stout, *Democracy and Tradition*.

8

✝

Payoff for Poor Countries

INTRODUCTION

This book has provided a framework for a careful and detailed theological and ethical reflection on money as a social relation. Most importantly, chapters 6 and 7 highlighted the need to transform and restructure the international monetary system in order to make it more supportive of the development of the Global South and resistant to imperial dominance. In this final chapter, I want to discuss potential payoff of the proposed triune model of the global monetary system for the poor Global South. Here I would attempt to show, only briefly, how the *Earth Dollar* monetary system addresses some of the radical economic needs of the dominated Global South, especially the African continent. Then I will discuss the importance of the whole study for theological-ethics and point to areas for further research.

BENEFITS OF *EARTH DOLLAR* FOR
DEVELOPING AND POOR ECONOMIES

It appears time is running out for Africa as poverty is freely roaming about in the whole of its territory and living rooms, devouring and seeking whom it may devour. In steadfast hope, we need to resist it and the involvement of the global monetary system in its sustenance, knowing that the same sufferings are experienced by too many people in the Global South. Even the most rudimentary discussion of poverty in Africa and how it inhibits economic development, its devastating social and economic effects, and its link with the global monetary system would easily double the size of this chapter, if not the whole book. With the space available we should still be able, however, to get some sense of the degree and intensity of poverty in the continent and appreciation of some of its more significant implications. We will consider only two of them which are closely related: population and food shortages.[1]

When the twenty-first century opened in 2000, the population of Africa was estimated at 793 million people. Experts then, estimating the growth rate at 2.2 percent per annum, predicted that the number will climb to 1.37 billion in 2025. This number in itself may not raise eyebrows. But once it is examined in the light of growth rates of food and other resources required to care for the population, which are not growing as fast as the population, all sorts of dire implications come to the fore for attention. For instance, with this kind of discrepancy in growth rates, the continent is faced with a huge dependency burden. Africans aged between 15 and 64, the active working age, are and will continue to support a huge number of dependents (children and nonworking adults over 64 years of old) for a very long time to come. Every worker supports at least one under-15 dependent. Add to this number the dependents over 64 years you get a sense of the burden that the labor force carries. The dependency ratio (the percentage of children under 15 years and adults over 64 in the overall population) is 46 percent in Africa as compared with only 34.2 percent in the United States. The difference in the dependency ratio between the United States and Africa is worse than what the statistics just presented are able to portray. One has to add the burden of unemployment to this picture. In most African countries, rates of unemployment among persons in the active labor force are in the double digits. This comparison has to be further extended to include the fact that often those lucky enough to get employment are paid comparatively low wages, are underemployed, or severely underutilized. Making matters worse, one has to add to the crushing burden of poverty and dependency, the death blows of HIV and its associated diseases, and crumbling health care systems that are ill-prepared to stem the tide of AIDS.

For some observers, it is quite easy to see the problem of a rapidly growing population as purely caused by internal factors such as high birth rates and the so-called Africans' propensity for large families or to argue that the high population growth rate is the cause of the underdevelopment of African economies. This is a very myopic way of looking at the problem. The connection between population and economic development is not as simple as that. Many experts argue that the population problem should be seen as a "problem of underdevelopment." Michael Todaro, a well-known development expert, noted in his book *Economic*

Development that "widespread poverty tends to sustain high birthrates for the obvious reasons that families living without adequate incomes, employment, health, education, and social services have little security for the future other than reliance on their children."[2] So whatever social phenomenon or mechanism that is implicated in the issue of economic underdevelopment in Africa cannot be readily ruled out in the explanation of poverty and high population growth rate. As we have argued in this study, one cannot fully comprehend the problem of poverty and underdevelopment in Africa and the rest of the Global South without paying attention to the imperial monarchical currency system and the overall global trade and payment system.

Now let us turn to the issue of food shortage. While in the 1960s, Africa was self-sufficient in food production; by the 1980s it was importing 14 percent of its food needs, and today Africans' failure to feed themselves from endogenous food supply has become alarming.[3] In general, population growth rate has tended to exceed rate of food production. This has raised or refocused the debate on Thomas Malthus' prediction about the negative effect of rapid population growth and dwindling food supply. Reverend Malthus, in his 1798 book, *Essay on the Principle of Population*, warned that "the perpetual tendency in the race of man to increase beyond the means of subsistence is one of the general laws of animated nature which [we] can have no reason to expect will change."[4] According to him, the discrepancy (the number of people surpassing the means of their subsistence) is a recipe for disasters from overpopulation. How are we to interpret the problem of food shortage? The likely answer to this question has to have two sides: the *supply of food* and the *price of food*. We have already looked at the food production and found out that indeed there is "too little food." What I have so far not brought to the attention of the reader is this: the relatively falling food production level must be firmly situated in its political context. Agricultural and economic productions have been (and are) disrupted in the continent by political upheavals, dictatorships, coups, civil unrest, and wars. Take for instance, the period between 1990 and 1997, sub-Saharan Africa lost an estimated 40 percent of its agricultural output owing to political conflicts, according to the United Nations Food and Agricultural Organization. The losses in output were estimated at $21 billion in 1995 prices. The FAO went on to remark that "for the conflict-affected countries, estimated agricultural losses were 75 percent of ODA [Official Development Assistance] for 28 years, a percentage that increased with each decade. Conflict [induced] losses in Sub-Saharan Africa were considerably greater than Foreign Direct Investment (FDI) in the countries."[5]

Let us now focus on the price of food as the second side of the issue of food shortage. No doubt food prices have been going up because of the

pressure of population. Many economists argue that the rising internal
food prices and declining food production will not be in themselves problems if the continent's economic production is on track. Why are manufacturing sectors in Africa in the doldrums? Many of the continent's
economies would have earned enough foreign earnings to buy the necessary food from the world market if there are vibrant manufacturing sectors or if economic production is not incessantly disrupted by wars (some
of which were proxy battles for imperial powers) and other political activities. After all, the world-market prices of basic food relative to manu-
factures have been falling.[6] We should, therefore, not hasten to assume
that the "balance between food and population" is only an economic or
agricultural one. It goes beyond the pale of narrow economic analysis. Sen
writes that "there is, indeed, no such thing as an apolitical food problem."[7] African scholars like Agnes Odejide have argued that the food crisis in Africa is political in character and in origin.[8] There is no space to
fully make the argument that African governments' agricultural policies
in postcolonial Africa deliberately manipulated the price of peasant production in favor of tax collection and bourgeois capital accumulation, and
not for developing program for food sufficiency or security. There is no
time to also describe the colonial-era imperial policies that particularly
targeted African agriculture to feed Western industries and, at the same
time, failing to modernize the peasant agricultural system. Walter Rodney, in his 1972 book *How Europe Underdeveloped Africa*, remarked that,
"the vast majority of Africans went into colonialism with a hoe. After
decades of colonialism, the hoe—not the tractor—remained the over-
whelmingly dominant agricultural implement."[9] Simply put, they went
in with hoe and came out with hoe. The whole question of agricultural development and food production can neither be divorced from the persistent effort to extract surplus from peasants for development of industries
that favor elite capital accumulation at the local level nor from the policies
at the international level that are also bent on extracting resources, debt
servicing and repayments, and seigniorage from the Global South. All this
is not to deny Africans' responsibility for their economic plight. While we
are urging Africans to accept their responsibility, we should not fail to
diligently nudge the global monetary system as we know it today to withdraw its abjectly Hobbesian hands from smothering development in
Africa and the Global South.

The question now is: in what ways will the proposed *Earth Dollar* monetary system help to address some of the economic needs of the Global
South or at least resist the Hobbesian hands of imperial domination? The
interpretation of the significance (beneficial potentials) of the idea and
model of the *Earth Dollar* has remained implicit in the exposition in chapter 7 and shall now be stated explicitly in a short discussion. The model

we have presented indicates potential benefits of a single world currency
to poor countries of Africa, South America, and Asia. The discussion of
the benefits should not be construed to imply that one expects that with
the implementation of single world money (*universal credit-money*) there
will be equilibrium of forces in the international economic order. It is only
to point to some potential shifts in the "immanent and predominant loci-
of-power with regard to the exchange and production of economic values" so that some nations will not win consistently and others lose consistently and persistently in international economic relations.

With the use of one world currency (*stateless money*) the locus of control
of the major vehicle of global economic relations is democratized and this
can lead to democratization of world resource use. This is how one
African economist, Peter Alex Egom, puts it:

> Simply put, a general theory of world economic orders states that world eco-
> nomic orders differ with regard to the locus of control over the determination
> and issue of international money. Since each world economic order has a cor-
> responding financial system then the financial system immanent in a world
> economic order is the operational embodiment of the wills and wiles of the
> national entities, or institutions, representatives and citizens thereof, who
> control the determination and issue of international money or monies. Cor-
> respondingly each world economic order embodies a pattern of world re-
> source use.[10]

This democratization, at the minimum, is not about transfer of resources
from the leading industrial countries of the West and Asia to poor countries so as to achieve some kind of equality. It is about giving the ability to
poor countries to have control over their own national resource use and
their degree of dependence on the international economy. When
economies subscribe, whether by choice, ignorance, *akrasia*, or force, to "a
world economic order in which the right to determine and issue the monetary vehicle of international exchange and production of economic values is vested in few national economies, [they] deprive themselves of control over their own national resource use and, what is more, of control
over their degree of dependence on the world economy."[11]

With the use of a global single currency managed by *Earth Central Bank*,
which is operating according to guidelines set forth in chapter 7, the international playing field would also become democratic because the advantages enjoyed by issuers of few national currencies, which are used as
the global vehicle of exchange, would be removed. Today a country like
the United States pays for its own international obligations in its own currency. This is an undemocratic, monarchical advantage. Besides, "relying
on national currencies to pay for international transactions makes less and
less sense in today's integrated [integrating] world economy, in which

most products no longer have a clearly national origin but are produced in several countries at the same time. . . . Globally integrated production networks and financial markets are better off with a truly international medium of exchange."[12]

Another advantage likely to accrue to poor countries would come from the design parameters of the *Earth Dollar* system. The proposed design of *Earth Dollar* has a mechanism for distribution of adjustment burdens and capital resources. The poor countries are what they are because, among other reasons, they are starved of investment capital, and with debt payments, as we have shown in chapter 1 with Susan George's statistics, they are also exporters of capital to the rich countries. The little foreign reserves they struggled to accumulate are kept mostly in U.S. financial houses. The United States, the richest country in the world, is also the biggest net importer of capital. This is not an equitable system. The changes envisaged in the design of the *Earth Dollar* system will result in a win-win scenario for both rich and poor economies. This is how economist Professor Guttmann explains it:

> The strength of the world economy depends on a reversal of [the] perverse flow of capital. The poorer countries need to import capital on a continuous basis and to use that influx of funds productively for balanced industrialization. Providing them with sufficient funds at reasonable terms also benefits rich nations in terms of larger export markets . . . and reduced illegal immigration. Even though industrialization in developing countries at times creates massive dislocation in the regions of the industrial nations that formerly depended heavily on labor-intensive manufacturing, it also frees resources there for new types of work. If those are higher value added than are the jobs lost, rich countries as a whole benefit from the new international division of labor.[13]

There is also the benefit from being shielded from virulent, violent foreign exchange-rate movements. Today, the poor countries of the Global South often suffer when exchange-rate markets move violently: their external debt burdens go up or down in terms of what is the amount of local resources that is required to service them, the value of their commodity exports are also affected, and overall their terms of trade catch cold when the "boys of Wall Street" sneeze and play their "casino games." But in the *Earth Dollar* system, each national currency circulates only within its own borders and national currencies are no longer exchanged directly but indirectly through the numeraire of the *Earth Dollar*. The relative prices of national currencies in the proposed system would reflect "differentials in purchasing power[14] between countries involved" and are subject to adjustments as national trade surpluses or deficits threaten the functioning of the overall system.[15]

Before proceeding any further, let me summarize some of the potential benefits from the implementation of the *Earth Dollar* monetary system: ✩

(a). democratization of the international monetary system and global economic relations;
(b). democratization of world resource use as the locus of control of the major vehicle of international economic relations is opened toward justice and equality;
(c). giving poor countries more control over their own national resources and degree of dependence on the international economy;
(d). providing a mechanism for the equitable distribution of adjustment burdens and capital resource in international monetary relations;
(e). addressing the problem of virulent, violent foreign exchange rate movements; and
(f). addressing the problem of inequality between poor and rich nations.

These advantages may appear all too general and abstract to some readers. I would, therefore, need to further highlight the crucial role the *Earth Dollar* monetary system can play in the economic development of developing countries with a *concrete example*. There is a burgeoning literature on the importance of monetary and financial development for the economic growth and national competitiveness of Global South economies. Often the monetary system and the investment patterns and horizon it authorizes and encourages are at the root, if not the root, of their major economic predicament. The *Earth Dollar* monetary system would not solve all national and international problems and social demonries in the Global South, but it is a veritable step toward working out the economic reasoning for liberating poor countries from the imperial currency system that have been dominating economic intercourse at the global level. Let me illustrate this point by examining its likely impact on the financial situation of the Global South. The *Earth Dollar* monetary system can be used to address the hydra-headed problem of financial instability (which is linked to the structure and operation of the global financial system that are largely beyond the control of poor nations which do not have key currency status) that have too frequently buffeted developing countries. I do not have a mastery of the technical econometric skills required to build large simulation models to personally estimate the probabilistic financial impact the *Earth Dollar* would make on the problem of financial instability. Even if I have such a set of skills it would require a major study all by itself to estimate and calibrate the impact and thus take me too far afield from my limited purpose here. So I will rely on the study done by a well-regarded professional economist at University of California, Berkeley to make my point. Professor Barry Eichengreen has studied the likely impact of various potential solutions to the problems of financial instability in developing economies. One solution he examined is that of single world currency, providing us an opportunity to show in hard monetary terms one of the potential benefits of the *Earth Dollar*. This obviates the need to speculate about its impact in the absence of reliable economic calculations.

It is germane to remind the reader that financial instability and currency and banking crises are some of the principal underlying concerns that provoked the thinking on the *Earth Dollar*. These problems are at the core of the development conundrum of the Global South as we saw with the Mexican and Brazilian debt crises in the 1980s, Indonesia in 1997–1998, and Argentina in 2001–2002. I have argued in chapter 7 that the international monetary system is flawed when viewed from the perspective of global debt crisis or sudden collapse of national currencies due to flight of "hot money." There I stated that private international banks' money creation, as the history of national and international debt crises has shown, is very prone to credit overextension and subsequent violent contractions. These crises exact enormous tolls on the economies of developing nations.

Economist Eichengreen's recent paper, "Financial Stability," presented on behalf of the *Copenhagen Consensus*,[16] shows that the annual average output losses per year from currency and banking crises in Asia and Latin America in the 1980s were 0.1 percent and 2.2 percent, respectively. The figures in the 1990s were 1.4 percent for Asia and 0.7 percent for Latin America.[17] These percentages may appear small to undiscerning eyes, but they are significant in economic terms. According to Eichengreen, losses like these are of first-order importance. What Latin America lost as a result of financial instability (currency and exchange rate crises) in the 1980s is enough to transform its living standards, "make incomes and living standard two-thirds higher in a generation [25 years]," providing resources to address critical social problems.[18] He goes on to suggest four alternative treatments (options) for the problem of financial instability and provides estimates of their costs and benefits: (1) regulate financial markets, (2) reimpose capital controls, (3) create a single world currency, and (4) have developing countries borrow in their own currencies.

The annual net benefit for his model of single world currency (somewhat like the *Earth Dollar* option advocated here) is $91 billion *per annum*. He assumes that eliminating currency crises by using a single world currency produces benefits to developing countries to the tune of 0.7 percent of gross domestic product, GDP (estimated from the share of developing countries in world GDP calculated at purchasing power parity).[19] This estimated amount of $91 billion per annum can go into poverty alleviation and industrialization in developing countries. For purposes of comparison, the U.S. Marshall Plan transferred $14 billion in 1948 dollars to war-ravaged Europe, about $70 billion in 1991 dollars.[20]

Eichengreen highlights the positive impact of a single world currency in this way: "the experience of the euro area illustrates how this response can eliminate the currency-crisis problem; just contrast the prevalence of currency crises in Europe in the 1980s and 1990s with their absence from the euro area today."[21] We can also go behind the sophisticated mathematical calculations that produced the yearly $91 billion figure (which is, by the way, not sacrosanct as it depends on the assumptions of Eichengreen's model) to link up with our earlier discussions on the food crisis in some areas of the Global South. One of the causes of food crises (viewing it from the angle of *food prices*) is the problem associated with currency mismatches. A currency mismatch occurs when countries or banks have assets in local currencies but liabilities in foreign denominated currencies such as the dollar. For instance, for a Nigerian corporation or bank, this means that incomes are in naira but debts in dollars and with the weakening of the naira exchange rate due to crises, assets (denominated in local currency) are no longer sufficient to service or pay off foreign liabilities. Recently some economists have coined a catchy phrase for the inability of developing economies to borrow abroad in their own currencies. They tagged it the "original sin."[22] The actual crises or fear of a crisis often lead to violent depreciation of national currencies of the Global South. Among the result of this weakening of exchange rate is this: the price of food imports drastically goes up and also the import of modern agricultural equipment to produce the food locally becomes much more prohibitive. This is not all. The effect of financial instability certainly extends beyond food crisis. Socioeconomic conditions generally worsen as in the case of South Korea in the 1990s. Eichengreen states that the number of poor in the country rose from 6 million in 1997 to more than 10 million in 1998.[23] The table below shows other social indicators relating to the financial crises of 1997–1998.

Given these dire effects, the potential ability of the *Earth Dollar* to stem the tide of financial crises (which by all accounts are becoming more frequent and virulent since 1971 when President Nixon delinked the dollar

Table 8.1.   South Korean Social Indicators Following the Crisis

Year	Divorces	Crimes	Crimes per 100,000	Drug Addicts per 100,000	Suicides
1996	79, 895	1,494,846	3,282	6,189	5,777
1997	91,159	1,588,613	3,454	6,947	5,957
1998	116,727	1,765,887	3,803	8,350	8,496
1999	118,014	1,732,522	3,697	10,589	7,014

Source: Joun-Woo Lee, "Social Impact of the Crisis," in Duck-Koo Chung and Barry Eichengreen (eds.), *The Korean Economy Beyond the Crisis* (Cheltenham: Edward Elgar, 2005) quoted in Eichengreen, "Financial Instability," 45.

from its gold standard anchor and cut off the moorings of the global financial system) recommends it for serious consideration.

One possible question an economic interlocutor could ask me is this: can you speak to the issue of whether your proposal for a single world currency is Pareto improving? Does it make poor countries better off without making the United States and other major players worse off?

One can respond to this question in three ways. First, argue that the insistence on Pareto optimality is considered problematic. If any time we think of resisting injustice and imperial domination, we limit ourselves to the issues of improving the welfare of the poor and increasing levels of equality as well as simultaneously making sure that the oppressors and privileged groups are not worst off; we may not go very far in transforming any polity. All I am asking for is a leveling of the playing field, and not tilting it in favor of some advanced countries. I think this is a perfectly legitimate democratic request that can (and should) stand on its own.

The second point is this: the proposed *Earth Dollar* monetary system will help address the financial instability that plagues developing countries and help to promote their growth. One would think that the U.S. economy and those of the major players stand to benefit from an expanding global economy. Third, without conducting a detailed econometric study one may not be able to answer this question in a formal way that may pass muster with neoclassical economists. But, I would like to mention again the study of Professor Barry Eichengreen which shows that there is a huge annual net benefit to the world in the single currency model. Three paragraphs below, I draw from the history of economic growth rates in the euro area to further and more specifically indicate that the *Earth Dollar* monetary system might be "pareto-improving."

Since there is, today, in the world a "successful" single currency (euro) for a very important area of the global economy and our proposal is about using a single global currency to improve the economies of poor countries, it makes sense to examine what is happening in the European Monetary Union. There is a question that suggests itself here: is there any evidence on whether the creation of the euro has helped relatively smaller European economies and not harmed the dominant European countries? This could be used to support the idea of going to "scale" with the single global currency. My response here would be made in two moves: an economic theoretical answer and the use of comparative economic growth rates of member states since the introduction of the euro in 1999.

Although entering a currency union like the European Monetary Union (EMU) involves costs and losses which depend on the extent to which a country in the union can withstand asymmetric shocks, there has been known to be a remarkable international trade creation. Currency union, according to several studies, can increase trade among members by a factor of two to three without trade diversion from non-currency-union members.[24] Currency union impacts not only trade, but also income, growth, and welfare. The benefits are likely to go to both rich and poor countries in the union—the size of an individual country's benefit depends on its economic mass, factor mobility, structural factors, demographics, etc.

Let us now examine how membership in the EMU has benefited the less dominant economies of Spain and Greece compared with Germany and Italy, the more advanced economies. For our very limited purpose here, the discussion will relate only to real GDP growth across euro area countries. In an European Central Bank's study led by Nicholai Benalal et al,[25] it was revealed that dispersion in real GDP growth rate (difference in output growth rates of member economies at a certain point in time) among member economies has narrowed in the past few years. More importantly for our purpose, Spain and Greece have experienced higher growth rates than the relatively more dominant Germany and Italy. Spain and Greece[26] from 1999 to 2004 grew respectively at 3.1 percent and 4.1 percent per annum. The average for the Euro area as a whole was 1.9 percent; Germany, 1.2 percent; and Italy had 1.4 percent.[27] The authors of the study attributed the performance of the two countries partly to "a catching-up process." It is what they said next about Germany and Italy that gives us at least some crude indication of how to respond to the second part of the question— the part about not harming the dominant European countries. (The indication is that the *Earth Dollar* monetary system might be "pareto-improving.") Benalal et al. wrote:

> It is important to note that, even prior to 1999, output growth in these two countries [Germany and Italy] was below the euro area average. In Germany, it has been persistently below the euro area average since 1995. In Italy, real GDP growth has been persistently below the euro area average since 1996, excluding the year 2001, when it was very close to the euro area average [3.0 versus 3.5]. Even prior to 1996, however, Italian growth was persistently weak. In fact, excluding the year 1995, output growth in Italy had been weaker than the euro area average since 1988.[28]

I would end this section by reiterating that I do not take lightly the huge problem of the political feasibility of establishing the *Earth Dollar* monetary system.[29] This potentially daunting difficulty should, however, not deter us from putting forward this option that can help us resist and subvert nimble, rhizomatic imperial monetary dominance, keep hope alive, and at the same time enhance the development prospects of the poor economies. There was a time the dream of euro was seen as a mere pipe dream, but today it is a reality. I believe, perhaps too optimistically, that if agitations by poor nations, popular demands by social movements, and the objective economic trend we have identified in the last chapter do not all conspire to move the international monetary system toward a single world currency, euro area's abiding interest to counter the dominance of the dollar and the likely (distant) future prospect of the U.S. *almighty dollar* losing its imperial dominance to the Chinese yuan may move Washington to embrace the single currency option as a face-saving strategic option. The point would be to stop China from exercising monetary dominance over the rest of the world as the United States is doing now and before it Britain. Today China appears, quite arguably, to be at the same cusp of history as United States was at the turn of the twentieth century when it was waiting in the wings to take over the imperial monetary dominant role from the declining British Empire. China (yes, still a "Third World" country) is fast growing economically, accumulating huge foreign exchange reserves at a furious pace, relentlessly securing petroleum energy sources, and steadily building the sophisticated military umbrella that may serve to render the yuan a key vehicular currency, if not straightforwardly the global imperial currency in our life time. Asia's China will not play the second fiddle forever.

CONTRIBUTIONS TO SCHOLARSHIP

We can now elaborate further on issues of this study's significance beyond points made in the introduction. This study has provided a comprehensive theological-ethical framework for expertly and incisive reflection on the complex issues of modern money. It undertook a technical theological investigation of money in order to interpret, evaluate, and aid the transformation of the social practice of money as proleptic anticipation of the eschatological new creation. As a result of this interest in facilitating the transformation of money and monetary system to approximate the dynamic relations of the triune God, this work clearly goes beyond merely interpreting the contemporary monetary situation to critically reflect on the practice and reorganization of the global financial system that can follow from the formulations engendered by a theology of money.

Up to now, there has not been an adequate theology to address the nature, workings, significance, and consequences of money and its related global financial system in a way that can guide Christian social ethics in contemporary society. In place of an ordered discussion of criteria for making theological distinctions between just and unjust monetary systems, there are scattered comments and hints on the contemporary monetary situation. The gap has now been filled, and this book has joined the reflection on the production, circulation, and control of money with those on poverty of Majority World economies, especially those in Africa.

The study also serves as a critique of existing theologies of money. Current theological studies of money do not adequately theorize what exactly is theology's contribution to the analysis of money. I have used a theological approach to set up a model for reconfiguring an understanding of money and set forth the need for methodological reflection on the role of a theological approach to money. The theological-ethical reflection undertaken in this study is in continuous correlation with economics, sociology, and philosophy.

Another important contribution of this book to theological-ethics or theological approach to economics (orthodox or heterodox) is that it makes arguments that are falsifiable—certainly some crucial parts of the *Earth Dollar* model are in principle falsifiable. Many so-called serious works in theological ethics or theological economics make arguments that are not falsifiable; no way for their authors to know what events, states, acts, data, and results can refute their positions. The position taken on single global currency is liable to refutation. We can always test if the single-global-currency arguments are valid or not by building econometric models to see if they are beneficial to adopt or by examining historical cases of currency unions. I tentatively showed that my arguments might accommodate falsifiability tests by pointing to the history of economic growth in the euro area and announcing the need for perspicacious minds in economics to set up the necessary econometric models to test the propositions of the *Earth Dollar* monetary system. By this methodological standpoint, I am not arguing that all arguments in theological ethics have to be ultimately judged in terms of their success in showing if their propositions are confirmable or in making accurate predictions. But it is a move only to suggest that economics ethics need to make arguments that are less vague, needs to encourage positions that are to an extent translatable into propositions that economists can test, and the results of such testing can possibly serve as a challenge to improve the overall quality of explanation and interdisciplinary dialogue in the field.

This study has also problematized the depoliticized nature of monetary theory, policy, and practices. The appearance of technical, rational, and scientific objectivity that monetary policy and global trade and payment system have acquired in twentieth and twenty-first centuries have cast the problem of both national-global monetary orders as a depoliticized, technical governance issue that is beyond discussion, debate, and contestability. In contrast, to repoliticize (monetary) practices, "would be to interrupt discourse, to challenge what have, through discursive practices, been constituted as normal, natural, and accepted way of carrying on."[30] This study has provided the narrative raw material and incisive analyses to shake up the discursive stability of modern monetary financial practices, "thus raising the possibility of alternative monetary arrangement."

Finally, this book, in my opinion, for the first time provides a theological-ethical argument for a single global currency. It does this by providing a theological (trinitarian) reflection on the global monetary system. The reflection is adequately supported and informed by a technical theory which shows that the logic and dynamics of the current monarchical currency system would do well to move toward trinitarian structures. This is not an approach usually taken by theologians and ethicists who use the doctrine of the Trinity in social analysis. Often their theological reflections on social issues are not supported by a technical theory which shows that the system or phenomenon they are analyzing has an inbuilt dialectics to move in the direction they are pointing out to us. In this book, we have shown that the tension between the universal and particular as played out in the global trade and payment is the underlying principle that is driving or is likely to drive particularistic national currencies toward universal and total integration as one global currency (*Earth Dollar*) and then will define the patterns of interaction between them.

AREAS OF FURTHER RESEARCH

There are five major directions that the theology of money provided in this book might take in future development. First, owing to space constraints, we have not traced the connection between money and personhood. The economic and sociological foundations necessary for crafting a robust systematic theology of money cannot be fully set in place without a concept of personhood that is capable of countering the narrow neoclassical concept of "rational" autonomous *homo economicus*. At the foundational level of every monetary/economic system or theory there is a conception of what a person is and an account of how persons are related to one another. In the neoclassical economics view of humans and human actions which dominates contemporary monetary thinking, the existence of a human person is regarded as only individuated but not communally located for the simple reason of generating reliable predictions and explanations. The individual is abstracted from her social context in which her decisions are made and actions take place.

Neoclassical economism does not require the individual to live a flourishing social life, nor even that she desires the good of her community. Rather it simply requires her to express her choice or preference rationally and match her means to her chosen values and ends. The way anyone can know her preference or is allowed to investigate her preference is to examine the way she votes with her money in the market. She is assumed to be a solitary, rational utility maximizer. She is *homo economicus*, quite similar to Martin Buber's "capricious man."[31] In this cold, neoclassical praxeological model of mainstream economists social relations are depersonalized; indeed solid relations have melted into the thin air and the world has been transformed into a chain of mathematical problems.

There is not much accent placed on understanding personhood (which is being plus being-in-relation) beyond mere broaching it as "transactors who are in a state of reciprocal independence."[32] But people are not monads, and thus theologians and ethicists who are serious about capturing the actual nature of personhood in their scholarship cannot just use the *homo economicus* concept of personhood in their theologizing about money. Therefore, any systematic theological investigation of the modern monetary system that seeks to transform human patterns of interaction within the economic system must also provide, from the beginning, a theory of personhood on which its vision is based.[33]

Second, if one understands personhood as being in communion, it has other implications for the way one theologizes about money. Like personhood, money also has its place only in the community. As Otto A. Piper put it, "there is no private money. As a means of exchange, money has its place [only] within a community."[34] Money enables person-in-relation communion everywhere. This person-in-relation communion that money enables is received as well as given. It is a shared participation in which each economic agent contributes and she is contributed by others. Because money is a social practice, as we have shown, the participation it creates through the giving and receiving is fully present only among all in the community. Behind every person with power to be in relationship is "capacity or minimum personal qualification which those exercising the power" to be in communion with others must possess. Thus, a systematic theology of money needs to provide an analysis of capabilities that every person will need in order to fully participate and flourish in his or her community and contribute to its preservation and progress.

Third, for a fuller understanding of money we need to analyze the spheres or the embedding milieus of the monetary process in an economy. The production and use of money is not only personal, it is relational, institutional, societal, and inevitably global. The channels of exchange by which people generate, mobilize, and distribute the monetary resources are socialized and these need to be tracked. One type of research program needs to examine the process at the household, family level, to show how money comes to be generated in the family and the moral issues pertaining to such production. Another needs to look at how corporations and financial institutions create, distribute, and control credit and credit-money in an economy. This is to draw out the profound ethical issues involved in the private control of a public resource in the production of money. The teaching of the church has been limited to stewardship or the control of capital (congealed form of money, equipment, factories, etc.) in the society and has not recognized or understood the processes that create, define, sustain, and distribute money in society. These processes get to define who ultimately has possession of the money and capital. By looking at the acquisition of physical assets and financial securities in a given time period and the sources of funds used to acquire them, we could get some idea of the level of participation of the various classes of household in the monetary process in America.[35]

Fourth, another direction of future research could focus on how the process of creation and allocation of money is deeply embedded in a vision of the moral order and in a framework of moral discourse. An investigation of the ethics of monetary policy and philosophy of central banking would show how central banks are implicated in a moral vision that favors well-heeled financial assets holders at the expense of ordinary people and hinders the participation of the poor and not-so rich in the communities. We began this process in chapter 5 when exploring the ambiguities and demonries of U.S. central banking practices, and when exposing, in chapter 6, the imperial center of today's global monetary systems.

Finally, there still remains a task for sociologists, political scientists, and political theologians to clearly and specifically identify the bearers of eschatological hopes and political agency to bring the *Earth Dollar* monetary system into reality. The jobs of the task are about the analysis of social movements to rival and contest the imperial monetary dominance and the development of the narratives of activists challenging imperial monetary regimes. These narratives may need to deftly present the prophetic tradition of agents expressing and embodying adversarial hope, expectation of the "underivably new," and practices of countering and reworking of empire's way of being that both stretch back into the deep past and forward in our time.[36]

NOTES

1. I draw most of my data from these sources: United Nations Population Division, World Bank, and *African Development 2000* (Oxford: Oxford University Press, 2000),

2. Michael Todaro, *Economic Development in the Third World Nation*, 4th ed. (White Plains, NY: Longman, 1989), 198.

3. Food and Agricultural Organization of United Nations, *FAOSTAT Database 2000* (Rome).

4. Thomas Robert Malthus, *Essay on the Principle of Population* (London: J. Johnson, 1798; repr. Penguin Classics, 1982), 198–99.

5. Food and Agricultural Organization of United Nations, *State of Food and Agriculture (SOFA) 2000* (Rome), 73, 79.

6. See UNCTAD VIII, *Analytical Report by the UNCTAD Secretariat to the Conference* (United Nations, 1992), Table V-S, 235.

7. Amartya Sen, "The Food Problem: Theory and Policy," *Third World Quarterly* 4, no. 3 (1982): 459.

8. Agnes Odejide, "Food Sufficiency in Africa," in *The Political Economy of Development: An Africa Perspective*, vol. 2, ed. Sadig Rasheed and Siyanbola Tomori (Nairobi: ICIPE Science Press, 1996), 42.

9. Walter Rodney, *How Europe Underdeveloped Africa* (London: Bogle L' Ouverture Publications, 1972; repr. Howard University Press, 1981), 219.

10. Peter Alexander Egom, *Money in the Theory of International Economic Activity: An Inquiry into the Nature and Causes of the Wealth and Poverty of Nations* (Guderup, Denmark: Adione, 1977), 7.

11. Egom, *Money in the Theory of International Economic Activity*, 13.

12. Robert Guttmann, *How Credit-Money Shapes the Economy* (Armonk, NY: M. E. Sharpe, 1994), 428.

13. Guttmann, *How Credit-Money Shapes the Economy*, 440.

14. "Purchasing power parity defines an exchange rate at which a currency buys approximately the same amount of goods and services in the domestic market and abroad having been exchanged for the local money." See Guttmann, *How Credit-Money Shapes the Economy*, 518n29.

15. Guttmann, *How Credit-Money Shapes the Economy*, 443.

16. Barry Eichengreen, "Financial Instability," paper written on behalf of the Copenhagen Consensus, presented in Copenhagen, May 25–28, 2004.

17. It should be noted that averages like this hide huge differences between economies. The financial crises that Argentina experienced in 2001–2002 or Indonesia in 1997–1998 reduced national output to the point of economic collapse and resulted in drastic reductions in living standards. The fall in output was upward of 20 percent. "Statistical analyses . . . provide a sanitized sense of the social consequences. To remind oneself of the immediacy of these effects, it is only necessary to observe that Indonesian and Argentina experienced larger falls in output and real incomes than that suffered by the United States in the Great Depression, an event that produced a revolution in social and economic policy." See Eichengreen, "Financial Instability," 9–10.

18. See Eichengreen, "Financial Instability," 1.

19. See Eichengreen, "Financial Instability," pp. 28–29. "Purchasing power parity defines an exchange rate at which a currency buys approximately the same amount of goods and services in the domestic market and abroad having been exchanged for the local money." See Guttmann, *How Credit-Money Shapes the Economy*, 518n29.

20. I am using 1991 dollars because Professor Barry Eichengreen's model used the financial crises data of the 1990s. In 2005 dollars (using the GDP deflator) the Marshall Plan value of $14 billion is worth about $96.36 billion and Eichengreen's single-currency model figure of $91 billion (assuming 1998 as the base year) is worth $106.35 billion.

21. See Eichengreen, "Financial Instability," 28.

22. Barry Eichengreen, Ricardo Hausmann, Ugo Panizza, "Currency Mismatches, Debt Intolerance, and Original Sin: Why They are not the Same and Why

They Matter," NBER Working Paper No. 10036, October 2003. Note that the economists' concept of "original sin" does not have anything to do with Adam and Eve in the Bible. It rather refers to the inability of a country to borrow abroad in its own currency due to the structure of the international financial system and that this inability precedes and provides the basis for the country's problem of currency mismatches. They regard this characteristic of emerging markets (or developing economies) as defining their place and differentiating them from advanced economies in the international system as well as the primary source of their recurring financial fragility. They argue that the fragility exists because of inadequate opportunities for international risk sharing—in other words, there is a kind of distortion in relationship in which some countries win consistently and others persist in losing. The point being made here is this: the radical inability is an inherent quality of the poor (less advanced) economies' as they act in the international market, a constitutive part of all financial decisions and actions on their part. But to limit our understanding and interpretation of what the economists have raised up here to the individual country, individual country's "sinfulness," is to miss the larger point they are making. (For their options for redemptions [their own words] or changing the system often involves transforming the whole international financial system as we know it.) Original sin in the financial system is something that is genuinely common to the system as whole. It is only in this corporate character that it can be fully understood. With the greatest degree of circumspection of a non-expert, one might venture to say that this way of interpreting "original sin" in the global monetary system would remind some theologians and ethicists of Friedrich Schleiermacher's understanding of "original sin," another issue of a global (universal) nature or concern. In *The Christian Faith*, vol. 1 (New York: Harper & Row, 1963), 288, he writes: "Whether, in fact, we regard it [original sin] as guilt and deed or rather as a spirit and a state, it is in either case common to all; not something that pertains severally to each individual and exists in relation to him by himself, but in each the work of all, and in all the work of each; and only in this corporate character, indeed, can it be properly and fully understood. . . . The distinctive form of original sin in the individual, as regards its quality, is only a constituent part of the form it takes in the circle to which he immediately belongs, so that, though inexplicably when taken by itself, it points to the other parts as complementary to it." On the whole, Schleiermacher's concept of original sin relies on a relational model of human existence, the interconnected nature of human existence; for him sin is therefore a distortion of relationships through the interaction of all with all in each.

23. See Eichengreen, "Financial Instability," 10.

24. For example, see Charalambos G. Tsangarides, Pierre Ewenczcy, and Michal Hulej, "Stylized Facts on Bilateral Trade and Currency Unions: Implications for Africa," Working Paper /06/31, International Monetary Fund, January 2006; and Francis Breedon and Thórarinn G. Pétursson, "Out in the Cold? Iceland's Trade Performance Outside of the EU," Working Paper No. 26, Central Bank of Iceland, December 2004.

25. Nicholai Benelal, Juan Luis Diaz del Hoyo, Beatrice Pierluigi, and Nick Vidalis, "Output Differentials across the Euro Area Countries," Occasional Paper No. 45, European Central Bank, May 2006.

26. Please note that Greece entered the EMU in 2001.

27. One must accept that these data points do not really answer the question. The answer would need a better study and assessment, which I do not have now. The information here at least gives us some sense of what is happening to economic growth in the monetary union.

28. Benalal et al., "Output Differentials," 14.

29. The imaginative framework of the *Earth Dollar* is important even if political and economic realities block its immediate implementation. A certain realism, such as the ability of the nations whose currencies serve as the global currencies of trade and central banks' foreign reserves to block moves toward a denationalized currency, compels us to acknowledge this skepticism. I wish to add that gathering the world economies into a single currency zone may not be as difficult as corralling cats in the midst of a hurricane or gathering up again water spilled on the ground. The economy of the United States was a smorgasbord of private and foreign national currencies until the establishment of the dollar as the national currency in 1790, not to mention that the history of European Union success in establishing the euro is still fresh in our minds. We also know the history of gold standard between years 1880–1913, a period regarded by many economists and historians as period of single world currency based on gold.

30. Jenny Edkins, *Poststructuralism and International Relations: Bringing the Political Back In* (London: Lynne Rienner, 1999), 12; quoted by Marieke De Goede, *Virtue, Fortune, and Faith* (Minneapolis: University of Minnesota Press, 2005), 3.

31. Martin Buber, *I and Thou* (New York: Scribner, 1958), 110.

32. Christopher A. Gregory, *Gifts and Commodities* (London: Academic Press, 1982), 12; quoted in Kathryn Tanner, *Economy of Grace* (Minneapolis, MN: Fortress Press, 2005), 50.

33. In a separate paper I have worked out this theory for my theology of money. I worked out a relational concept of personhood by relying on an African conception of person which holds the possibility of more mutually participative economic life than the neoclassical economic concept of personhood. The major argument in this paper is that relations are constitutive of personhood.

34. Otto A. Piper, "That Strange Thing Money," *Theology Today* 6, no. 2 (July 1959): 219.

35. See Board of Governors of the Federal Reserve System, *Guide to the Flow of Funds Accounts* (Washington, DC, 1993), 7.

36. For examples of how this has been done with regard to other spheres of resistance against empire see Mark Taylor's book, *Religion, Politics and the Christian Right* (Minneapolis, MN: Fortress Press, 2005); and Taylor's *The Executed God* (Minneapolis: Fortress Press, 2001).

Bibliography

Abram, David. *The Spell of the Sensuous.* New York: Vintage Books, 1996.

African Development Bank. *African Development Report 2000.* (Oxford: Oxford University Press, 2000).

Akyüz, Yulmaz, and Heiner Flassbeck. "Exchange Rate Regimes and the Scope for Regional Cooperation," in *Reforming the Global Financial Architecture: Issues and Proposals,* edited byYulmaz Akyüz and Heiner Flassbeck. Penang, Malaysia: Third World Network, 2002, 81–116.

Alesina, Albertto, Rafael di Tella, and Robert MacCulloch. "Inequality and Happiness: Are Europeans and Americans Different?" National Bureau of Economic Research Working Paper 8198. Cambridge, Massachusetts, April 2001.

Altvater, Elmar. "The Foundations of Life (Nature) and the Maintenance of Life (Work)," *International Journal of Political Economy* 20, (1990): 10–34.

Alvey, James. "Lisa Hill's Discovery of Adam Smith's Hidden Theology." Paper presented at the Australian Political Studies Association Conference, University of Adelaide, Adelaide, September 29–October 1, 2004.

Amjad-Ali, Charles, W. "A Theory of Justice for an Ecumenical Praxis: A Critique of Eurocentric Pseudo-Universals." Unpublished Ph D dissertation, Princeton Theological Seminary, 1985.

Anidjar, Gil. "Christians and Money (The Economic Enemy)," *Ethical Perspective: Journal of the European Ethics*12, no. 4 (2005): 497–519.

Arendt, Hannah. *The Human Condition.* Chicago: University of Chicago Press, 1958.

Arrighi, Giovanni. "Lineages of Empire," *Historical Materialism* 10, 3 (Summer 2002): 3–16.

———. *The Geometry of Imperialism: The Limits of Hobson's Paradigm.* 2d ed. London: Verso, 1985.

Auerback, Marshall. "Last Orders for the U.S. dollars." *Critique* 12, Japan Policy Research Institute, March 2005, http: //www.jpri.org/publications/critiques/critigue_XII_2.html (accessed May 3, 2006).

Badiou, Alain. *Being and Event*, translated by Oliver Feltham. London: Continuum, 2006.

Baker, Wayne E. "What is Money? A Social Structural Interpretation," in *Intercorporate Relations: The Structural Analysis of Business*, edited by Mark S. Mizruchi and Michael Schwartz. New York: Cambridge University Press, 1987, 109–44.

Barker, Ernest. *The Politics of Aristotle*. London: Oxford University Press, 1958.

Barth, Karl. *Church Dogmatics*, vol. 1, edited by G. W. Bromiley and T. F. Torrance. Edinburgh: T. & T. Clark, 1936, part 1.

Bell, Stephanie A., and Edward J. Nell, eds. *The State, the Market and the Euro: Chartalism versus Metalism in the Theory of Money*. Cheltenham, UK: Edward Elgar, 2003.

Bell, Stephanie. "The Role of the State and the Hierarchy of Money," *Cambridge Journal of Economics* 25, no. 3 (2001): 149–63.

Bellah, Robert N. *Beyond Belief: Essay in Religion in a Post-Traditional World*. New York: Harper & Row, 1970.

Benelal, Nicholai, Juan Luis Diaz del Hoyo, Beatrice Pierluigi, and Nick Vidalis, "Output Differentials across the Euro Area Countries." Occasional Paper Number 45, European Central Bank, May 2006.

Bernstein, Peter L. *Against the Gods: The Remarkable Story of Risk*. New York: John Wiley & Sons, 1996.

———. *Capital Ideas: The Improbable Origins of Modern Wall Street*. New York: Free Press, 1992.

Bhagwati, Jagdish, *In Defense of Globalization*. New York: Oxford University Press, 2004.

Billings, David. "Natality or Advent: Hannah Arendt and Jürgen Moltmann on Hope and Politics," in *The Future of Hope: Christian Tradition Amid Modernity and Postmodernity*, edited by Miroslav Volf and William Katerberg. Grand Rapids, MI: William B. Eerdmans Co., 2004), 125–45.

Blank, Rebecca M., and Alan S. Blinder. "Macroeconomics, Income Distribution, and Poverty," in *Fighting Poverty: What Works and What Doesn't*, edited by Sheldon H. Danziger and Daniel H. Weinberg. Cambridge, MA: Harvard University Press, 1986, 180–208.

Blaug, Mark. *The Methodology of Economics or How Economists Explain*. Cambridge: Cambridge University Press, 1992.

Bloch, Ernest. *The Principle of Hope*, vols. 1–3, translated by Neville Plaice, Stephen Plaice, and Paul Knight. Cambridge. MA: MIT Press, 1995.

Bloch, Ernest, and Jonathan Parry, eds. *Death and Regeneration of Life*. Cambridge: Cambridge University Press, 1982.

Bloch, Maurice. *Ritual, History and Power: Selected Papers in Anthropology*. New York: Berg, 1989.

Block, Robert. "Some Muslim Nations Advocate Dumping the Dollar for the Euro," *Wall Street Journal*, April 15, 2003.

Boff, Leonardo. "The Liberating Design of God," in *Mysterium Liberations: Fundamental Concepts of Liberation Theology*, edited by Ignacio Ellacuria and Jon Sobrino. Maryknoll, NY: Orbis Books, 1993, 389–403.

———. *Trinity and Society*, translated by Paul Burns. Maryknoll, NY: Orbis, 1988.

Board of Governors of the Federal Reserve System. *Guide to the Flow of Funds Accounts*. Washington, DC, 1993.

Breedon, Francis, and Thórarinn G. Pétursson. "Out in the Cold? Iceland's Trade Performance Outside of the EU." Working Paper No. 26, Central Bank of Iceland, December 2004.

Buber, Martin. *I and Thou*. New York: Scribner, 1958.

Buchan, James. *Frozen Desire: The Meaning of Money*. New York: Welcome Rain, 2001).

Buffet, Howard. "Human Freedom Rests on Gold Redeemable Money." Reprinted from *The Commercial and Financial Chronicle*, May 6, 1948.

Bush, Randall B. *Recent Ideas of Divine Conflict: The Influence of Psychological and Sociological Theories of Conflict upon the Trinitarian Theology of Paul Tillich and Jürgen Moltmann*. San Francisco: Mellen Research University Press, 1991.

Callinicos, Alex. *The New Mandarins of American Power: The Bush Administration's Plans for the World*. Cambridge, MA: Polity Press, 2003.

Carlino, Gerald, and Robert DeFina. "The Differential Regional Effects of Monetary Policy: Evidence from the U.S. States," *Journal of Regional Science* 39, no. 2 (1999): 339–58.

———. "Monetary Policy and the U.S. States and Regions: Some Implications for the European Monetary Union," *National Bureau of Economic Research*, Working Paper No. 98-17, July 1998.

———. "The Differential Regional Effects of Monetary Policy." *Review of Economics and Statistics* 80, no. 4 (1998): 572–87.

Carnegie, Andrew. "Wealth," *North American Review*, 148, no. 391 (June 1889): 653–64.

Carpenter, S., and William M. Rodgers III. "The Disparate Labor Market Impacts of Monetary Policy," *Journal of Policy Analysis and Management* 23, no. 4 (2004): 813–30.

Carruthers, Bruce. "The Sociology of Money and Credit," in *The Handbook of Economic Sociology*, 2nd ed., edited by N. J. Smelser and R. Swedberg. Princeton, NJ: Princeton University Press, 2005, 355–78.

Choi, Young B. "Conventions and Economic Change: A Contribution Towards a theory of Political Economy," *Constitutional Political Economy* 10 (1999): 245–64.

Chung, Duck-Koo, and Barry Eichengreen, eds. *The Korean Economy Beyond the Crisis*. Cheltenham, UK: Edward Elgar, 2005.

Clark, William, R. *Petrodollar Warfare: Oil, Iraq and the Future of the Dollar*. Gabriola Island, Canada: New Society Publishers, 2005.

Clayton, Philip. "Eschatology as Metaphysics under the Guise of Hope," in *World without End: Christian Eschatology from a Process Perspective*, edited by Joseph A. Bracken, S.J. Grand Rapids: William B. Eerdmans Co., 2005, 128–49.

———. *Mind and Emergence: From Quantum to Consciousness*. Oxford: Oxford University Press, 2004.

Collins, Randall. *Interaction Ritual Chains*. Princeton, NJ: Princeton University Press, 2004.

Columbia Business School. *Columbia Ideas at Work: Connecting Research to the Practice of Business*. New York: Summer 2006.

Conradie, Ernst M. "In Search of a Vision of Hope for a New Century," *Journal of Religion and Society*, 1 (1999), available at http: //moses.creighton.edu/JRS/ 1999/1999-1.html (accessed August 22, 2006).

Cooper, Richard N. "Proposal for a Common Currency among Rich Democracies," Working Paper No. 127. Oesterreichische Nationalbank, available at http: www.oenb.at (accessed September 13, 2006).

Cowen, Tyler, and Randall Kroszner. *Explorations in the New Monetary Economics.* Cambridge, MA: Blackwell, 1994.

Daly, Herman E., and John B. Cobb Jr. *For the Common Good: Redirecting the Economy toward Community, the Environment, and a Sustainable Future,* 2nd ed. Boston: Beacon, 1989.

Deflem, Mathieu. "The Sociology of the Sociology of Money: Simmel and the Contemporary Battle of the Classics," *Journal of Classical Sociology* 3, no.1 (2003): 67–96.

D' Arista, Jane. "Another Year Awash in Liquidity," *Capital Flows Monitor* (April 27, 2006): 1–8.

———. "Causes and Consequences of the Buildup in Global Liquidity, Part 2," *Capital Flows Monitor* (April 27, 2005): 1–8.

———. "Reforming the Privatized International Monetary and Financial Architecture," *Financial Markets and Society* (November 1999): 1–22.

De Goede, Marieke. *Virtue, Fortune, and Faith.* Minneapolis: University of Minnesota Press, 2005.

Derrida, Jacques. *Specters of Marx: The State of Debt, the Work of Mourning, and the New International,* translated by Peggy Kamuf. New York: Routledge, 1994.

Diulio, Eugene A. *Theory and Problems of Macroeconomic Theory.* New York: McGraw-Hill, 1990.

Dodd, Nigel. "Reinventing Monies in Europe," *Economy and Society* 34 no. 4 (November 2005): 588–83.

———. "Globalization of Money?: National Sovereignty and the management of Risk," in *Nation-States and Money: The Past, Present and Future of National Currencies,* edited by Emily Gilbert and Eric Helleiner. London: Routledge, 1999, 182–95.

Dourley, John. "Tillich's Appropriation of Meister Eckhart: An Appreciative Critique," *Bulletin of the North American Paul Tillich Society* 31, no. 1 (Winter 2005): 9–17.

Duchrow, Ulrich, and Frank J. Hinkelammert. *Property for People, Not for Profit: Alternative to the Global Tyranny of Capital.* London: Zed Books, 2004.

Dunn, Kevin C. "Africa's Ambiguous Relation to Empire and Empire," in *Empire's New Clothes: Reading Hardt and Negri,* edited by Paul A. Passavant and Jodi Dean. New York: Routledge, 2004, 143–62.

Edkins, Jenny. *Poststructuralism and International Relations: Bringing the Political Back In.* London: Lynne Rienner, 1999.

Edwards, Denis. *The God of Evolution: A Trinitarian Theology.* New York: Paulist Press, 1999.

Egom, Peter Alexander. *NEPAD and the Common Good.* Lagos, Nigeria: Global Market Forum, 2004.

———. *Globalization at the Crossroads: Capitalism or Communalism.* Lagos, Nigeria: Global Market Associates, 2002.

———. *Money in the Theory of International Economic Activity: An Inquiry into the Nature and Causes of the Wealth and Poverty of Nations.* Guderup, Denmark: Adione, 1977.

Eichengreen, Barry. "Financial Instability." Paper presented at Copenhagen Consensus Conference, May 25–28, 2004, available at http: //www.econ.berkeley .edu/~eichengr/policy.html (accessed September 5, 2006).

———. Ricardo Hausmann, Ugo Panizza, "Currency Mismatches, Debt Intolerance, and Original Sin: Why They are not the Aame and Why They Matter," NBER Working Paper No. 10036, October 2003.

Eliade, Mircea, ed. *The Encyclopedia of Religion*, vol. 11. New York. Macmillan Publishing Co., 1987.

Ellis, Stephen, and Gerrie Ter Haar. *Worlds of Power: Religious Thought and Political Practice in Africa.* New York: Oxford University Press, 2004.

Escobar, Arturo. *Encountering Development: The Making and Unmaking of the Third World.* Princeton, NJ: Princeton University Press, 1995.

Falola, Toyin, ed. *Africa*, vol. 5, *Contemporary Africa.* Durham, NC: Carolina Academic Press, 2003.

Feldstein, Martin. "Stabilize Price, Not the Dollar," *Wall Street Journal*, March 17, 1995, p. A10.

Felms, Joachim. "Global: Pondering the Composition of Central Bank Reserves, Part 1," Global Economic Forum, Morgan Stanley, October 18, 2005, http: //www .morganstanley.com/GEFdata/digests/20051018-tue.html (accessed May 3, 2006).

Fine, Ben, and Costas Lapavitsas. "Markets and Money in Social Theory: What Role for Economics?," *Economy and Society* 29, no. 3 (2000): 357–82.

Food and Agricultural Organization of United Nations. *State of Food and Agriculture (SOFA) 2000.* Rome.

———. FAOSTAT Database 2000. Rome.

Ford, Lewis S. "Tillich's Tergiversations toward the Power of Being," *Scottish Journal of Theology* 28 (1975): 323–40.

Foucault, Michel. "Structuralism and Post-Structuralism: An Interview with Michel Foucault," *Telos* 55 (Spring 1983): 195–211.

Friedman, Milton. *Money Mischief: Episodes in Monetary History.* New York: Harvest/HBJ Books, 1994.

———. "The Resource Cost of Irredeemable Paper Money," *Journal of Political Economy* 94, no. 3 (June 1986): 642–47.

———. *A Program for Monetary Stability.* New York: Fordham University Press, 1992.

———. *Capitalism and Freedom.* Chicago: University of Chicago Press, 1962.

———. *Essays in Positive Economics.* Chicago: University of Chicago Press, 1953.

Gadamer, Hans-Georg. *Truth and Method.* London: Continuum, 1975.

Galbraith, John Kenneth. *Money: Whence it Came, Where it Went.* Boston: Houghton Mifflin Co., 1975.

Gay, Craig. M. *Money and the Erosion of Meaning in Today's Society.* Grand Rapids, MI: William B. Eerdmans Co., 2004.

Ganssman, Heiner. "Book Review: Geoffrey Ingham, 'The Nature of Money,'" *Economic Sociology, European Electronic Newsletter* 6, no. 1 (October 2004): 29–32.

George, Susan. "How the Poor Develop the Rich," in *The Post-Development Reader*, edited by Majid Rahnema with Victoria Bawtree. London: Zed Books, 1997, 207–13.

Gilbert, Emily, and Eric Helleiner, eds. *Nation-States and Money: The Past, Present and Future of National Currencies*. London: Routledge, 1999.

Giovanni Arrighi. *The Long Twentieth Century: Money, Power, and the Origins of our Times*. London: Verso, 1994.

Goodchild, Philip. "Capital and Kingdom: An Eschatological Ontology," in *Theology and the Political: The New Debate*, edited by Creston Davies, John Milbank, and Slavoj Zizek. Durham, NC: Duke University Press, 2005, 127–52.

———. "Debt, Epistemology and Ecotheology," *Ecotheology* 9, no. 2 (2004): 151–77.

Goodhart, Charles. A. "What is the Essence of Money?" *Cambridge Journal of Economics* 29 (2005): 817–25.

Goux, Jean-Joseph. *Symbolic Economies: After Marx Freud*. Ithaca, NY: Cornell University Press, 1990.

Grau, Marion. *Of Divine Economy: Refinancing Redemption*. New York: T & T Clark, 2004.

Gregory, Christopher A. *Gifts and Commodities*. London: Academic Press, 1982.

Grenz, Stanley J. *Rediscovering the Triune God: The Trinity in Contemporary Theology*. Minneapolis, MN: Fortress Press, 2004.

Grierson, Philip. *The Origins of Money*. London: Athlone Press, 1977.

Gunton, Colin E. *Father, Son and Holy Spirit: Toward a Fully Trinitarian Theology*. London: T & T Clark, 2003.

Guttmann, Robert. *How Credit-Money Shapes the Economy*. Armonk, NY: M. E. Sharpe, 1994.

Hallward, Peter. *Badiou: A Subject to Truth*. Minneapolis: University of Minneapolis Press, 2003.

Hamel, Gary, and C. K. Prahalad. "Strategy as Stretch and Leverage," *Harvard Business Review* (March–April 1993): 75–84.

Hardt, Michael, and Antonio Negri. *Multitude: War and Democracy in the Age of Empire*. New York: Penguin Press, 2004.

———. *Empire*. Cambridge, MA: Harvard University Press, 2000.

Hardy, Daniel W. *Finding the Church: The Dynamic Truth of Anglicanism*. London: SCM Press, 2001.

Harrison, Beverly Wildung. *Making the Connections: Essays in Feminist Social Ethics*, edited by Carol S. Robb. Boston: Beacon Press, 1985.

Hart, H. L. A. *The Concept of Law*, 2nd ed. Oxford: Oxford University Press, 1994.

Hart, Keith. *Money in an Unequal World: Keith Hart and his Memory Bank*. New York & London: Profile Books, 2000.

Hassert, Paul. "Theology and Money," *Explore* 4, no. 2 (Fall 1978): 21–32.

Hayek, Friedrich. *Denationalization of Money—The Argument Refined*, 3rd. ed. London: Institute of Economic Affairs, 1990.

Hegel, G. W. F. *Philosophy of Right*, translated by T. M. Knox. New York: Oxford University Press, 1969.

Hill, Lisa. "The Hidden Theology of Adam Smith," *European Journal of the History of Economic Thought* 8, no.1 (2001): 1–29.

Hirschman, Albert O. *The Passions and the Interest: Political Arguments for Capitalism before its Triumph.* Princeton, NJ: Princeton University Press, 1977.

Hol, Antoine M. "Adjudication and the Public Realm: An Analysis Based on the Work of Hannah Arendt," *Utrecht Law Review* 1, no. 2 (December 2005): 40–55.

Hoppe, Hans-Hermann. "How is Fiat Money Possible? or, The Devolution of Money and Credit," *Review of Austrian Economics* 7, no. 2 (1994): 49–74.

Horton, Robin. *Patterns of Thoughts in Africa and the West: Essays on Magic, Religion and Science.* Cambridge: Cambridge University Press, 1993.

Huber, Joseph. "Plain Money: A Proposal for Supplying the Nations with the Necessary Means in a Modern Monetary System," October 1999, http: //www.soziologie.uni-halle.de/publikationen/index.html (accessed April 30, 2005).

Hudson, Michael. "The Archaeology of Money: Debt vs. Barter Theories of Money," in *Credit and State Theories of Money,* edited by Randall Wray. Cheltenham, UK: Edward Elgar, 2004, 99–127.

———. "The Credit/Monetarist Debate in Historical Perspective," in *The State, the Market and the Euro: Chartalism versus Metalism in the Theory of Money,* edited by Stephanie A. Bell and Edward J. Nell. Cheltenham, UK: Edward Elgar, 2003, 38–76.

———. *Super Imperialism: The Economic Strategy of American Empire.* London: Pluto Press, 2003.

Hunter, James Davison, and Joshua Yates. "In the Vanguard of Globalization: The World of American Globalizers," in *Many Globalizations: Cultural Diversity in the Contemporary World,* edited by Peter L. Berger and Samuel P. Huntington. Oxford: Oxford University Press, 2002, 323–57.

Hutchinson, Roger C. "Mutuality: Procedural Norm and Foundational Symbol," in *Liberation and Ethics,* edited by Charles Amjad-Ali and W. Alvin Pitcher. Chicago: Center for the Scientific Study of Religion, 1985, 97–110.

Ingham, Geoffrey. *The Nature of Money.* Cambridge, MA: Polity Press, 2004.

———. "The Nature of Money," *Economic Sociology, European Electronic Newsletter* 6, no.1 (October 2004): 18–28.

———. "Schumpeter and Weber on the Institutions of Capitalism: Solving Swedberg's Puzzle," *Journal of Classical Sociology* 30, no. 3 (2003): 297–309.

———. "Fundamentals of a Theory of Money: Untangling Fine, Lapavitsas and Zelizer," *Economy and Society* 30, no. 3 (2001): 304–23.

———. "Class Inequality and the Social Production of Money," in *Renewing Class Analysis,* edited by Rosemary Crompton, Fiona Divine, Mike Savage, and John Scott. Oxford: Blackwell Publishers, 2000, 66–86.

———. "Money is a Social Relation," in *Critical Realism in Economics: Development and Debate,* edited by Steve Fleetwood. London: Routledge, 1999, 103–24.

Innes, A. Mitchell. "What is Money?" *Banking Law Journal* 30 (1913): 377–408.

———. "The Credit Theory of Money," *Banking Law Journal* 31 (1914): 151–68.

Jens, Stephen L. "USD: Is Reserve Diversification Negative for the Dollar?" *Global Economic Forum,* September 16, 2005, http: //www.morganstanley.com/GEF-data/digests/2005916-fri.html (accessed May 3, 2006).

Jevons, William Stanley. *Money and the Mechanism of Exchange*. New York: Appleton, 1986.

Kärkkäinen, Veli-Matti. *Trinity and Religious Pluralism: The Doctrine of the Trinity in Christian Theology of Religions*. Aldershot, UK: Ashgate Publishing, 2004.

Keynes, John Maynard. *The Collected Writings of John Maynard Keynes*, vol. 25, *Activities 1940–1944: Shaping the Post-War World, The Clearing Union*, edited by D. Moggridge. London: Macmillan, 1980.

———. *A Treatise on Money*. London: Macmillan, 1930.

———. *Economic Consequences of Peace*. New York: Harcourt, Brace & Howe, 1920.

Kilby, Karen. "Perichoresis and Projection: Problems with the Doctrines of Trinity," *New Blackfriars* 81, no. 965 (October 2000): 432–45.

Knapp Georg F. *The State Theory of Money*, abridged and translated by H. E. Batson. London: Routledge & Kegan Paul, 1924.

Kopytoff, Igor. "The Cultural Biography of Things: Commoditization as Process," in *The Social Life of Things: Commodities in Cultural Perspective*, edited by Argun Appadurai. Cambridge: Cambridge University Press, 1988, 64–90.

Krugman, Paul. *The Accidental Theorist and Other Dispatches from the Dismal Science*. New York: W. W. Norton & Co. 1998.

———. *The Age of Diminished Expectations: U.S. Economic Policy in the 1990s*. Cambridge, MA: MIT Press, 1994.

Lacugna, Catherine Mowry. "The Practical Trinity," *Christian Century* 109, no. 22 (July 15–22, 1992): 678–82.

Lamb, Matthew. "Theology of Money: Rationality, Religion, and Economics," *American Behavioral Scientist* 35, no. 6 (July 1992): 735–55.

Lapavitsas, Costas. "The Social Relations of Money as Universal Equivalent: A Response to Ingham," *Economy and Society* 34, no. 3 (2005): 389–403.

Lawrence, Frederick G., Patrick H. Byrne, and Charles C. Hefling Jr. "Introduction," in Bernard Lonergan, *Collected Works*, vol. 15, *Macroeconomic Dynamics: An Essay in Circulation Analysis*. Toronto: Lonergan Research Institute, 1999.

Lietaer, Bernard. *The Future of Money: A New Way to Create Wealth, Work, and Wiser World*. London: Century, 2001.

Little, Daniel. *Varieties of Social Explanation: An Introduction to the Philosophy of Social Sciences*. Boulder, CO: Westview Press, 1991.

Liu, Henry C. K. "More on the US Experience," *Asia Times Online*, November 27, 2002, http://www.atimes.com/atimes/printN.html (accessed June 8, 2005).

Lonergan, Bernard. *Collected Works*, vol. 15, *Macroeconomic Dynamics: An Essay in Circulation Analysis*. Toronto: Lonergan Research Institute, 1999.

———. *Insight: A Study of Human Understanding*. Toronto: Toronto University Press, 1992.

Maclister, Terry. "Iran Takes on West's Control of Oil Trading," *Guardian*, June 16, 2004, http://business.guardian.co.uk/story/0,3604,1239644,00.html (accessed July 13, 2006).

MacIntyre, Alasdair. *After Virtue*. Notre Dame, IN: University of Notre Dame Press, 1984.

Maclennan, Ronald Bruce. *The Doctrine of the Trinity in the Theology of Paul Tillich*. Unpublished Ph D Dissertation, Lutheran School of Theology, Chicago, 1991.

Macmurrray, John. *Persons in Relation*. London: Faber & Faber, 1961.

Madsen, Richard. *Morality and Power in a Chinese Village*. Berkeley: University of California Press, 1984.

Mansfield, Edwin. *Managerial Economics: Theory, Applications, and Cases*. New York: W. W. Norton & Co., 1990.

Marx, Karl *Capital*, vol. 1. London: Penguin, 1976.

———. *Grundrisse: Foundations of the Critique of Political Economy*, translated by Martin Nicolaus. New York: Penguin Books, 1973.

———. *Writings of the Young Marx on Philosophy and Society*, translated by Lloyd Easton and Kurt Guddat. New York: Doubleday, 1967.

———. *The Economic and Philosophical Manuscript of 1844*. Moscow: Foreign Language Publishing, 1956.

Malthus, Robert Thomas. *Essay on the Principle of Population*. London: J. Johnson, 1798; repr. Penguin Classics, 1982.

McFague Sallie. *Models of God: Theology for an Ecological, Nuclear Age*. Philadelphia: Fortress University Press, 1982.

———. *Metaphorical Theology: Models of God in Religious Language*. Philadelphia: Fortress University Press, 1982.

Meeks, M. Douglas. *God the Economist: The Doctrine of God and Political Economy*. Minneapolis, MN: Fortress, 1989.

Menger, Carl. "On the Origin of Money," *Economic Journal* 2 (June 1892): 239–55.

Mignolo, Walter D. *Local Histories/Global Designs: Coloniality, Subaltern Knowledges, and Border Thinking*. Princeton, NJ: Princeton University Press, 2000.

Mises, Ludwig von. *Theory of Money and Credit*. Irvington-on-Hudson, NY: Foundation for Economic Education, 1971.

Mishkin, Frederic S. *The Economics of Money, Banking, and Financial Markets*. Glenview: Scott, Foresman & Company, 1989.

Moltmann, Jürgen. *The Coming of God: Christian Eschatology*. Minneapolis, MN: Fortress Press, 1996.

———. *The Trinity and the Kingdom*. Minneapolis, MN: Fortress Press, 1993.

———. *Theology of Hope*. Minneapolis, MN: Fortress Press, 1993.

Mouw, Richard J. *He Shines in all that's Fair: Culture and Common Grace*. Grand Rapids, MI: William B. Eerdmans Co., 2001.

Mundell, Robert. "The International Monetary System and the Case for a World Currency," Leon Kozminski Academy of Entrepreneurship and Management (WSPiZ) and Tiger Distinguished Lecture Series 12, Warsaw, October 23, 2003.

———. "Currency Areas and International Monetary Relations at the Dawn of a New Century," *Review of International Economics* 9, no. 4 (2001): 595–607.

———. "Gold Would Serve into the 21st Century," *Wall Street Journal*, September 30, 1981, p. 28.

———. "The Theory of Optimum Currency Area," *American Economic Review* 15, no. 4 (1961): 509–17.

Needleman, Jacob. *Money and the Meaning of Life*. New York: Doubleday, 1991.

Nelson, Robert H. *Economics as Religion from Samuelson to Chicago and Beyond*. University Park: Pennsylvania State University Press, 2001.

———. *Reaching for Heaven on Earth: The Theological Meaning of Economics*. (Savage, MD: Rowman & Littlefield, 1991).

Niebuhr, Reinhold. *Love and Justice: Selection from the Shorter Writings of Reinhold Niebuhr*, edited by D. B. Robertson. Louisville, KY: Westminster/John Knox Press, 1957.

———. *Nature and Destiny of Man*, vol. 1 and 2. Upper Saddle River, NJ: Prentice Hall, 1941.

Norris, Thomas. "The Symphonic Unity of His Theology: An Overview," in *Beauty of Christ: An Introduction to the Theology of Urs Von Balthasa*, edited by Bede McGregor and Thomas Norris. Edinburgh: T & T Clark, 1994, 213–52.

Odejide, Agnes. "Food Sufficiency in Africa," in *The Political Economy of Development: An African Perspective*, vol. 2, edited by Sadig Rasheed and Siyanbola Tomori. Nairobi: ICIPE Science Press, 1996.

Olson, Mancur. *The Rise and Decline of Nations: Economic Growth, Stagflation, and Social Rigidities*. New Haven, CT: Yale University Press, 1982.

Oslington, Paul. "Natural Theology as an Integrative Framework," St. Marks Day Public Lecture, St Marks National Theological Center, May 2005.

Oyebade, Adebayo, ed. *The Transformation of Nigeria: Essays in Honor of Toyin Falola*. Trenton, NJ: African World Press, 2002.

Pannenberg, Wolfhart. "The God of Hope," in *Basic Questions in Theology*. London: SCM Press, 1971, 234–49.

Parks, Lawrence. "To Revive U.S Manufacturing, Reform Our Monetary System," http: //www.fame.org/HTM/Revive%20U.S.%20Manufacturing%20Reform%20OUr%20 (accessed December 29, 2004).

Parks, Lawrence. "Questions and Answers About Money, Public Policy and Informational Issues." Foundation for the Advancement of Monetary Education. New York City, February 17, 2001.

Parry, Jonathan, and Maurice Bloch, eds., *Money and the Morality of Exchange*. Cambridge: Cambridge University Press, 1989.

Parsons, Talcott. *Politics and Social Structure*. New York: Free Press, 1969.

———. *Structure and Process in Modern Societies*. New York: Free Press, 1960.

Passavant, Paul A., and Jodi Dean, eds. *Empire's New Clothes: Reading Hardt and Negri*. New York: Routledge, 2004.

Pauck, Wilhelm, and Marion Pauck. *Paul Tillich: His Life and Thought*, vol. 1, *Life*. New York: Harper & Row, 1976.

Paul, Ron. "The End of the Dollar Hegemony," http: //www.house.gov/paul/congrec2006/cr021506.htm (accessed July 13, 2006).

———. "Paper Money and Tyranny," House of Representatives, September 5, 2003.

Peters, Rebecca Todd. *In Search of the Good Life: The Ethics of Globalization*. New York: Continuum, 2004.

Phillips, Kevin. *Boiling Point. Republicans, Democrats, and the Decline of Middle-Class*. New York: Random House, 1993.

Piper, Otto A. "That Strange Thing Money," *Theology Today*, 16, no. 2 (July 1959): 215–31.

Pixley, Jocelyn. *Emotions in Finance: Distrust and Uncertainty in Global Finance*. Cambridge: Cambridge University Press, 2004.

Polanyi, Karl. *The Great Transformation: The Political and Economic Origins of Our Time*. Boston: Beacon Press, 2001.

Prychitko, David, ed. *Individuals, Institutions, Interpretation: Hermeneutics Applied to Economics*. Avebury, UK: Aldershot, 1995.

Quinby, Lee. "Taking the Millennialist Pulse of Empire's Multitude: A Genealogical Feminist Diagnosis," in *Empire's New Clothes: Reading Hardt and Negri*, edited by Paul A. Passavant and Jodi Dean. New York: Routledge, 2004, 231–51.

Rajan, Ramkishen S., and Jose Kiran. "Will the Greenback Remain the World's Reserves Currency?" Unpublished paper, January 2006.

Rakodi Carole, ed. *The Urban Challenge in Africa: Growth and Management of its Large Cities*. Tokyo: United Nations University Press, 1997.

Reiss, Julian. "Explanatory Mechanism and the Aims of the Social Science," http://reiss.org/papers.html (accessed July 25, 2006).

Rockoff, Hugh. "The 'Wizard of Oz' as a Monetary Allegory," *Journal of Political Economy* 98, no. 4 (1990): 739–60.

Rodgers III, William M. "The Impact of Monetary Policy on the Distribution and Type of Unemployment," *John J. Heldrich Center for Workforce Development and National Poverty Center*. Rutgers: State University of New Jersey, July 2004.

Rodney, Walter. *How Europe Underdeveloped Africa*. London: Bogle L'Ouverture Publications, 1972.

Romer, Christina D., and David H. Romer. "Choosing the Federal Reserve Chair: Lessons from History." Working Paper No. 10161, National Bureau of Economic Research, December 2003.

Romer, Christina D., and David H. Romer. "Monetary Policy and the Well-being of the Poor." Working Paper No. 6793, National Bureau of Economic Research. November 1998.

Rosecrance, Richard. *The Rise of the Trading States: Commerce and Conquest in the Modern World*. New York: Basic Books, 1986.

Rosenberg, Alexander. *Philosophy of Social Science*. Boulder, CO: Westview Press, 1995.

Samuelson, Paul A. *Economics*, 9th ed. New York: McGraw-Hill, 1973.

———. "Proof that Properly Anticipated Prices Fluctuate Randomly," *Industrial Management Review* 6 (Spring 1965): 41–49.

Sassen, Saskia. "The Repositioning of Citizenship: Emergent Subjects and Spaces for Politics," in *Empire's New Clothes: Reading Hardt and Negri*, edited by Paul A. Passavant and Jodi Dean. New York: Routledge, 2004, 175–98.

———. *The Global City*. Princeton, NJ: Princeton University Press, 2001.

Sapir, Jacques. "Seven Theses for a Theory of Realist Economics; Part I: Theses One to Four," *Post-Autistic Economic Review* 21 (September 13, 2003), http://www.btinternet.com/~pae_news/review/issue/21.htm. (accessed November 1, 2004).

Schleiermacher, Friedrich. *The Christian Faith*, vol. 1. New York: Harper & Row, 1963.

Schumpeter, Joseph A. *History of Economic Analysis*. New York: Oxford University Press, 1994 [1954].

Schweiker, William. "The Spirit of Life and the Reverence for Life," in *God's Life in Trinity*, edited by Miroslav Volf and Michael Welker. Minneapolis, MN: Fortress Press, 2005, 22–32.

———. *Theological Ethics and Global Dynamics: In the Time of Many Worlds.* Oxford: Blackwell, 2004.

———. *Responsibility and Christian Ethics.* Cambridge: Cambridge University Press, 1995.

Schweitzer, Albert. "The Ethics of Reverence for Life," *Christendom* 1 (1936): 225–39. It is also available at http: //www.chapman.edu/schweitzerInstitute/revRead/ethics.asp.

Schwobel, Christoph, and Colin E. Gunton. *Persons, Divine and Human: King's College Essays in Theological Anthropology.* Edinburgh: T & T Clark, 1991.

Scott, James C. "Domination, Acting and Fantasy," in *The Paths to Domination, Resistance and Terror,* edited by Carolyn Nordstrom and JoAnn Martin. Berkeley: University of California Press, 1992, 55–84.

Searle, R. "Social Ontology and the Philosophy of Society," *Analyse and Kritik* 2 (1998): 143–58.

———. "Social Ontology and Political Power," www.law.berkeley.edu/centers/kadish/searle.pdf (accessed July 26, 2006).

Selby, Peter. *Grace and Mortgage: The Language of Faith and the Debt of the World.* London: Darton, Longman & Todd, 1997.

Sen, Amartya. *Development as Freedom.* New York: Random House, 2000.

———. *On Ethics and Economics.* Malden: Blackwell, 1988.

———. "The Food Problem: Theory and Policy," *Third World Quarterly* 4, no. 3 (1982): 447–59.

Serequeberhan, Tsenay. *The Hermeneutics of African Philosophy: Horizon and Discourse.* New York: Routledge, 1994.

Shell, Marc. *Art and Money.* Chicago: University of Chicago Press, 1995.

Shuman, Michael. *Going Local: Creating Self-Reliant Communities in a Global Age.* New York: Free Press, 1998.

Sirico, Robert A. "Examining the Moral Dimensions of Monetary Policy," *Economic Insights* 1, no. 1 (February 25, 1994): 4

Simmel, Georg. *The Philosophy of Money,* translated by Tom Bottomore and David Frisby. London: Routledge & Kegan Paul 1978 [1900].

Smith, Adam. *An Inquiry into the Nature and Causes of the Wealth of Nations,* Bantam Classic Edition. New York: Random House, 1776, [2003].

———. *The Principles Which Lead and Direct Philosophical Enquiries Illustrated by the History of Astronomy,* in *Essays on Philosophical Subjects,* vol. 3, edited by W. P. D. and J. C. Bryce. Oxford: Oxford University Press, 1980, 2.

———. *The Theory of Moral Sentiments,* ed. by D. D. Raphael and A. L. Macfie (Oxford: Clarendon Press, 1976).

Speidell, Todd. H. "A Trinitarian Ontology of Persons in Society," *Scottish Journal of Theology* 47 (1994): 283–300.

Spindler, Z. A. "Public Choice Perspectives on Monetary Regimes," unpublished paper dated January 15, 2004. Department of Economics, Simon Fraser University, Burnaby, Canada.

Spiro, David E. *The Hidden Hand of American Hegemony: Petrodollar Recycling and International Markets.* Ithaca, NY: Cornell University Press, 1999.

Stackhouse, Max L. "Introduction: Foundations and Purposes," in *On Moral Business: Classical and Contemporary Resources for Ethics in Economic Life,* edited by

Stackhouse, Dennis P. McCann, and Shirley J. Roels, with Preston N. Williams. Grand Rapids, MI: William B. Eerdmans Co., 1995), 10–34.

———. *Public Theology and Political Economy: Christian Stewardship in Modern Society*. Grand Rapids, MI: William B. Eerdmans Co., 1987.

Stark, Rodney. *The Victory of Reason: How Christianity Led to Freedom, Capitalism, and Western Success*. New York: Random House, 2005.

Stevenson, Taylor W. *Soul and Money: A Theology of Wealth*. New York: Episcopal Church Center, 1991.

Stout, Jeffrey. *Democracy and Tradition*. Princeton, NJ: Princeton University Press, 2004.

———. *Ethics After Babel: The Languages of Morals and their Discontents*. Boston: Beacon Press, 1988.

Sturm, Douglas. "The Prism of Justice: E Pluribus Unum?" *Selected Papers, The Annual of the Society of Christian Ethics* (1981): 1–28.

Sutcliffe, Bob. "Development After Ecology," in *From Modernization to Globalization: Perspectives on Development and Social Change*, edited by T. Roberts and A. Hite. Oxford: Blackwell, 1995, 328–39.

Swedberg, Richard. "Answer to Geoffrey Ingham," *Journal of Classical Sociology* 30, no. 3 (2003): 311–14.

Todaro, Michael. *Economic Development in the Third World Nation*, 4th ed. White Plains, NY: Longman, 1989.

Tanner, Kathryn. *Economy of Grace*. Minneapolis, MN: Fortress Press, 2005.

Tavlas, George S. "The Internal Use of Currencies: The U.S. Dollar and the Euro," *Finance and Development* 35, no. 2 (June 1998): 46–49.

Taylor, Mark C. *Confidence Games: Money and Markets in a World without Redemption*. Chicago: University of Chicago Press, 2004.

Taylor, Mark Lewis. "Empire and Transcendence: Hardt and Negri's Challenge to Theology and Ethics." Unpublished paper dated October 22, 2005.

———. "Polyrhythm in Worship," in *Making Room at the Table: An Invitation to Multicultural Worship*, edited by Brian K. Blount and Leonara Tubbs Tisdale. Louisville, KY: Westminster John Knox, 2001, 108–28.

———. *The Executed God: The Way of the Cross in Lockdown America*. Minneapolis, MN: Fortress Press, 2001.

———. *Paul Tillich: The Theologian of Boundaries*. Minneapolis, MN: Fortress Press, 1991.

———. *Religion, Politics and the Christian Right*. Minneapolis, MN: Fortress Press, 2005.

Thaler, Richard H. "Mental Accounting Matters," *Journal of Behavioral Decision Making* 12, (1999): 183–206.

Thrift, Nigel, and Andrew Leyshon. "Moral Geographies of Money," in *Nation-States and Money: The Past, Present and Future of National Currencies*, edited by Emily Gilbert and Eric Helleiner. London: Routledge, 1999, 159–81.

Tillich, Paul. *The Courage to Be*. New Haven, CT: Yale University Press, 1952.

———. *Dynamics of Faith*. New York: Harper & Row, 1957.

———. *The Interpretation of History*. New York: Charles Scribner's Sons, 1936.

———. *Love, Power, Justice*. New York: Oxford University Press, 1960.

———. *Morality and Beyond*. Louisville, KY: Westminster John Knox Press, 1963.

———. *Political Expectation*. New York: Harper & Row, 1971.

———. *The Protestant Era*. Chicago: University of Chicago Press, 1948.

———. *The Religious Situation*, translated by H. Richard Niebuhr. New York: Meridian Books, 1956.

———. *The Socialist Decision*, translated by Franklin Sherman. New York: Harper & Row, [1933] 1977).

———. *Systematic Theology*, vol. 1, *Reason and Revelation, Being and God*. Chicago: University of Chicago Press, 1951.

———. *Systematic Theology*, vol. 2, *Existence and the Christ*. Chicago: University of Chicago Press, 1957.

———. *Systematic Theology*, vol. 3, *Life and the Spirit, History and the Kingdom of God*. Chicago: University of Chicago Press, 1965.

———. *Theology of Culture*. New York: Oxford University Press, 1959.

Tobin, James, and S. S. Golub. *Money, Credit, and Capital*. New York: Irwin/McGraw Hill, 1998.

Torrance, T. F. *The Trinitarian Faith: The Evangelical Theology of the Ancient Catholic Church*. London: T & T Clark, 1995.

Tsangarides, Charalambos G., Pierre Ewenczcy, and Michal Hulej. "Stylized Facts on Bilateral Trade and Currency Unions: Implications for Africa." Working Paper /06/31, International Monetary Fund, January 2006.

Tucker, Robert C. *The Marx-Engels Reader*. New York: W. W. Norton & Co., 1978.

UNCTAD VIII. *Analytical Report by the UNCTAD Secretariat to the Conference*. United Nations, 1992.

United Nations. *UN Millennium Development Goals Report 2005*. New York: United Nations, 2005.

———. *Investing in Development: A Practical Plan to achieve the Millennium Development Goals*. New York: United Nations Development Program, 2005.

United States Treasury Department. *The Use and Counterfeiting of United States Currency Abroad*, Part 2. Washington, DC, March 2003.

van Huyssteen, J. Wentzel. *The Shaping of Rationality: Toward Interdisciplinarity in Theology and Science*. Grand Rapids, MI: William B. Eerdmans Co., 1999.

Volcker, Paul A. "An Economy on Thin Ice," *Washington Post*, April 10, p. B7.

Volf. Miroslav, and Dorothy C. Bass, ed. *Practicing Theology: Beliefs and Practices in Christian Life*. Grand Rapids, MN: William B. Eerdmans Co., 2002.

———. *After Our Likeness: The Church as the Image of the Trinity*. Grand Rapids, MN: William B. Eerdmans Co., 1998.

———. "'The Trinity is Our Social Program'": The Doctrine of the Trinity and the Shape of Social Engagement" *Modern Theology* 14, no. 3 (July 1998): 403–23.

———. *Exclusion and Embrace*. Nashville, TN: Abingdon Press, 1996.

———. "The Church as a Prophetic Community and a Sign of Hope," *European Journal of Theology* 2, no. 1 (1993): 9–30.

———. *Work in the Spirit: Toward Theology of Work*. New York: Oxford University Press, 1991.

Wallace, Laura. "Ahead of His Time," *Finance and Development* 43, no. 3 (September 2006): 4–7.

Wariboko, Nimi. "Urbanization and Cities in Africa," in *Contemporary Africa*, vol. 5, edited by Toyin Falola. Durham, NC: Carolina Academic Press, 2003, 633–55.

———. "State-Corporation Relationship: Impact on Management Practice," in *The Transformation of Nigeria: Essays in Honor of Toyin Falola*, edited by Adebayo Oyebade. Trenton, NJ: African World Press, 2002, 289–327.

Waterman, Anthony M. C. *Political Economy and Christian Theology Since the Enlightenment*. New York: Palgrave Macmillan, 2004.

———. "Economics as Theology: Adam Smith's Wealth of Nations," *Southern Economic Journal* 68, no. 4 (2000): 673–86,

Weatherford, Jack. *The History of Money: From Sandstone to Cyberspace*. New York: Three Rivers Press, 1997.

Weber, Max. *Economy and Society*. Berkeley: University of California Press, 1978.

———. "Religious Rejections of the World and their Directions," in *From Max Weber: Essays in Sociology*, edited by H. H. Gerth and C. W. Mills. New York: Oxford University Press, 1958, 323–59.

Weintraub, E. Roy. "Neoclassical Economics," in *The Fortune Encyclopedia of Economics*, edited by David R. Henderson. New York: Warner Books, 1993, 135–38.

Wennerlind, Carl C. "The Humean Paternity to Adam Smith's Theory of Money," *History of Economic Ideas* 8 (2001): 77–97.

———. "The Link between David Hume's *Treatise of Human Nature* and His Fiduciary Theory of Money," *History of Political Economy* 33, no. 1 (2001): 139–60.

———. "Money Talks, but What is it Saying? Semiotics of Money and Social Control," *Journal of Economic Issues* 35, no. 3 (September 2001): 557–69.

Winter, Gibson. *Community and Spiritual Transformation: Religion and Politics in a Communal Age*. New York: Crossroad Co., 1989.

———. *Elements for a Social Ethics*. New York: MacMillan, 1966.

Wolf, Martin. *Why Globalization Works*. New Haven, CT: Yale University Press, 2004.

———. "We need a Global Currency," *Financial Times*, August 3, 2004, http: //search .ft.com/ftArticle?queryText=We+Need+a+Global+Currency&y=10&aje=true& x=19&id=040803008394&ct=0 (accessed December 8, 2004).

Wolf, Susan. "Sanity and the Metaphysics of Responsibility," in *Responsibility, Character, and the Emotions: New Essays in Moral Psychology*, edited by Ferdinand Schoeman. New York: Cambridge University Press, 1987, 46–62.

———. "Asymmetrical Freedom," *Journal of Philosophy* 77, no. 3 (March, 1980): 151–66.

Wright, Robert. *NonZero: The Logic of Human Destiny*. New York: Vintage Books, 2001.

Yapa, Lakshman. "Reply: Why Discourse Matters, Materially," *Annals of the Association of American Geographers* 87, no. 4 (1997): 717–22.

———. "What Causes Poverty?: A Postmodern View," *Annals of the Association of American Geographers* 86, no. 4 (1996): 707–28.

Zafirovski, Milan. *Exchange, Action, and Social Structure: Elements of Economic Sociology*. Westport, CT: Greenwood Press, 2001.

Zarlenga, Stephen A. *The Lost Science of Money: The Mythology of Money—The Story of Power*. Valatie, NY: American Monetary Institute, 2002.

Zelizer, Viviana. *The Purchase of Intimacy*. Princeton, NJ: Princeton University Press, 2005.

————. "Missing Monies: Comment on Nigel Dodd, 'Reinventing monies in Europe,'" *Economy and Society* 34, no. 4 (November 2005): 584–88.

————. "Circuits within Capitalism," in *The Economic Sociology of Capitalism*, edited by Victor Nee and Richard Swedberg. Princeton, NJ: Princeton University Press, 2005, 289–322.

————. "Circuits of Commerce," in *Self, Social Structure, and Beliefs: Exploration in Sociology*, edited by C. Williams. Berkeley: University of California Press, 2004, 122–44.

————. "Sociology of Money," in *International Encyclopedia of the Social and Behavioral Sciences* 15 (2001): 1991–94.

————. "Fine Tuning the Zelizer View," *Economy and Society* 29, no. 3 (2000): 383–89.

————. "Payments and Social Ties," *Sociological Forum* 11 (September 1996): 481–95.

————. *The Social Meaning of Money: Pin money, Paychecks, Poor Relief, and Other Currencies*. New York: Basic Books, 1994.

Zizioulas, John. *Being and Communion: Studies in Personhood and the Church*. Crestwood, NY: St. Vladimir's Seminary Press, 1985.

Zucker, Wolfgang M. "The Demonic: From Aeschylus to Tillich," *Theology Today* 26 (April 1969): 34–50.

Index

About the Author

Nimi Wariboko is the Katherine B. Stuart Associate Professor of Christian Ethics at Andover Newton Theological Seminary. He was educated at Columbia University (MBA, Finance/Accounting) and Princeton Theological Seminary (Ph. D, Ethics). His research, teaching, and writing focus on economic ethics, the intersection of religion and economic activities, money, economic development, and social theory. He has experience in investment banking and strategy consulting to banks on Wall Street and expertise in financial analysis. Wariboko has excellent understanding of the history and working of the global monetary system. He taught as an adjunct faculty member at New York University ("African Civilization"), The New York Institute of Finance ("Security Analysis," and "Advanced Mergers and Acquisitions."), and the Frank G. Zarb School of Business, Hofstra University ("International Business").

Wariboko has published extensively on social ethics, finance, management, economic history, and social sciences. His books include *The Depth and Destiny of Work: An African Theological Interpretation* (2008); *Pattern of Institutions in the Niger Delta: Economic and Ethological Interpretations of History and Culture* (2007); *The New Rules of Bank Strategy in Nigeria: A Paradigm Shift* (2001); *The Mind of African Strategists: A Study of Kalabari Management Practice* (1997); *Principles and Practice of Bank Analysis and Valuation* (1994), and *Financial Statement Analysis: A Workbook* (1993).

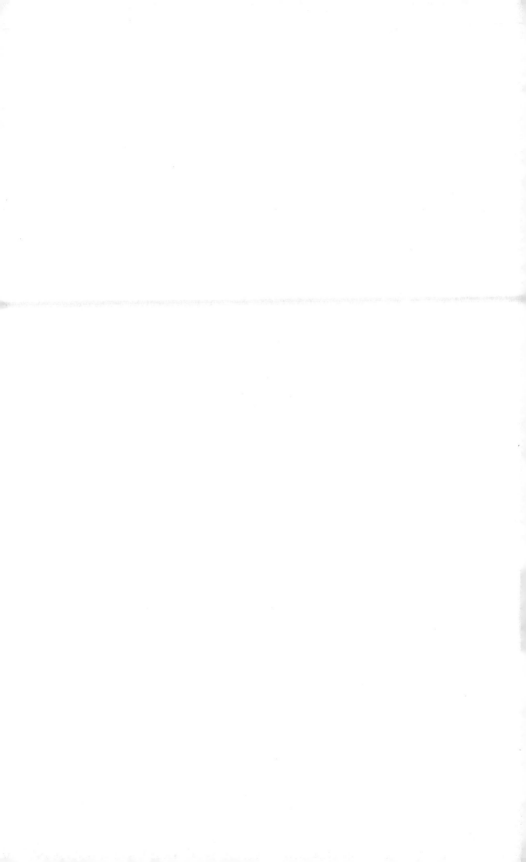

Made in the USA
Lexington, KY
26 February 2014